eBay®
For Seniors
FOR
DUMMIES®

eBay® For Seniors

FOR

DUMMIES®

by Marsha Collier

WILEY

Wiley Publishing, Inc.

eBay® For Seniors For Dummies®

Published by
Wiley Publishing, Inc.
111 River Street
Hoboken, NJ 07030-5774

www.wiley.com

Copyright © 2010 by Wiley Publishing, Inc., Indianapolis, Indiana

Published by Wiley Publishing, Inc., Indianapolis, Indiana

Published simultaneously in Canada

For general information on our other products and services, please contact our Customer Care Department within the U.S. at 877-762-2974, outside the U.S. at 317-572-3993, or fax 317-572-4002.

For technical support, please visit www.wiley.com/techsupport.

Wiley also publishes its books in a variety of electronic formats. Some content that appears in print may not be available in electronic books.

Library of Congress Control Number: 2009935836

ISBN: 978-0-470-52759-7

10 9 8 7 6 5 4 3 2

WILEY

About the Author

Marsha Collier spends a good deal of time on eBay. She loves buying and selling (she's a PowerSeller with her own eBay store) as well as meeting eBay users from around the world. As a columnist, an author of three best-selling books on eBay, and an invited lecturer at eBay Live, she shares her knowledge of eBay with millions of online sellers. *eBay For Dummies* is published in special versions for the United Kingdom, Canada, Germany, China, and Australia. Currently, she has 15 books in print on her favorite subject — eBay.

Marsha is one of the foremost eBay experts and educators in the world, and the top-selling eBay author. In 1999, Marsha created the first edition of *eBay For Dummies*, the bestselling book for eBay beginners. She followed up the success of the first book with *Starting an eBay Business For Dummies*, a book targeting individuals interested in making e-commerce their full-time profession. That book became an instant nationwide hit, making several notable best seller lists. These books are updated regularly to keep up with site and market changes.

Marsha's books have sold over 1,000,000 copies (including the special editions in foreign countries — two in Australia, two in Canada, and two in the United Kingdom — as well as translations in Spanish, French, Italian, Chinese, and German).

Along with her writing, Marsha is an experienced e-commerce educator. She was the lead instructor at eBay University (teaching seminars all over the United States), as well as a regular presenter at the eBay Live national convention since its inception. Marsha also hosted "Make Your Fortune Online," a PBS special on online business that premiered in 2005. The show was the basis for her PBS premium five DVD set, "Your Online Business Plan." In 2006, she was invited to address the Innovations Conference in Singapore to present the ideas of e-commerce to a new market. In 2008, she was dubbed one of twenty influential iCitizens in

Kelly Mooney's *The Open Brand: When Push Comes to Pull in a Web-Made World*, and was invited to speak at a leading e-commerce conference attended by representatives of Coca-Cola, Hewlett Packard, Procter & Gamble, Victoria's Secret, and prominent e-commerce leaders.

During the holiday season, she does several national satellite-media tours to explain the safety of shopping online. She hosts Computer & Technology Radio on KTRB 860 AM in San Francisco as well as on the Web at www.computerandtechnologyradio.com. She also makes regular appearances on television, radio, and in print to discuss customer needs and online commerce.

Marsha currently resides in Los Angeles, CA. She can be reached via her Web site, www.marshacollier.com. Or find her on Twitter @MarshaCollier.

Author's Acknowledgments

This book couldn't have been written without the input from thousands of eBay sellers and buyers that I've spoken to from all over the country. You inspire me to work harder and do my best to help all of you.

I must acknowledge the best of the best at Wiley Publishing, Inc.: Leah Cameron, who taught me how to make this book the best it can be; super-wordsmith Barry Childs-Helton, whose stamp is all over this book in the best of ways (even if we sometimes differed on hyphenation rules); and my super technical editor Louise (aunt*patti) Ruby who double-checks for the latest changes in eBay policies.

It's time I seriously acknowledged someone very special to me at Wiley: Steven Hayes. I've worked with Steve on my books for over ten years. Sometimes we fight like an old married couple, but he gets me and supports me — I guess that's what good relationships are all about. Thank you, Steve, for everything.

I can't forget Andy Cummings, my publisher, who, after all these years still takes my calls and puts up with my idiosyncrasies!

Thank you all!

Dedication

In all my years teaching eBay, the most serious students have always been those "of a certain age." And let's face it! Who has more stuff to sell than those who have been around long enough to accumulate a bunch of really great stuff?

I dedicate this book to all those of us out there who need a little bit larger print; those who want just the facts and no BS to get them straight to making money. This book is dedicated to you.

Publisher's Acknowledgments

We're proud of this book; please send us your comments through our online registration form located at http://dummies.custhelp.com. For other comments, please contact our Customer Care Department within the U.S. at 877-762-2974, outside the U.S. at 317-572-3993, or fax 317-572-4002.

Some of the people who helped bring this book to market include the following:

Acquisitions, Editorial, and Media Development

Editors: Leah Cameron and Barry Childs-Helton

Executive Editor: Steven Hayes

Technical Editor: Patti Louise Ruby

Media Development Manager: Richard Graves

Editorial Assistant: Amanda Graham

Sr. Editorial Assistant: Cherie Case

Cartoons: Rich Tennant
   (www.the5thwave.com)

Composition Services

Project Coordinator: Patrick Redmond

Layout and Graphics: Samantha K. Cherolis, Julie Trippetti, Christine Williams

Proofreader: Betty Kish

Indexer: Rebecca R. Plunkett

Publishing and Editorial for Technology Dummies

   Richard Swadley, Vice President and Executive Group Publisher

   Andy Cummings, Vice President and Publisher

   Mary Bednarek, Executive Acquisitions Director

   Mary C. Corder, Editorial Director

Publishing for Consumer Dummies

   Diane Graves Steele, Vice President and Publisher

Composition Services

   Debbie Stailey, Director of Composition Services

Contents at a Glance

Table of Contents

Introduction

I've been teaching, writing, and selling on eBay for over 12 years. I've taught thousands of people how to use eBay and to succeed doing it. Some of the most pointed questions I've been asked come from some of the sharpest students I've ever taught — those of a "certain age." People with a little graying. I don't like the word *senior*; I prefer the word *experienced*.

After all, who has more experience on this planet? Who has bought more merchandise in their lifetime? Who knows a good deal from a lousy one? Who has a better idea of what good customer service is like? That's right, you do, not those cocky kids. Living longer — and experiencing more — gives us an advantage in this world.

Lessons learned from the school of hard knocks leave impressions on us; good and bad. Hopefully we've learned that certain things just don't work in the long run. But here we are, in the Digital World, with an entirely new set of rules (just when we thought we had it all figured out)! Who knew we'd want to know how to buy and sell online?

Each day goes by and we realize there's something cool out there that we're not part of. We don't like that. Not one bit.

Anyone born before 1960 grew up in an analog age. Televisions were big bulky affairs, and the first remote controls ca-chunked each time you changed the channel (and they had only four buttons). We woke up and went to sleep seeing a test pattern. Cameras (the good ones) were solid, heavy devices, and movie cameras whirred along with a comfortable mechanical hum. Typewriters clacked in a danceable rhythm.

Then life turned digital without our permission, sometimes even without our noticing until after it happened. Many comfortable mechanical sounds went away, replaced with electronic buzzing, beeping, and twittering. Everything got more complex: The button count on my remote control went from four to a gazillion! Everything got smaller — some of those little cameras look so small and cheesy that I'm shocked they can take good pictures, but they do. (They take great ones.) Even, it seems, type on a page has shrunk, which is why my publisher has graciously set this book in a type that's easy on the eyes so you can read something on the page and then glance at your computer without having to pick your glasses off the top of your head.

If you count yourself among those business-savvy, experienced, graying folks who still feel some trepidation on the Internet — especially when selling on eBay — you've come to the right place.

Why eBay?

Excitement for shopping and selling on eBay has spread to so many corners of the world. The site has become part of our culture. It's a safe place to buy and sell, unlike some of those online classified sites with no built-in security. eBay users (such as you and I) total close to 200 million — that's quite a community. It's a community of buyers who don't have the time to find discounts locally — and of shrewd sellers who find used and wholesale items to sell online and supplement their income — or even make a full-time living. This makes eBay the one-and-only international marketplace that combines this kind of access, consistency, and safety; the best part is that eBay is available to anyone who wants to take the time to figure out how it works.

In this book, you get the goods on how to make money on eBay, whether you're new to the Internet or already Web-savvy. You see how to turn your everyday household clutter into cold, hard cash, and how to look for items that you can sell on eBay. If you're looking to save money buying items you need, I show you how to find the bargains, how to make smart bids, and how to win the auctions.

 How much money you earn (or spend) depends entirely on how *often* and how *smartly* you conduct your eBay transactions. *You* decide how often you want to run sales and make purchases; I'm here to help with the *smart* part by sharing tips I've learned over my past 12 years on eBay.

I'm writing this book so you can add eBay savvy to your list of successes. Read this book closely — it gives you everything you need to know to get your business done without getting outsmarted by the kids. (And don't tell them you read it. Make 'em think you've always been just too cool!) And remember...

⟶ eBay is a constantly evolving Web site. It isn't too hard to master, but it's just like any tool — when you know the ins and outs, you're ahead of the game. You can get the deals when you shop, and you can make the most money when you sell. You've come to the right place to find out all about eBay. This book is designed to help you understand the basics about buying and selling on eBay, the world's most successful trading community.

⟶ A Web site as complex as eBay has many nooks and crannies that may confuse users. Think of this book as a roadmap that can help you find your way on eBay, getting just as much or as little as you want from it. Unlike an actual road map, however, you won't have to fold it back to its original shape (whew). Just close the book and come back any time you need a question answered.

I have five other eBay books available for you, and this is the one to start with. This book gives you the solid foundation you need to go on to my other, more advanced books on eBay selling.

About This Book

Remember those open-book tests that teachers sprang on you in high school? Well, sometimes you may feel like eBay is pop-quizzing you while you're online. Think of *eBay For Seniors For Dummies* as your open-book-test cheat sheet with the answers. You don't have to memorize anything; just keep this book handy and follow along as you need to.

With all this in mind, I've divided this book into pertinent sections to help you find your answers fast. I'll show you how to

➠ Get online and register to do business on eBay and PayPal.

➠ Bid on and *win* eBay auctions.

➠ Choose an item to sell, pick the right time for your listing, market it so that a bunch of bidders see it, and make a nice profit.

➠ Communicate well and close deals without problems, whether you're a buyer or a seller.

➠ Handle problems with finesse, should they crop up.

➠ Become a part of a unique community of people who like to collect, buy, and sell items of just about every type!

 If you see a blur where a name should be in a figure, don't reach for your glasses. To shield the privacy of eBay users, screen images (commonly called *screen shots*) that I've used in this book blur user IDs to protect the innocent (or not-so . . .).

Foolish Assumptions

I'm thinking that you've picked up this book because you've heard that people are making huge money selling on eBay, and you want to find out how to cash in. Or perhaps you heard about the bargains you can find. If either of these assumptions is true, this is the right book for you.

Here are some other foolish assumptions I've made about you (I'm famous for my foolish assumptions — you too?):

➠ You have access to a computer and the Internet so that you can do business on eBay.

➠ You have an interest in selling or buying stuff, and you want to find out more about doing that online.

➠ You want tips to help save money when you bid or buy, and to make money when you sell. (You too? I can relate. We have a lot in common.)

➠ You're concerned about maintaining your privacy and staying away from scammers.

How This Book Is Organized

This book has four parts. The chapters stand on their own, meaning you can read what you need — say, skim Chapter 5 after you read Chapter 10 or skip Chapter 3 altogether. Whatever works. It's all up to you.

If you've already dipped your toe into the eBay pool, you can fly ahead to get good tips on advanced strategies to enhance your sales. Don't wait for permission from me — feel free to go for it.

Part I: Joining the Crowd on eBay

In Part I, I tell you what eBay is and set you up to use it. I take you through the registration process on both eBay and PayPal, guide your way through the many links and pages of the eBay Web site, and help you organize your eBay transactions and interactions using the My eBay page.

Part II: Shopping at the eBay Marketplace

If you're ready to start shopping, check out Part II, which gives you the lowdown on searching for exactly what you want, buying, and winning auctions.

That old cliché, "Let the buyer beware," (*caveat emptor* for the literati among you) *became* a cliché because even today (er, especially today?) it's sound advice. Use my tips to help you decide when to buy or bid — and when to take a pass on an offered item.

Part III: Making Your Mark on eBay

Becoming a buyer or seller on eBay makes you part of an online community. In this part, I tip you off to the interesting parts of the site, as well as some of the rules. You've no doubt heard about feedback; it's the core of the eBay community. I show you how to boost your own. As in life, so on eBay: Your reputation is everything.

Part IV: Taking the Plunge: Running a Sale

In Part IV, it's time to take off the gloves and find your first item for sale. I show you how to get the goods out of your house and put cash in your pocket. I take you through all the different forms of sales on eBay and show you how to take the best advantage of each and every one.

I also show you how to make your item photography and shipping (two of the tasks that sellers rue the most) a simple, quick part of your selling day.

Get Going, Already!

Like everything else in the world, eBay changes. (Wow, isn't that annoying?) eBay tries to improve things — such as the look of the site and its ease-of-use — on a regular basis. My job is to arm you with a feel for the soul of eBay so you won't be thrown by any minor course corrections on eBay's part. If you hit rough waters, just look up the problem in the index in this book. I either help you solve it or let you know where to go on eBay for some expert advice.

Most of all, don't get frustrated! Keep reviewing topics so you feel fully comfortable to take the plunge on eBay. After all, I've heard that Albert Einstein once said something about never committing to memory what you can look up in a book (though I forget when he said that . . .). Now you've got the book.

Feedback, Please

I'd love to hear from you: your successes and your comments. Contact me at talk2marsha@coolebaytools.com. I can't answer each and every question you send. But do know that I promise to read each e-mail and answer when I can.

Check out my Web site at www.coolebaytools.com. And follow me on Twitter.com for my seller tips and comments; http://twitter.com/marshacollier.

You can also call in and speak to me live on my radio show. Every Saturday from noon to 2:00 p.m. Pacific Time, I co-host the *Computer and Technology Show* with Marc Cohen. Call 877-474-3302 if we can ever help you with your computer problems. The show is live on KTRB 860 AM in San Francisco, live online at www.computerand technolgyradio.com, and archived on iTunes.

Getting Comfy with the Spirit of eBay

Chapter 1

The online world is spawning all kinds of businesses (known as *e-commerce* to the technorati), and eBay is the superstar. You've probably got the drift about eBay by now. Since its beginnings in Pierre Omidyar's kitchen, eBay has become a household word. Even if you're not into pop culture, you still find mentions of eBay all over the place. Pierre and his buddy, Jeff Skoll, had a pretty great idea back in 1995; they created a safe and fun place for folks to shop from the comfort of their homes.

Originally, the site grew — person by person — across the country (and soon around the world) as people peddled their own stuff from their homes and collections. Now, eBay is also a marketplace for new merchandise. People figured out a way to buy at wholesale and resell merchandise online for a profit. Nowadays you can purchase new and useful items, such as alarm systems, fancy electronic toothbrushes, batteries, clothing, cars, homes — just about anything you can think of.

Take a look around your house. Vintage designer dresses? Elegant antique shaving set? Great-looking clock! Not to mention all the other way cool stuff you own. All these great fashions, household appliances, and collectibles are fabulous to own, but when was the last time your clock turned a profit? When you connect to eBay, your PC or Mac can magically turn into a money machine. Just visit eBay and marvel at all the items that are just a few mouse clicks away from being bought and sold.

In this chapter, I clue you in to what eBay is and how it works. Not only can you buy and sell stuff in the privacy of your home, but you can also meet people who share your interests. The people who use the eBay site are a friendly bunch, and soon you'll be buying, selling, swapping stories, and trading advice with the best of them. It's like Cousin Joyce's giant online potluck party — but instead of bringing a dish, you sell it!

Check Out What Happens on eBay

1. Start with this important fact: eBay *doesn't* sell a thing. Instead, the site does what all good hosts do: It creates a comfy environment that brings together people with common interests. eBay puts buyers and sellers in an online store and lets them transact business safely within its established rules.

    Think of eBay as the buddy who set you up on your last blind date — except the results may be a lot better. Your matchmaking friend doesn't perform a marriage ceremony but does get you in the same room with your potential soul mate.

2. Join eBay's online marketplace; all you need to do is fill out a few forms online and click. You can become a member with no big fees, silly hats, or secret handshakes. After you register, you can buy and sell anything that falls within the eBay rules and regulations. (Chapter 2 guides you through the registration process.)

3. Understand that the eBay home page is where the general public first visits eBay. The visitors conduct searches, find out what's happening, and begin to browse the site. Because you're *not* the GP, I show you my favorite place to start the day on eBay: the My eBay page, shown in **Figure 1-1**. From the My eBay page that you create, you can keep track of every item you have up for sale or have a bid on.

Look here for items you're buying ...

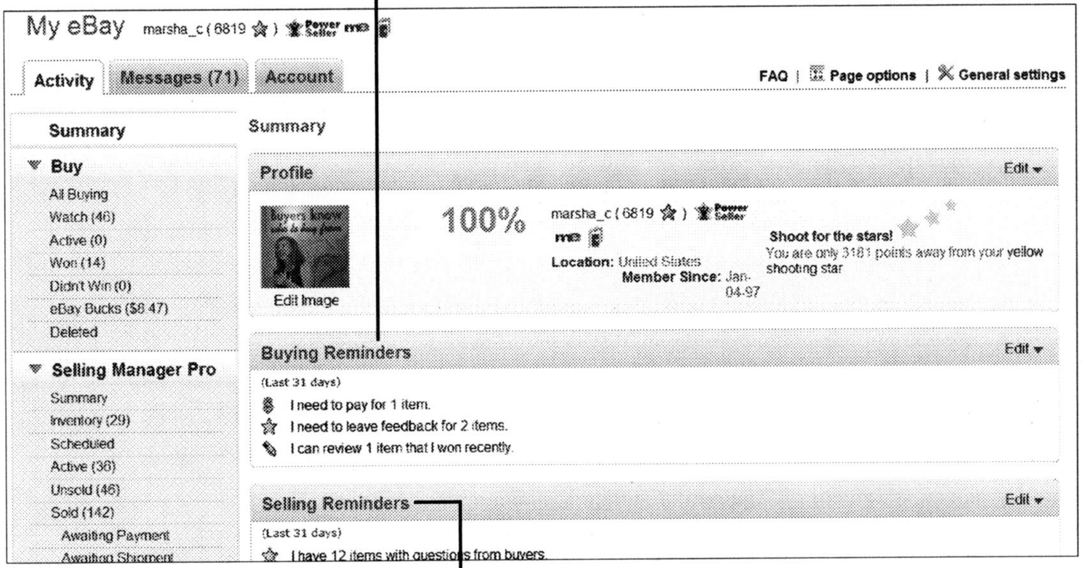

Figure 1-1: My eBay page showing Activity, Messages (71), and Account tabs. Summary shows Buy section (All Buying, Watch (46), Active (0), Won (14), Didn't Win (0), eBay Bucks ($8.47), Deleted) and Selling Manager Pro section (Summary, Inventory (29), Scheduled, Active (36), Unsold (46), Sold (142), Awaiting Payment, Awaiting Shipment). Profile shows 100%, marsha_c (6819), Location: United States, Member Since: Jan-04-97. Buying Reminders and Selling Reminders sections.

... and here for items you're selling.

Figure 1-1

You can read more about the eBay home page and find out more about My eBay in Chapter 3.

4. Embrace item listings; you see lots of those on eBay (and one example in **Figure 1-2**). If you're looking to become a seller, creating an item listing page on eBay is as simple as filling out a form. (Maybe not *so* simple, but that's why you bought this book. Chapters 12 and 13 run you through the entire process.) Merely type the name of your item and a short description, add a crisp digital picture, set your price, and voilà — it's money time. Keep in mind these characteristics of selling an item:

- **eBay charges a small fee** (sometimes it's even free during promotions) for the privilege of putting your item on the site. When you list your item, millions of people (eBay has over 100 million registered users) from all over the world can check out your goods and buy or place bids if you've listed an auction.

- **Other eBay members must bid on your item** for you to make money on an auction listing. With a little luck, a bidding war may break out and drive the bids up high enough for you to turn a nice profit. After the auction, you deal directly with the buyer, who sends you the payment either through a PayPal or with a credit card through a payment service. Then you ship the item. Abracadabra — you just turned your item (everyday clutter, no doubt) into cold, hard cash.

- **You can run as many listings as you want,** all at the same time. To get info on deciding what to sell, leaf through Chapter 11, and to find out how to set up a listing, jump to Chapter 13.

5. Discover the process for finding what you want on eBay. If you're a collector or you just like to shop for bargains on everyday goods, you can browse 24 hours a day through the items up for auction in eBay's tens of thousands of categories, which range from Antiques to Writing Instruments (see **Figure 1-3**). Use eBay's search feature — available from any eBay page — to find the item you want. Then do a little research on what you're buying and who's selling it, place your bid, and keep an eye on it until the auction closes.

Item picture   Item name   Price   Seller information

Cloud Dome Photo Stage Studio w/2 5000°k Lights Kit NEW

Item condition: New

Quantity: 1   12 available

Price: **US $84.95**   [Buy It Now]

This item is being tracked in My eBay.

Shipping: **$12.50** US Postal Service Priority Mail
| See all details
Estimated delivery within 4-8 business days

Returns: 3 day money back, buyer pays return shipping |
Read details

Coverage: Pay with *PayPal* and your full purchase price is covered | See terms

Enlarge

Top-rated seller

marsha_c (6819 ☆)

me 100%

✓ Consistently receives highest buyers' ratings

✓ Ships items quickly

✓ Has earned a track record of excellent service

Ask a question

See other items

Visit store: 🏪 Marsha Collier's Fabulous Finds

Other item info

Item number: 350116884828
Item location: Los Angeles, United States
Ships to: United States
Payments: PayPal See details
History: 3 sold

☑ Share   🖨 Print   ⚑ Report item

Figure 1-2

Click any More button for more categories.

ebaY   Hi, marsha_c! (Sign out)   ⊙⊙⊙ You currently have $8.47 eBay Bucks!   Site Map

Buy   Sell   My eBay   Community   Help

[ ]   All Categories ▾   [Search]   Advanced Search

Categories ▾   Motors   Stores   Daily Deal   eBay Security & Resolution Center

Home > **Buy**

All Categories

Antiques	Art	Baby	Books
Antiquities	Direct from the Artist	Baby Gear	Accessories
Architectural & Garden	Art from Dealers & Resellers	Baby Safety & Health	Antiquarian & Collectible
Asian Antiques	Wholesale Lots	Bathing & Grooming	Audiobooks
Books & Manuscripts		Car Safety Seats	Catalogs
More ▾		More ▾	More ▾

Business & Industrial	Cameras & Photo	Cell Phones & PDAs	Clothing, Shoes & Accessories
Agriculture & Forestry	Binoculars & Telescopes	Cell Phones & Smartphones	Costumes & Reenactment Attire
Businesses & Websites for Sale	Camcorders	Bluetooth Accessories	Cultural & Ethnic Clothing
Construction	Camcorder Accessories	Cell Phone & PDA Accessories	Dancewear & Dance Shoes
Electrical & Test Equipment	Camera Accessories	PDAs & Pocket PCs	Infants & Toddlers
More ▾	More ▾	More ▾	More ▾

Coins & Paper Money	Collectibles	Computers & Networking	Crafts
Bullion	Advertising	Apple Computers & Components	Art Supplies

Figure 1-3

When I wrote *Santa Shops on eBay* (Wiley), I had a great time visiting the different categories and buying a little something here and there — it's amazing just how varied the selection is. I even bought some parts for my pool cleaner!

Take a look at Chapter 4 for the easy way to find items to buy. When you see an item you like, you can set up a bidding strategy and let the games begin. Chapter 6 gives you bidding strategies that can make you the winner.

Know eBay's Role in the Action

1. Recognize eBay as your online auctioneer. Throughout the auction process, eBay's computers keep tabs on what's going on. When the auction or sale is over, eBay takes a percentage of the final selling price and enables the buyer to check out and pay for the item. At this point, eBay's job is pretty much over, and eBay steps aside.

2. Use eBay's expertise to find solutions. Most of the time, everything works great, everybody's happy, and eBay never has to step back into the picture. But if you happen to run into trouble in paradise, eBay can help you settle the problem, whether you're the buyer or the seller.

3. Get familiar with eBay's feedback system. eBay regulates members with a detailed system of checks and balances known as member-to-member *feedback*, which I describe in Chapter 5. The grand plan is that the community polices itself under eBay's guidance, as follows:

- eBay jumps in when shady activity comes to light. But those who keep eBay most safe are the community members, the buyers and sellers who have a common stake in conducting business honestly and fairly.

- Every time you sell something or buy an item, eBay members have a chance to leave a comment about you. You should do the same for them. If they're happy, the feedback is positive; otherwise, the feedback is negative. Either way, your feedback sticks to you like glue. As a preview, posted feedback looks like **Figure 1-4**.

All positive feedback!

7,650 Feedback received (viewing 1-25)			Revised Feedback: 0
Feedback		**From / Price**	**Date / Time**
Cool product. A+++		Buyer ████████ (403 ⭐)	Aug-19-09 09:20
Museum Putty QUAKE HOLD Wax Quakehold Earthquake LARGE (#360171729835)		US $7.75	View Item
Just beautiful. Fast shipping. Pleasure to do business with.		Buyer ████████ (195 ⭐)	Aug-16-09 16:51
...		...	Private
Just beautiful! Fast and great shipping. Pleasure to do business with.		Buyer ████████ (195 ⭐)	Aug-16-09 16:39
MINT Vintag Barbie Repro SILKEN FLAME 977 RED FLARE 939 (#360172612674)		US $24.99	View Item
Thank you		Buyer ████████ (227 ⭐)	Aug-13-09 19:01
Museum Putty QUAKE HOLD Wax Quakehold Earthquake LARGE (#360171729835)		US $7.75	View Item
Arrived well packed & quickly - autographed to ME!! WOW! D :)		Buyer ████████ (82 ⭐)	Aug-13-09 11:17
NEW 2009 eBay For Dummies 6 MARSHA COLLIER Signed Book (#350236161863)		US $24.99	View Item
Great selling experience, great product!!!		Buyer ████████ (100 ⭐)	Aug-13-09 09:33
Museum Putty QUAKE HOLD Wax Quakehold Earthquake LARGE (#360171729835)		US $7.75	View Item
I am crazy for this stuff! Everything is finally straight and secure.		Buyer ████████ (395 ⭐)	Aug-13-09 07:11
Museum Putty QUAKE HOLD Wax Quakehold Earthquake LARGE (#360171729835)		US $7.75	View Item
This stuff can do anything. All pictures in house are now straight!!!!!		Buyer ████████ (395 ⭐)	Aug-13-09 07:09

Figure 1-4

 Building a great reputation with positive feedback ensures a long and profitable eBay career. Negative feedback, like multiple convictions, is a real turnoff to buyers and can make it hard to do future business on eBay.

Understand the Auction Process

1. eBay offers several kinds of auctions, but for the most part, they all work the same way. An *auction* is a unique sales event where the exact value of the item for sale is not known (it's determined by how much someone is willing to spend), as shown in **Figure 1-5**. As a result, an element of surprise is involved — not only for the bidder (who may end up with a great deal) but also for the seller (who may end up making a killing).

There's still time to beat this bid.

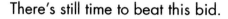

NWT DIANE VON FURSTENBERG SOPHIA LOREN BUSTIER DRESS

Item condition:	New: With Tags
Time left:	1h 46m 55s (Jul 28, 2009 15:36:53 PDT)
Bid history	3 bids
Current bid:	**US $113.00**
Your max bid:	**US $** [ ] **Place bid**
	(Enter US $115.50 or more)
You can also:	**Watch this item**

You'll earn **$2.26** in eBay Bucks. See conditions

Shipping:	**$6.95** US Postal Service Priority Mail	See all details
	Estimated delivery within 6-7 business days
Returns	No Returns Accepted
Coverage	Pay with **PayPal** and your full purchase price is covered	See terms

Figure 1-5

2. See how an auction works from both the seller's and bidder's perspective:

- **Seller:** A seller pays a fee, fills out a form, and sets up the auction, listing a *minimum bid* he or she is willing to accept for the item. Think of an auctioneer at Sotheby's saying, "The bidding for this diamond necklace begins at $5,000." You might *want* to bid $4,000, but the bid won't be accepted. Sellers can also set a *reserve price* — sort of a safety net that protects them from losing money on the deal.

- **Bidder:** Bidders duke it out over a period of time (the minimum is one day, but most auctions last a week or even longer) until one comes out victorious.

Big surprise, the highest bidder wins! The tricky thing about participating in an auction is that no one knows the final price an item goes for until the last second of the auction.

 Unlike "traditional" live auctions that end with the familiar phrase "Going once, going twice, sold!" eBay auctions are controlled by the clock. The seller pays a fee and lists the item on the site for a predetermined period of time; the highest bidder when the clock runs out takes home the prize.

Know How a Reserve Price Works

1. Reserve-price auctions have an extra feature. In addition to a minimum bid, which is required in any eBay auction, a *reserve price* protects sellers from having to sell an item for less than the minimum amount they want for it. An auction with a reserve is shown in **Figure 1-6**.

Notice the reserve has not been met.

Figure 1-6

Suppose you see a 1968 Jaguar XKE sports car up for auction on eBay with a minimum bid of only a dollar. It's a fair bet that the seller has put a reserve price on this car to protect himself from losing money. The reserve price allows sellers to set lower minimum bids, and lower minimum bids attract bidders. Unfortunately, if a seller makes the reserve price too high and it isn't met by the end of the auction, no one wins.

2. Nobody knows (except the seller and the eBay computer system) what the reserve price is until the auction is over, but you can tell from the auction page whether you're dealing with a reserve-price auction. You have to open the specific auction page to find out whether it has a reserve. If bids have been made on an item, the auction page also shows a message telling you if the reserve price hasn't been met. (Refer to Figure 1-6.)

Discover Listings That Not Everyone Sees

1. If you're interested in bidding on items of an adult nature, look for eBay's Adults Only category where *restricted-access* auctions show up. These auctions are run like the typical timed auctions, but with access restricted to those eBay members over 18 and these additional requirements:

- **A credit card on file.** Although you can peruse the other eBay categories without having to submit credit card information, you must have a credit card number on file on eBay to view and bid on items in this category.

- **A terms of use agreement.** To bid on adult items, you first need to agree to a terms of use page after entering your user ID and password. This page pops up automatically when you attempt to access this category.

2. Some sellers choose to hold *private listings* (they can be either auctions or fixed price listings) because they're selling sensitive or expensive items. For example, a seller may know that some buyers are embarrassed to be seen bidding on a box of racy neckties in front of the rest of the eBay community. (I, also, am not crazy about the community knowing I'm buying Star Trek memorabilia — or even what lingerie I choose to buy.) And when selling big-ticket items, the seller may go the private route so that bidders don't have to disclose their financial status.

Private listings are run like the typical eBay listing except that each bidder's identity is kept secret. At the end of the auction, eBay provides contact info to the seller and to the high bidder, and that's it.

Bypass Bidding with Buy It Now

1. You don't have to participate in an auction on eBay to buy something. If you want to make a purchase — if it's something you *must* have — you can usually find the item and buy it immediately.

 Of course, using Buy It Now (*BIN* in eBay speak) doesn't come with the thrill of an auction, but purchasing an item at a fraction of the retail price without leaving your chair or waiting for an auction to end has its own warm and fuzzy kind of excitement.

2. If you seek this kind of instant gratification on eBay, browse the listings (see the Buy It Now button in **Figure 1-7**) or visit eBay Stores. You can also isolate these items by clicking the Buy It Now tab when browsing categories or performing searches.

3. Visiting eBay Stores (the home page is showing in **Figure 1-8**) is as easy as finding a store item in an eBay search or clicking the eBay Stores link from the home page.

Thousands of eBay sellers have set up stores with merchandise meant for you to Buy It Now. eBay Stores classify merchandise in categories just like eBay, and you can buy anything from socks to jewelry to appliances.

Feel free to buy now.

Cloud Dome Photo Stage Studio w/2 5000°k
Lights Kit NEW

Item condition: New

Quantity:	1	12 available
Price:	US $84.95	Buy It Now

This item is being tracked in My eBay.

Shipping: **$12.50** US Postal Service Priority Mail |
See all details
Estimated delivery within 4-5 business days

Returns: 3 day money back, buyer pays return shipping |
Read details

Coverage: Pay with *PayPal* and your full purchase price is
covered | See terms

Seller info

marsha_c (6622 ☆) 🌟 Power Seller

me 100%

Ask a question

See other items

Visit store: 🏪 Marsha Collier's
Fabulous Finds

Other item info

Item number: 350116884828

Item location: Los Angeles, United
States

Ships to: United States

Payments: PayPal See details

History: 3 sold

✉ Share 🖶 Print ⚑ Report item

Figure 1-7

Sellers who open an eBay Store have to meet a certain level of experience on eBay, and when you buy from an eBay Store, you're protected by the same fraud protection policy that covers you in an eBay auction.

4. More and more sellers are listing auctions with a *Buy It Now (BIN)* option, which is available for single-item auctions. This feature allows buyers who want to purchase an item *now* to do so. Have you ever wanted an item really badly and didn't want to wait until the end of an auction? If the seller offers Buy It Now, you can purchase that item immediately. If you're the seller, you can entice your bidders to pay just a tad more to have the satisfaction of walking away with the item free and clear.

eBay has stores as well as auctions.

Figure 1-8

 But there's a twist to the BIN option: The listing begins as an auction (see **Figure 1-9**). If the item receives a bid, the BIN option disappears, and the item goes through the normal auction process. If you want the item now, just click the Buy It Now button and the item is yours for the Buy It Now price.

5. Sellers with merchandise they're ready to sell often list an item at a fixed price. When they do, you can buy an item as soon as you see one at a price that suits you. For a variation on a fixed-price listing, the seller adds the *Make Offer* option, which enables buyers to make an offer for the item.

You can choose to bid or buy.

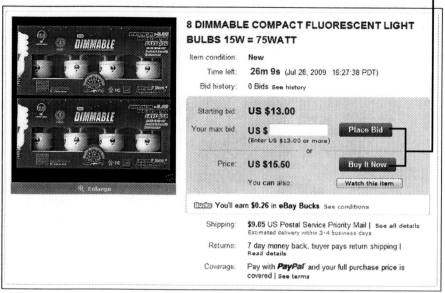

Figure 1-9

 With the Make Offer option, the seller doesn't have to accept the offer: They can also turn you down (sad face) or make you a counteroffer. For more on how these sales work, check out Chapter 6.

Getting Ready for eBay Action

Chapter 2

*T*he mere fact that business is transacted online and that eBay is a technology is what makes many people shy away. This book is written to take away the mystery and make selling on eBay as easy as downing a cold drink on a hot summer day.

You don't have to know a lot of fancy computer tech stuff to do well on eBay, but you must *have* a computer — either a desktop or laptop variety. If you're in the market for a computer, you can buy or lease a new, used, or refurbished system, depending on your computing needs and budget. The information in this chapter is geared mainly toward the purchase of new PCs (which you can get for around 600 bucks), but you should read this info even if you're thinking of buying a used computer.

Okay, so now you have a computer, and you're ready to surf eBay. Hold on a minute — before you start surfing, you need *access* to the Internet (a petty detail, I know). The way to access the Internet is through an ISP, or *Internet service provider*, such as Earthlink, Comcast, or Road Runner. If you don't already belong to one of these, don't worry. Joining is easy, and I tell you how in this chapter.

When you have an active Internet connection, you can browse eBay all you want without registering. But before you transact any sort of business on eBay, you must register. (I recommend registering while you're reading this book.)

 It's not a big deal to register at eBay. The only hard-and-fast rule is that you have to be 18 or older. Don't worry, the Age Police won't come to your house to card you; they have other ways to discreetly ensure that you're at least 18 years old. (*Hint:* Credit cards do more than satisfy account charges.)

Get Your Computer in Shape for eBay

1. Computers come in various shapes, sizes, and configurations (see some examples in **Figure 2-1**). Whatever style you go for, look for a computer with a good memory capacity. The more time you spend using your computer, the more stuff you want to save on your hard drive. Remember that 1950s horror movie, *The Blob?* The more stuffed your hard drive, the more Blob-like it becomes. A hard drive with at least 60 gigabytes (GB) of storage space should keep your computer happy, but you can get hard drives as big as 400GB and more.

Desktop   Laptop   Netbook

Figure 2-1

 I recommend you buy the biggest hard drive you can afford because no matter how large your hard drive is, you'll find a way to fill it up.

2. Make sure the computer's central processing unit (CPU) is fast. A CPU (also known as a "chip") is your computer's brain, and it should have the fastest processing speed you can afford. You can always opt for the top-of-the-line, but even a slower 900MHz (megahertz) processor could suffice.

 One of my computers is an antique slowpoke, but it's still fast enough that it won't choke when I ask it to do some minor multitasking. If you want lightning-fast speed (imagine a Daytona 500 race car with jet assist), you have to move up to a chip with at least a 3GHz (gigahertz) processing speed.

3. Make sure you have a top-quality modem if you have a dial-up connection. Your modem connects your computer to the Internet using your telephone line. Even if you have a broadband connection (see the next task in this chapter), you should have a modem (usually built in to most computers) that can connect you on the off-chance that your high-speed service is down.

 A modem transfers data over phone lines at a rate called *kilobytes per second*, or just plain *K*. A 56K modem is standard equipment and is especially important if you plan on using a lot of digital images (photographs) to help sell your items.

4. Get a big screen. Having an LCD monitor with at least a 17-inch screen can make a huge difference after several hours of rabid bidding or proofreading your auction item descriptions. Get anything smaller, and you'll have a hard time actually seeing the listings and images.

5. You must have a keyboard. No keyboard, no typing. The basic keyboard is fine. Some manufacturers do make funky ergonomic models that are split in the middle. But if the good old standard keyboard feels comfortable to you, stick with it.

Different keyboards have different feels to them. I like "clicky" keys that let my fingers know that the letters I type actually appear. Test out several keyboards and see which one suits your typing style.

6. You need a pointing device, usually a mouse. Some laptops come with touchpads or trackballs designed to do the same thing — give you a quick way to move the pointer around the screen so you can select options by clicking.

Set Up an Internet Connection

1. Decide which of the two main types of Internet connections you want. You can go with a slower, but less expensive dial-up connection. Or if you have a need for speed and your time is worth a bit more than an increase in ISP cost, you may want to look into getting a broadband connection.

Broadband, or high-speed, connections can be a boon to your eBay business. Here's the story on the different types:

- **DSL** *(Digital Subscriber Line)***:** For as little as $9.95 a month, you can avoid a pokey, analog dial-up connection and always be connected to the Internet. A DSL line can move data as fast as 6MB per second — that's six *million* bits per second, or 140 times as fast as a 56K modem. At that speed, a DSL connection can greatly enhance your eBay and Internet experiences. For more information about what DSL is and how to get it, use your neighbor's Internet connection and visit www.dslreports.com.

- **Cable:** An Internet cable connection is a reliable method for Internet access if you have digital cable TV. Your Internet connection runs through your television cable and is regulated by your cable TV provider. With the advent of digital cable, this reliable and speedy Internet connection is an excellent alternative. (See my speed report from my wireless network in **Figure 2-2.**) Most cable accounts include several e-mail addresses *plus* space to store your images.

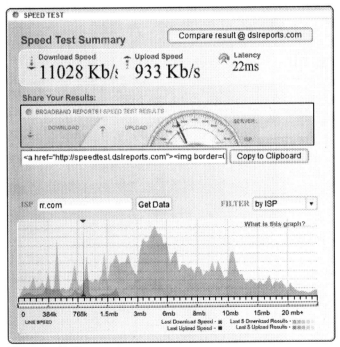

Figure 2-2

2. To join a telephone dial-up ISP (because dial-up uses the modem that resides in your computer and requires no additional equipment or connections), just load the freebie software that comes with a computer (or free at the computer store) into your CD drive and follow the registration steps that appear on your computer screen.

Have your credit card and lots of patience handy. With a little luck and no computer glitches, you'll have an active account and instant access to e-mail and the Internet in less than an hour.

3. Check out any information you can find about broadband connections available where you live. The quality of different broadband types (DSL and cable) can vary greatly from area to area and even from street to street. Pester your neighbor (again) to use his or her Internet connection and type www.broadbandreports.com in the browser's address bar. Click the Reviews tab, type your ZIP code in the appropriate text box, and read the reports from other users in your area (see **Figure 2-3**). You can send messages, post questions, and get all the information you need to decide what kind of high-speed connection will work best for you.

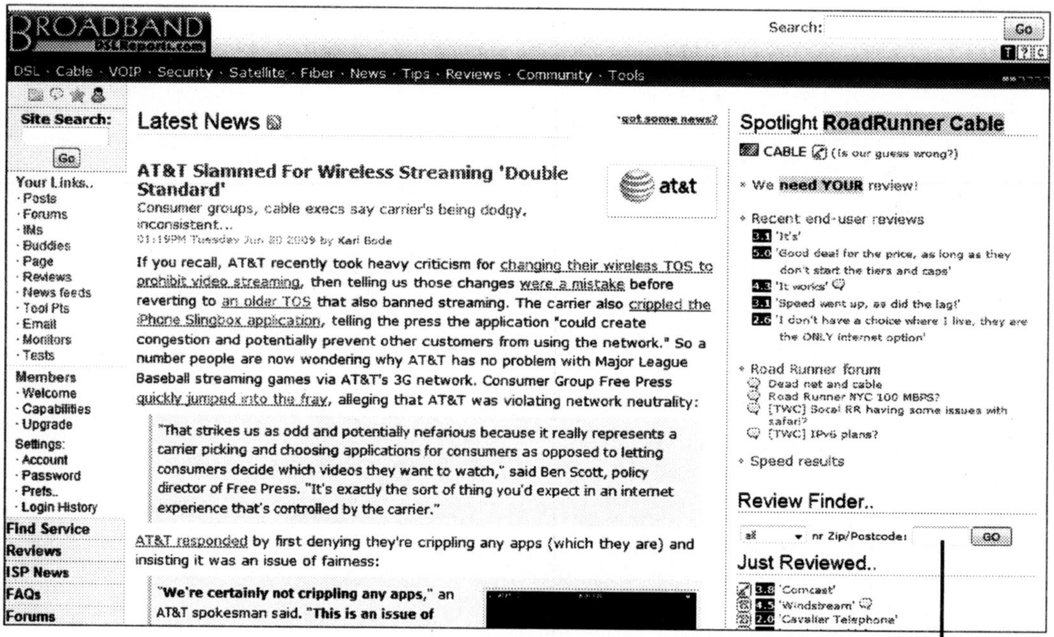

Type your ZIP code here for local reviews.

Figure 2-3

4. If you decide to get a broadband connection, contact the ISP you chose, make an appointment, and let them handle installing and setting up the equipment needed for connections.

Decide On an eBay User ID

1. Before you jump into eBay's registration process, think about how you'd like to be known on the site. Making up a user ID is always a pleasant chore. If you've never liked your real name or never had a nickname, here's your chance to correct that situation. Choose an ID that tells a little about you. Of course, if your interests change, you may regret choosing a user ID that's too narrow.

2. You can call yourself just about anything, but remember that this ID is how other eBay users will know you. Members' user IDs shows up on all listings, bids, and personal pages, as shown in **Figure 2-4**. Here are some guidelines that combine eBay's rules about user IDs and my suggestions:

- I say, "Don't use a name that would embarrass your mother," and eBay tells you to avoid user IDs that are offensive (such as *&*#@guy*).

- Don't use a name with a negative connotation, such as *scam-guy*. If people don't trust you, they won't buy from you.

- Don't use a name that's too weird, you know, something like *baby-vampire-penguin*. People may chuckle, but they may also question your sanity.

- Don't use names with *eBay* in them. (It makes you look like you work for eBay, and eBay takes a dim view of that.)

A user ID on My eBay

My eBay marsha_c (6807 ☆) 🏆 Power Seller ⬛

| Activity | Messages (85) | Account | 🖥 Page options | ✂ General settings |

🖶 Print | Help

Selling Manager Pro Summary
Last updated: Aug-06-09 20:39:38 PDT*

Summary

[Select a view ▼] [_____ ▼] [_____] [Search]

Buy
All Buying
Watch
Active
Won
Didn't Win
eBay Bucks
Deleted

At a glance Edit ▼

$5750 .... $5688.00
$4600
$3450 .... $3268.00
$2300 .... $1735.49
$1150 $37.73 $414.70
GMS(USD)
24 hrs 7 30 90 120
Time in days

Selling Manager Pro
Inventory (29)
Scheduled
Active (43)
Unsold (52)
Sold (148)
 Awaiting Payment
 Awaiting Shipment
 Paid & Shipped
Archived (27)
Reporting
Automation Preferences

Seller Dashboard Summary Edit ▼

Status

Search standing — Raised
PowerSeller discount — 20%
PowerSeller status —
Policy compliance — High
Buyer satisfaction — Good
Account status — Current

Go to your dashboard

Listing Activity Edit ▼

	Sales	# of Listings
Active Listings	$0.00	43
Listing with offers		0
Ending within the next hour		0
Ending today		0
Listings with questions		14
Listings with bids		0

Sold (last 90 days) Edit ▼

	Sales	# of Listings
All	$3,244.26	148
Awaiting Payment	$29.98	4

Figure 2-4

- Don't begin your user ID with an *e* followed by numbers, an underscore, a hyphen, a period, or *dot* (as in dot.com).

- Don't use names consisting of one letter (such as *Q* from *Star Trek*).

- eBay doesn't allow spaces in user IDs, so make sure that the ID makes sense when putting two or more words together. A friend of mine intended to register as "gang of one." She forgot the hyphens, so her ID reads *gangofone*.

- eBay also doesn't allow certain special characters, including & (even if you do have both *looks&brains*), @ (such as *@Aboy*), the greater than or less than symbols (> <), and consecutive underscores (__).

 Your ID can reflect your name too, or a nom de plume (if you're highly security minded). In these days of transparency, a buyer may feel more comfortable buying from *Steves-plumbing* than from *PlumbingGuy*. Whatever you choose as your user ID can become your brand. Once you get to selling in earnest, you can promote your brand (or name, if that's your ID) on social networking sites such as Facebook.

3. You can change your user ID once every 30 days if you want to, but I don't recommend it because people come to know you by your user ID. If you change your ID, your past does play tagalong and attaches itself to the new ID. But if you change your user ID too many times, people may think you're trying to hide something.

 If you change your user ID, an icon of a little blue character changing into a gold one appears next to your user ID. This icon stays next to your user ID for 30 days. Double-check when you see others with this icon. The world being what it is, they may have just changed their user IDs to mask a bad reputation. They can't hide it completely, though. You can find the dirt on anyone on eBay by reading their feedback profile.

 When you choose your user ID, make sure that it isn't a good clue for your password. For example, if you use *Natasha* as your user ID, don't choose *Boris* as your password. Even Bullwinkle could figure that one out.

Pick a Pickproof Password

1. Choosing a good password is not as easy (but is twice as important) as it may seem. Many passwords can be cracked by the right person in a matter of seconds. Your goal is to set a password that takes too much of the hackers' time. With the number of available users on eBay or PayPal, odds are they'll go to the next potential victim's password rather than spend too many minutes (or even hours) trying to crack yours.

2. As with any online password, you should follow these common-sense rules to protect your privacy:

- **Don't** choose anything too obvious, such as your birthday, your first name, contact numbers like your phone number or address (Got a phone book? So do the hackers...), and (*never* use this) your Social Security Number. (**Hint:** If it's too easy to remember, it's probably too easy to crack.) Also, don't use your, last name, your dog's name, or anyone's name. Again, it's common knowledge and easy to find out.

- **Don't** use strings of numbers, like Ringo Starr's birthday or your best friend's anniversary. Not only are these dates common knowledge, but so is this truism: A series of numbers is easy to crack.

- **Don't** give out your password to anyone — it's like giving away the keys to the front door of your house.

- **Don't** use the obvious: The word *password*. D'oh!

- **Don't** use any of the lousy (easily cracked and most frequently used) passwords in **Table 2-1**. The words in this table have been gleaned from password dictionaries available from hackers. *Note:* This is *not* a complete list by any means; there are thousands of common (lousy) passwords, and "unprintable" ones are a lot more common than you may think.

Table 2-1		Passwords to Avoid		
!@#$%	!@#$%^&	!@#$%^&*(	0	0000
00000000	0007	007	01234	123456
02468	24680	1	1101	111
11111	111111	1234	12345	1234qwer
123abc	123go	12	131313	212
310	2003	2004	54321	654321
888888	A	aaa	abc	abc123
action	absolut	access	admin	admin123
access	administrator	alpha	asdf	animal
biteme	computer	eBay	enable	foobar
home	internet	Login	love	mypass
mypc	owner	pass	password	passwrd
papa	peace	penny	pepsi	qwerty
secret	sunshine	temp	temp123	test
test123	whatever	whatnot	winter	windows
xp	xxx	yoda	mypc123	powerseller
sexy	jesus	firstname	faith	

3. Now that you know what not to do, try constructing a password by using whatever combination of letters and numbers you can come up with — only alternate CaPItal letters with lowercase. (Passwords are case sensitive.) And remember the following goals for setting and maintaining a strong, pickproof password:

- **Do** make things tough on the bad guys — combine numbers and letters (use uppercase and lowercase) or create nonsensical words.

- **Do** change your password *immediately* if you ever suspect someone has it. You can change your password by going to the Account Information area of your My eBay.

 Whoever has your password can (in effect) "be you" at eBay — running auctions, bidding on auctions, and leaving possibly litigious feedback for others. Basically, such an impostor can ruin your eBay career — and possibly cause you serious financial grief.

- **Do** change your password every few months just to be on the safe side.

 It should go without saying, but what the hey: Don't use any of the sample passwords shown here. It's safe to say that lots of people will be reading this book, and anything seen by lots of people isn't secret. (I know you know that, but still.)

Register to Deal on eBay

1. Before you can sign up on eBay, you have to be connected to the Web, so now's the time to fire up your computer. After you open your Internet browser, you're ready to sign up. In the address box of your browser, type www.ebay.com and press Enter.

2. Your next stop is the eBay home page. Under the Sign In button, where you can't miss it, is the Register link — it's "fast and free!" Click this link and let the sign-up process begin. You can get to the Registration form also by clicking the Register link next to the eBay logo at the top of the page. When you're at the Registration form, you go through a four-step process. Here's an overview:

    1. Enter the basic required info.

    2. Read and accept the User Agreement.

    3. Confirm your e-mail address.

 Hey, AOL users, this one's for you. If you have Internet e-mail blocked, you may need to update your AOL Mail Controls to receive e-mail from eBay. To do so, enter the AOL keyword **Mail Controls**.

    4. Breeze through the optional information.

3. You register on eBay through an encrypted connection called SSL (Secure Sockets Layer). You can tell because the normal `http` at the beginning of the Web address is now `https` and a small closed padlock may appear at the bottom-left (or bottom-right) corner of your screen.

 The padlock icon means that eBay has moved you to a secure place on their site that is safe from unauthorized people seeing or receiving your information. Your information is treated with the highest security and you can fill out these forms with the utmost confidence. I could tell you how SSL works, but instead, I'll just give you the bottom line: It *does* work; so trust me and use it. The more precautions eBay (and you) take, the harder it is for some hyper-caffeinated high-school kid to get into your data.

Fill In Required Information

1. After you click Register, you go to the first registration page. At the top of the page, eBay asks you to fill in some required identification information (see **Figure 2-5**), as follows:

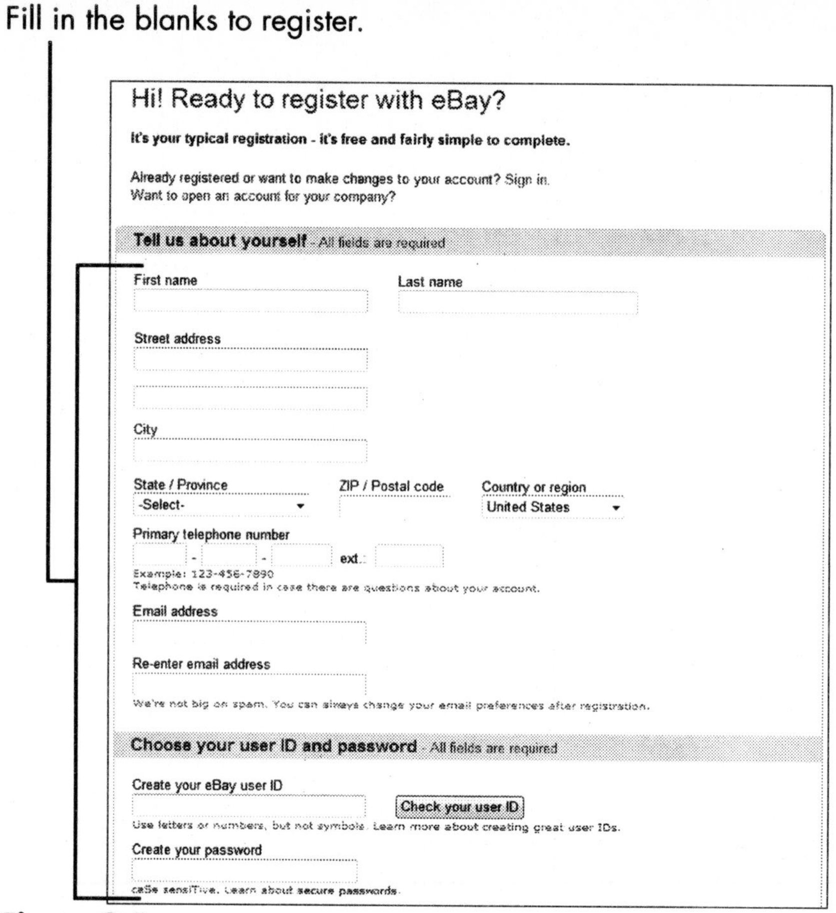

Fill in the blanks to register.

Hi! Ready to register with eBay?

It's your typical registration - it's free and fairly simple to complete.

Already registered or want to make changes to your account? Sign in.
Want to open an account for your company?

Tell us about yourself - All fields are required

First name

Last name

Street address

City

State / Province
-Select-

ZIP / Postal code

Country or region
United States

Primary telephone number

ext.

Example: 123-456-7890
Telephone is required in case there are questions about your account.

Email address

Re-enter email address

We're not big on spam. You can always change your email preferences after registration.

Choose your user ID and password - All fields are required

Create your eBay user ID

Check your user ID

Use letters or numbers, but not symbols. Learn more about creating great user IDs.

Create your password

caSe sensiTive. Learn about secure passwords.

Figure 2-5

- Your full name, address, and primary telephone number. eBay keeps this information on file in case the company (or a member who is a transaction partner) needs to contact you.

- Your e-mail address (*yourname@myISP.com*). If you register with an *anonymous e-mail service* such as Yahoo! Mail, Gmail, or Hotmail, you go to a page that requires additional information for authentication. You must provide valid credit-card information for identification purposes. Your information is protected by eBay's privacy policy, and your credit card won't be charged.

 It's safe to use your personal e-mail address for eBay registration. You will not be put on any spurious e-mail lists.

• Your new eBay user ID (see the earlier task, "Decide On an eBay User ID" for ideas on creating your user ID). If your chosen ID is already taken, eBay has a handy tool to help you select another one, as shown in **Figure** 2-6.

See eBay's recommended IDs here.

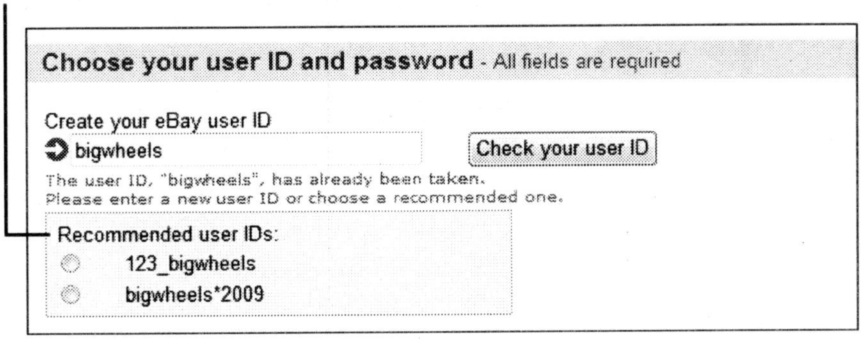

Choose your user ID and password - All fields are required

Create your eBay user ID

⟳ bigwheels   [Check your user ID]

The user ID, "bigwheels", has already been taken.
Please enter a new user ID or choose a recommended one.

┌ Recommended user IDs:
    ◯   123_bigwheels
    ◯   bigwheels*2009

Figure 2-6

• Your chosen password (see the earlier task, "Pick a Pickproof Password"). Type the password in the Create Your Password box and then type it a second time in the Re-enter Your Password box to confirm it.

2. Next, eBay prompts you for information it uses for verification purposes.

• Pick your secret question and input the answer. eBay uses the secret question you select here as a security test should you need help to remember your password.

You have six choices for your secret question. I suggest you do not select the "What is your mother's maiden name?" question because banks and financial institutions often use this question for identification. Guard your mother's maiden name and don't give it out to anyone blithely. Select one of the other questions and fill in the answer.

- Fill in your date of birth. eBay needs your birth date for two reasons. First, they want to be sure that you are of legal age to do business on eBay, and second, they may want to send you a nice birthday e-mail!

3. Make sure all the info you entered is correct. Think back to your grade school teacher, who kept saying, "Class, check your work." Remember that? She's still right! Review your answers.

 If eBay finds a glitch in your registration, such as an incorrect area code or ZIP code, you'll see a warning message on the next page. This is part of eBay's security system to ward off fraudulent registrations. Use the Back button to correct the information — if you put in a wrong e-mail address, for example, eBay has no way of contacting you. So you won't hear a peep from eBay regarding your registration until you go through the entire process all over again.

4. Click the link to see the eBay User Agreement and Privacy Policy. At this page, you take an oath to keep eBay safe for democracy and commerce. You promise to play well with others, to not cheat, and to follow the golden rule. No, you're not auditioning for a superhero club, but don't ever forget that eBay takes this stuff seriously.

5. I encourage you to read the User Agreement thoroughly when you register. So that you don't have to put down this riveting book to read the legalese right this minute, I show you part of the agreement (as found in eBay's Help area) in **Figure 2-7** and provide the nuts and bolts here.

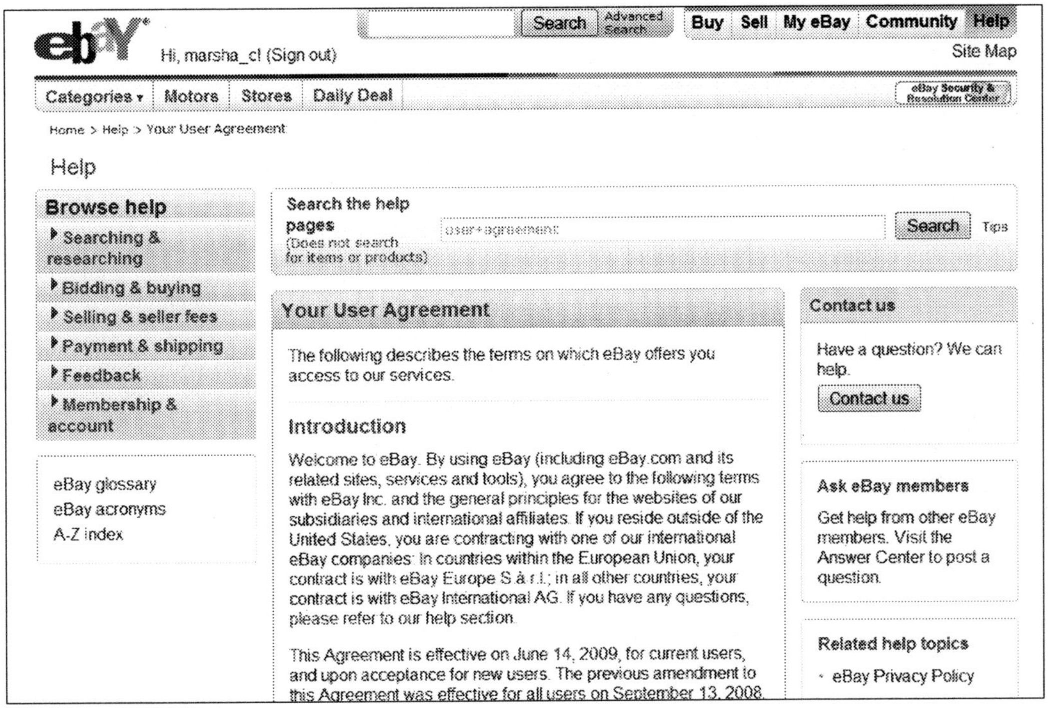

Figure 2-7

Be sure

- You understand that every transaction is a legally binding contract. (Click the User Agreement link at the bottom of any eBay page for the current eBay rules and regulations.)

- You agree that you can pay for the items you buy and the eBay fees that you incur.

- You understand that you're responsible for paying any taxes.

- You're aware that if you sell prohibited items, eBay can forward your personal information to law enforcement for further investigation.

 In the eBay User Agreement, eBay makes clear that it is just a *venue*, which means it's a place where people with similar interests can meet, greet, and do business. When everything goes well, the eBay Web site is like a school gym that opens for Saturday swap meets. At the gym, if you don't play by the rules, you can get tossed out. And if you don't play by the rules at eBay, the venue gets un-gymlike in a hurry. But fair's fair; eBay keeps you posted by e-mail of any updates in the User Agreement.

6. If you're a stickler for fine print, head to this link for all the *Ps* and *Qs* of the latest policies `http://pages.ebay.com/help/policies/privacy-policy.html`. Before you can proceed, you have to click a check box that indicates you really, really understand what it means to be an eBay user — and agree to the terms. Then, because I know that you (as a law-abiding eBay member) will have no problem following the rules, go ahead and click the Continue button at the bottom of the page — which takes you to a screen stating that eBay is sending you an e-mail at the e-mail address you supplied earlier in the registration process. You're almost finished.

7. When you receive the confirmation e-mail, click the Complete eBay Registration link to continue your registration. If your e-mail doesn't support links, go to this address:

```
http://cgi4.ebay.com/ws/eBayISAPI.
  dll?RegisterConfirmCode
```

You see the page shown in **Figure 2-8**. After you recon-
nect with eBay and type your e-mail address and confirmation code from the e-mail you received from eBay.
Then click Create My Account. Once eBay knows your
e-mail address is active, you'll be heartily congratulated
with a welcome screen.

Type your confirmation code from eBay here.

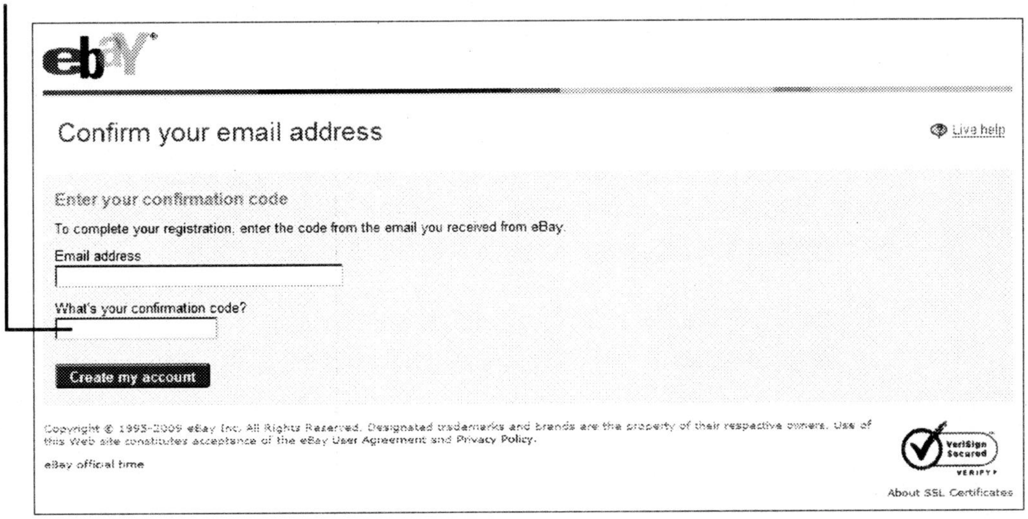

Figure 2-8

8. You are now officially a *newbie*, or eBay rookie. The only
problem is that you're still at the window-shopping level.
If you're ready to go from window shopper to item seller,
just click the Sell button in the navigation bar. You'll
have to fill out a few more forms, and before you know
it, you can start running your own auctions at eBay.

9. Now that you're a full-fledged, officially registered member of the eBay community, you may see an eBay pop-up
window, giving you the option to provide more information about yourself. These optional questions allow you
to fill in your self-portrait for your new pals at eBay. See
Chapter 9 for more information on adding your personal
touch with an About Me page and your My World page.

Until you've been a member of eBay for 30 days, a picture of a beaming, golden cartoonlike icon is next to your user ID wherever it appears on the site. This doesn't mean you've been converted into a golden robot; the icon merely indicates to other eBay users that you're new to eBay.

Redo Registration (If You Mess Up Your E-Mail Address)

1. In the unlikely event that you don't receive your eBay registration confirmation e-mail within 24 hours, your e-mail address most likely contains an error. At this point, the customer-support folks can help you complete the registration process. Go to the following address

```
http://pages.ebay.com/services/
    registration/reqtemppass.html
```

and enter your e-mail address. Click Resend Email. You will receive another e-mail with a special one-time confirmation password.

2. If, for some reason (brain cramp is a perfectly acceptable excuse), you incorrectly type the wrong e-mail address, you have to start the registration process all over again with a different user ID (eBay holds the previous ID for 30 days).

3. If at any time you run into a snag, you can click the Contact Us link that appears on the eBay home page. You will then arrive at the Contact Us page shown in **Figure 2-9**; then follow these steps:

Type here and click Ask.

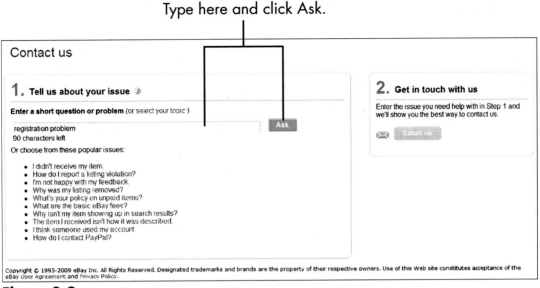

Figure 2-9

1. *Type* **Registration Problem** *into the query box.*

2. *Click* Ask.

3. *From the suggested list of problems, click on the one that says* I'm having registration problems.

4. *You will then be presented with a link to click that goes to the most common problems, as show in* **Figure 2-10**.

5. *If you'd prefer, you can look to the right side of the page and click* Chat with Us *to open a chat window. It will allow you to talk (through typing) to a real person in real time.*

6. *You can also click the* Call Us *box which will present you with a toll free number to call, along with a PIN number that will be good for only one hour. You will have to key the PIN number into your phone once you've connected to eBay.*

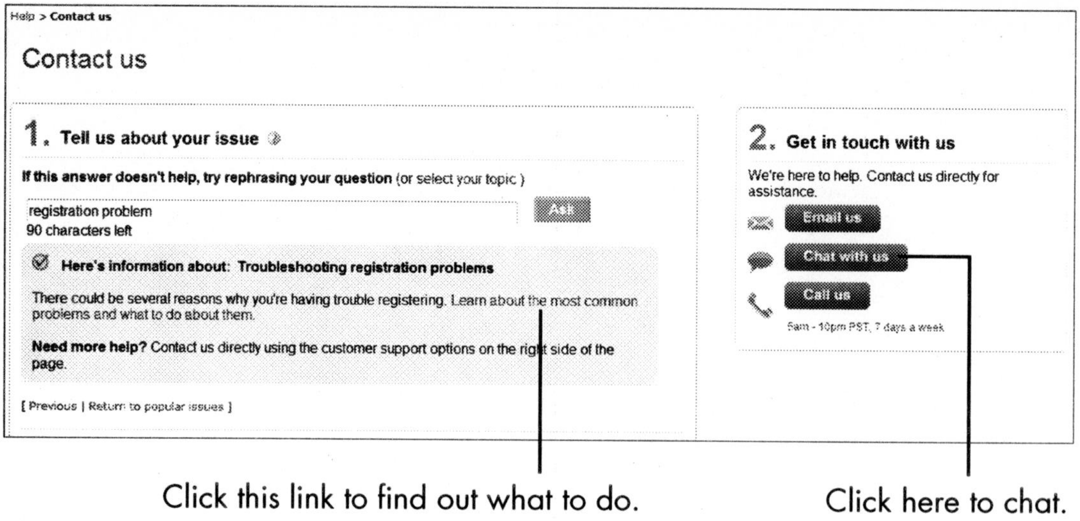

Help > **Contact us**

Contact us

1. Tell us about your issue ✎

If this answer doesn't help, try rephrasing your question (or select your topic)

registration problem
90 characters left   Ask

✅ **Here's information about: Troubleshooting registration problems**

There could be several reasons why you're having trouble registering. Learn about the most common problems and what to do about them.

Need more help? Contact us directly using the customer support options on the right side of the page.

[Previous | Return to popular issues]

2. Get in touch with us

We're here to help. Contact us directly for assistance.

✉ Email us

💬 Chat with us

📞 Call us

5am - 10pm PST, 7 days a week

Click this link to find out what to do.   Click here to chat.

Figure 2-10

Know Your Payment Options

1. Several payment options are available for your eBay purchases, but eBay only allows sellers to show electronic payment methods. The seller is not required to accept any form of payment except PayPal or one of the other electronic payment options (ProPay, Paymate, Moneybookers or a merchant account).

 If you want to make a payment in the form of a check or money order, use the Ask a Question link that you find on an item listing (see Chapter 3) — and ask if you can!

2. Take a minute and get familiar with the forms of payment available to you. Then you can decide whether you want to register with PayPal (which I talk about in the next section). You can pay by

- **Credit card:** Paying with a credit card is a favorite payment option for many buyers, one that's offered mainly by businesses and dealers. I like paying with credit cards because they're fast and efficient. In addition, using a credit card offers you another ally, your credit card company, if you're not completely satisfied with the transaction. Credit cards can also be used for payment through the other electronic payment options (such as PayPal, which I prefer) that a seller may offer.

 Sometimes sellers use a friend's company to run credit card payments for eBay auctions. So don't be surprised if you buy a vintage Tonka bulldozer and your credit card is billed from Holly's Hair-o-Rama.

- **PayPal:** I pay for all my eBay purchases through PayPal. Owned by eBay, PayPal is the largest Internet-wide payment network. Sellers who accept PayPal are identified in the Seller Info box and a PayPal logo in the item description, as shown in **Figure 2-11**. PayPal allows these sellers to accept MasterCard, Visa, American Express, and Discover as well as electronic checks and debits. The service is integrated directly into eBay auctions, so paying is a mouse click away.

 After you register with PayPal to pay for an item, PayPal debits your credit card or your bank checking account and sends the payment to the seller's account. PayPal does not charge buyers to use the service. Buyers can use PayPal to pay any seller within the United States (and around the world in over 55 countries).

Portable INFINITY Backdrop Photo STAGE
Cloud Dome 18x28
Authorized CLOUD DOME Dealer - POWERSELLER - 100% FB

Item condition: **New**

Quantity	1	3 available
Price:	**US $40.99**	**Buy It Now**
	This item is being tracked in My eBay.	

Shipping: **FREE** US Postal Service Parcel Post See more services ▾ | See all details
Estimated delivery within 3-10 business days

Returns: 7 day exchange, buyer pays return shipping | Read details

Coverage: Pay with **PayPal** and your full purchase price is covered | See terms

Top-rated seller
marsha_c
(6804 ☆) 100%

✓ Consistently receives highest buyers' ratings
✓ Ships items quickly
✓ Has earned a track record of excellent service

Ask a question
See other items
Visit 🔲 Marsha Collier's Finds

Other item info

Item number:	180291360698
Item location:	Los Angeles, US
Ships to:	Worldwide
Payments:	PayPal, merchant credit card See all
Purchase:	251 See history

This seller accepts PayPal.

Figure 2-11

Your credit card information is known only to the PayPal service; the seller never sees it. You also have protection behind you when you use PayPal. When you use PayPal to pay for a qualified eBay item from a Verified PayPal member, you are covered by PayPal's Buyer Protection program for the full purchase price.

- **Money order:** As a seller, my second-favorite method of receiving payment is the money order. Sellers love money orders because they don't have to wait for a check to clear. Money orders are the same as cash. As soon as the seller gets your money order, he or she has no reason to wait to send the item. You can buy money orders at banks, supermarkets, convenience stores, and your local post office. The average cost is about a dollar.

- **Personal or cashier's check:** Again, you have to ask the seller whether he or she will accept a check. Paying by check is convenient but has its drawbacks. Most sellers won't ship you the goods until after your check clears, which means a lag time of a couple of weeks or more. The good news about checks is that you can track whether or not they've been cashed. The bad news about checks is that you're revealing personal information, such as your bank account number, to a stranger. Cashier's checks are available at your bank but often cost much more than a money order. It's not worth the extra money — have fun and buy more eBay items instead.

Never use a form of payment that doesn't let you keep a paper trail. **Don't wire money, and never send cash in the mail!** If a seller asks for cash, quote Nancy Reagan and just say *no*. Chances are that you may never see the item or your money again. Oh, yeah, here's something else — if a seller asks you to send your payment to a post office box, get a phone number. Many legitimate sellers use post office boxes, but so do the bad guys.

Set Up a PayPal Account

1. The convenience of PayPal's integration with eBay shines when you (or your buyer) clicks the Pay Now button that shows up at the end of a transaction or on an invoice. If you aren't registered with PayPal yet, you'll find a convenient link on the left side of your My eBay page in the Shortcuts box, as shown in **Figure 2-12**. To register, just click the PayPal link. The PayPal Seller Overview page appears. Click the Sign Up button, and you arrive at the beginning of the PayPal registration process.

Figure 2-12

 Signing up with PayPal is safe. PayPal has had my credit cards and bank accounts on file since its inception, and I've never had a security breach. PayPal uses the extra security measure (called CVV2 and provided by Visa and MasterCard) that involves the three additional numbers found on the back of your credit card. I not only pay for my eBay purchases through this safe, handy account, but I also pay other people (who, like my plumber, don't normally accept credit cards), too. It's a great service that's convenient for both buyers and sellers.

2. Now it's time to decide the type of PayPal account you want. This decision isn't as simple as it might seem from **Figure 2-13**. Everyone I speak to always wants to click the Personal account, because they figure they will just want to shop online.

 Signing up for a Premier account at this point makes sense. You can register more than one credit card and more than one bank account (one for personal transactions and one for business). This way, when you start to sell, you'll have a history of transactions with PayPal, and you won't be treated like a newbie.

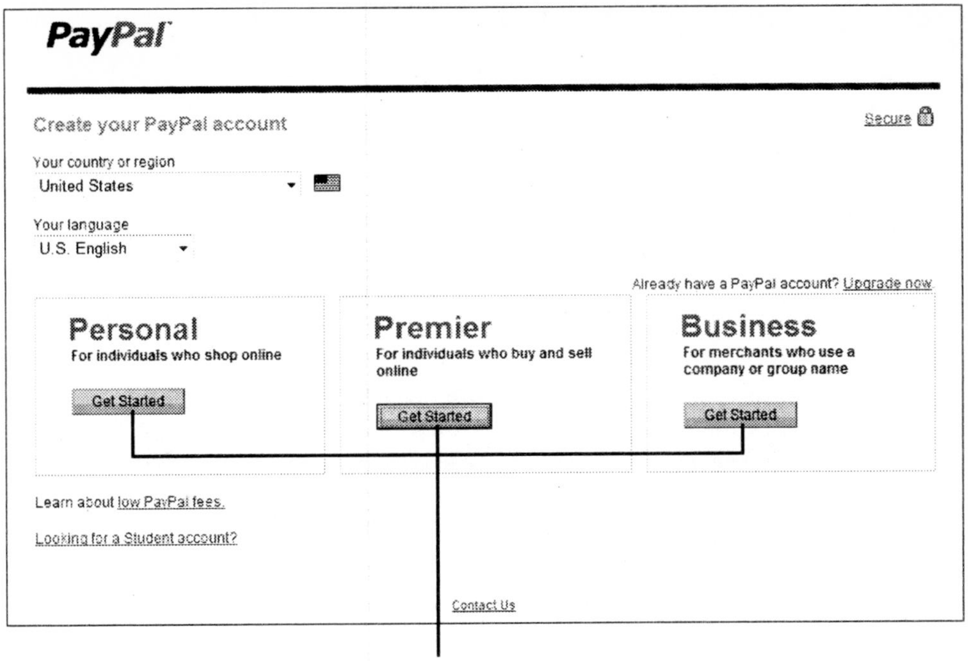

PayPal

Create your PayPal account   Secure 🔒

Your country or region
United States   ▾ ▦

Your language
U.S. English   ▾

Already have a PayPal account? Upgrade now

Personal
For individuals who shop online

[Get Started]

Premier
For individuals who buy and sell online

[Get Started]

Business
For merchants who use a company or group name

[Get Started]

Learn about low PayPal fees.

Looking for a Student account?

Contact Us

Choose one of the account types.

Figure 2-13

3. Choose your account type and follow the steps to enter your personal information, and add a credit card (or cards) for shopping and bank account information for the accounts you intend to use. Your bank account information is needed for a couple of reasons.

1. *PayPal needs to verify that you are indeed, you.* So they will deposit small change into your checking account. Once they do that, you go back to the PayPal site and confirm the amounts.

2. *Your bank account is where PayPal will need to deposit the money you'll be making when selling on the site* — or withdraw money from should you prefer not to use a credit card for your purchases.

Navigating the eBay Site

*W*hen you first get to the eBay site, you might think you have to be Ferdinand Magellan to find your way around. It's a huge site with lots of twists and turns, but have no fear! Follow the leads in this chapter, and you'll be zooming around like a pro.

I give you the inside scoop on finding your way around, including

➡ **The navigation bar:** eBay has some key places to visit, and generally, the navigation bar (which I describe in this chapter's first task, "Tune In to the eBay Home Page") is the quickest way to get from hither to yon.

➡ **Shortcuts and insights:** Although the eBay home page may seem like the best place to start, I'll give you some easy-to-use alternatives, as well as showing you a few of the fun, hidden features of eBay.

So loosen your fingers. I'm going to show you the way to find just what you're looking for on the eBay site!

Chapter 3

Get Ready to...

Tune In to the eBay Home Page

1. Starting at beginning is the most sensible place, so why not point your browser to the eBay home page (type www.ebay.com in your browser's address bar and press Enter). Do not attempt to adjust your computer monitor if the home page doesn't look exactly like **Figure 3-1**.

 You're not going crazy. eBay changes the home page from minute to minute to reflect what's going on — not just on the site, but in the world as well. Today you may notice that a link that was on the eBay home page yesterday is gone. That's normal.

2. Check out the key areas from the eBay *home page* via the master navigation bar at the top of the page. Its five link boxes can take you directly to many of the important eBay areas. If you *hover* your mouse pointer (that means to put the pointer over the link and let it sit there), you see a drop-down menu; **Figure 3-2** shows the menu that appeared when I hovered over the My eBay link. Click these various links — at least once — just to see what's available to you. Here's what you find:

- **Buy** takes you to the page that lists all the main eBay categories, as well as links to popular stores and eBay promotions that vary from time to time.

- **Sell:** Takes you to a page where you can start the process of listing an item for sale. (I explain how to navigate this form in Chapter 13.) The links at the bottom of the page direct you to various Seller Guides. (Mosey on now, there's not much to see there.)

- **My eBay:** Takes you to your personal My eBay page, where you keep track of all your buying and selling activities, account information, and favorite categories. (There's more about My eBay later in the chapter.)

Choose categories to shop.

Click here to sign in or register.

Navigation bar

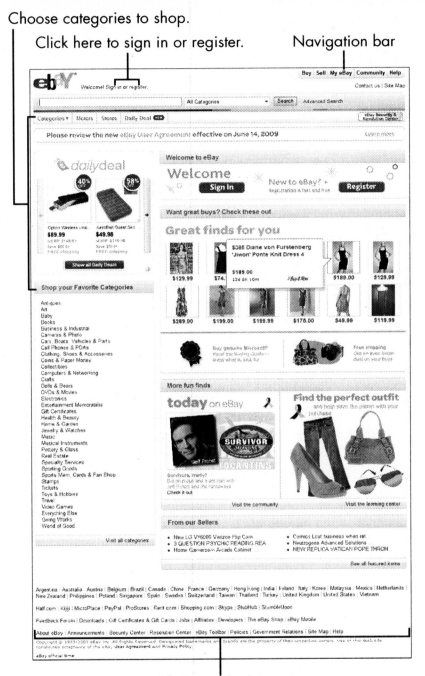

Tons of links on the home page

Figure 3-1

Hover on a link for the drop-down list.

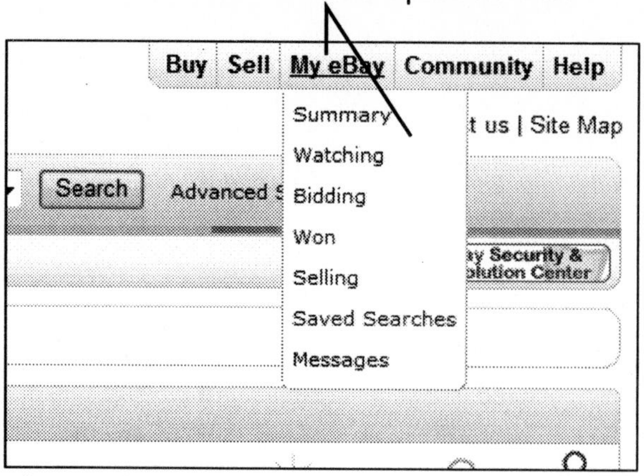

Figure 3-2

- **Community:** Takes you to a page where you can find the latest news and announcements, chat with fellow traders in the eBay community, find charity auctions, and find out more about eBay.

- **Help:** Takes you to one of the most valuable areas of the eBay site. **Figure 3-3** shows the Help area where you can get answers to many of your questions, as well as stay apprised of eBay's rules and regulations that govern trading on the site. The eBay Help overview page consists of a search box, where you can type your query, links for browsing help topics, an A–Z index, a list of the top five questions on eBay, and a link to the eBay Answer Center.

3. Check out the links at the top of the eBay home page. There you find several powerful links (below the navigation bar, as in **Figure 3-4**) that are just as important as the links on the navigation bar. These are

- **eBay Logo:** Click the eBay logo from any page on the site, and it takes you right back to the home page.

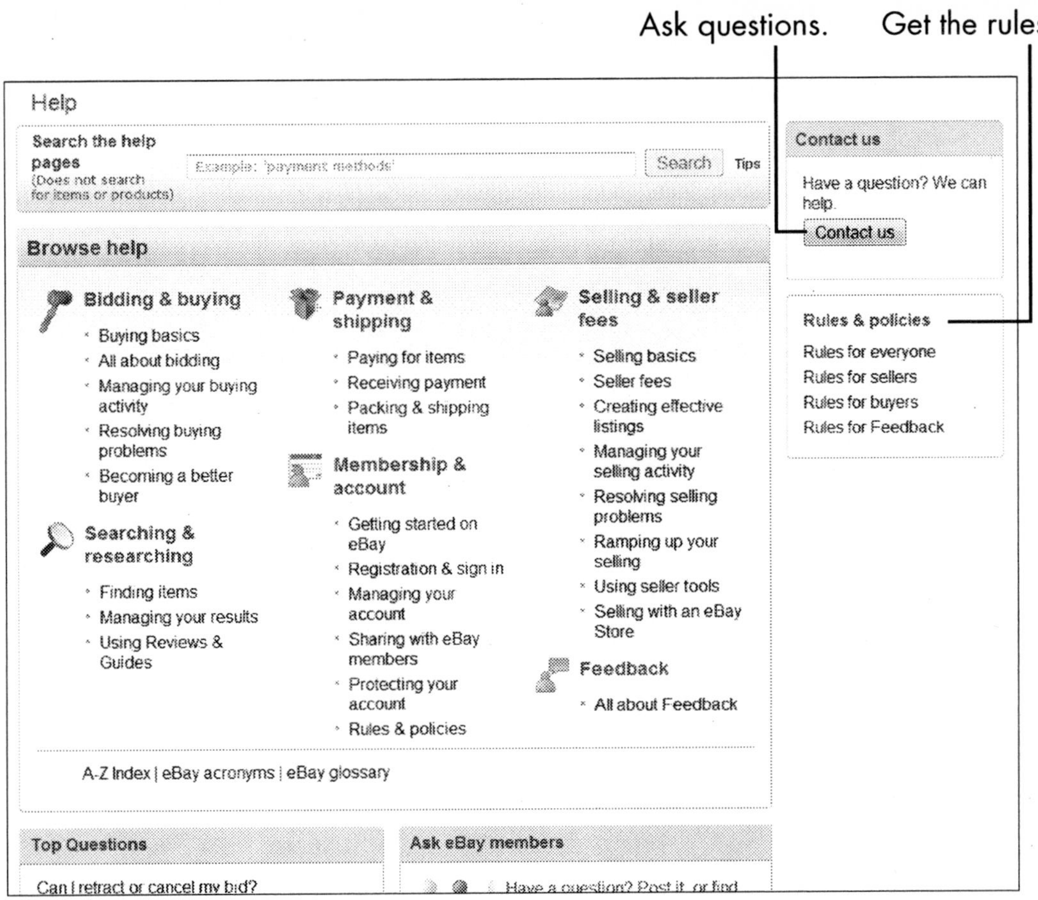

Ask questions.   Get the rules.

Help

Search the help pages
(Does not search for items or products)

Example: 'payment methods'   [Search]   Tips

Contact us

Have a question? We can help.

[Contact us]

Browse help

Bidding & buying
- Buying basics
- All about bidding
- Managing your buying activity
- Resolving buying problems
- Becoming a better buyer

Searching & researching
- Finding items
- Managing your results
- Using Reviews & Guides

Payment & shipping
- Paying for items
- Receiving payment
- Packing & shipping items

Membership & account
- Getting started on eBay
- Registration & sign in
- Managing your account
- Sharing with eBay members
- Protecting your account
- Rules & policies

Selling & seller fees
- Selling basics
- Seller fees
- Creating effective listings
- Managing your selling activity
- Resolving selling problems
- Ramping up your selling
- Using seller tools
- Selling with an eBay Store

Feedback
- All about Feedback

Rules & policies
Rules for everyone
Rules for sellers
Rules for buyers
Rules for Feedback

A-Z Index | eBay acronyms | eBay glossary

Top Questions

Can I retract or cancel my bid?

Ask eBay members

Have a question? Post it, or find

Figure 3-3

Click here for the home page.

ebay®   Welcome! Sign in or register.

Buy | Sell | My eBay | Community | Help

Contact us | Site Map

All Categories ▾   [Search]   Advanced Search

Categories ▾ | Motors | Stores | Daily Deal NEW   eBay Security & Resolution Center

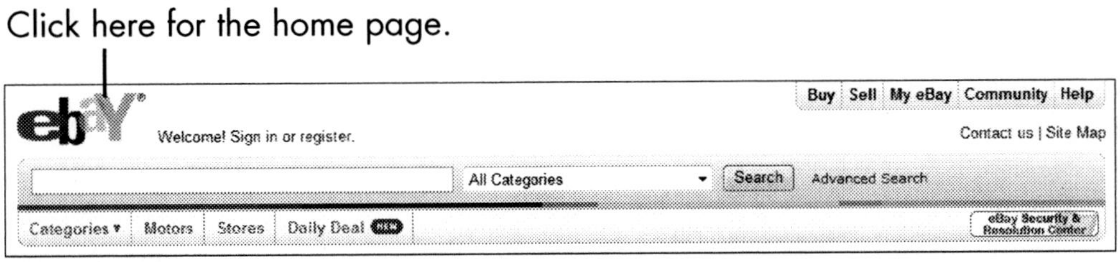

Figure 3-4

- **Sign In or Register:** Click Register to become a member of the eBay community (as I describe in Chapter 2). If you're already a member and signed in, the Register link isn't visible. If you click the Sign In link, go to the

Sign In page, and then sign in, you may not have to enter your user ID again that day (for details, see the later section "Sign In Before You Look Around").

- **Contact Us:** Click this link and you'll either have to sign in (on the resulting page) or use a bold link that says *I'm a Guest* to get you into eBay. Click there, and you're taken to the Contact Us page.

- **Site Map:** Provides you with a bird's-eye view of the eBay world. Every *top-level* (that is, main) link available on eBay is listed here. If you're ever confused about finding a specific area, try the Site Map first. I use this page all the time.

Get Around by Using the Drop-Down Menus

1. You can go where you want on eBay in a more direct fashion by using the drop-down menu.

 Keep in mind that all informational links provided to you by eBay in these drop-down menus are just that: *from eBay.* They may be influenced by advertising deals, alliances with providers . . . get the drift? Do not ever consider the information you get as unbiased. Know that this book is unbiased — I have no sponsors or advertisers to please.

2. Try hovering your mouse pointer over the Buy link in the navigation bar. As shown in **Figure 3-5**, here's what you find:

- **Browse Categories:** This option takes you to a list of all categories and their first-level subcategories. Browsing categories takes a lot of time. In Chapter 4, I show you how to search for just what you want.

- **Help with Buying and Bidding:** You already have that, right? After all, you bought this book — and I can guarantee that I've bought more on eBay than almost any eBay employee. Just jump over to Chapter 6 for the inside scoop.

- **Buyer Tools:** Hmmm, the only "buyer tools" I'm interested in are a credit card and my PayPal account. Keep in mind that anything you download to your computer will track what you do. "Free" tools are not created purely out of the goodness of any company's heart; they're written to sign people up, get data, and then sell such data at a profit. Get it?

- **Reviews & Guides:** Here's where you can participate in the eBay community by writing guides and reviewing products (even fine books like this one). If you're here to make money, perhaps you might be better spending your time honing your sales skills and selling items? Just a thought. . . .

- **eBay Mobile:** You want eBay to call you on your cell phone? They will do it for a fee, so perhaps you might pass. You can check your eBay listings for free on a Web-enabled cell phone by going to m.ebay.com.

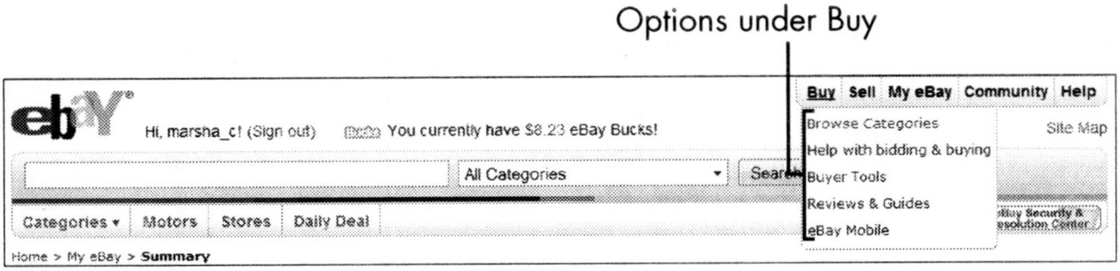

Options under Buy

Figure 3-5

3. The Sell drop-down menu gives you the following options through convenient links:

- **Sell an Item:** Here's your direct link to the Sell an Item form. Try to remember to click here directly when you want to list an item for sale — one step is easier than two, especially when the first step has promotional information.

- **Selling Tips:** You have this one covered. Let's just say that whoever wrote these tips probably read an earlier edition of this book.

- **What's Hot:** This connects you to eBay Pulse (`pulse.ebay.com`). It's a fun area that lets you view (by category, if you want) the most popular searches on eBay. Treat this information as a market gauge rather than as gospel. There's a sample in **Figure 3-6**.

See popular searches in any category.

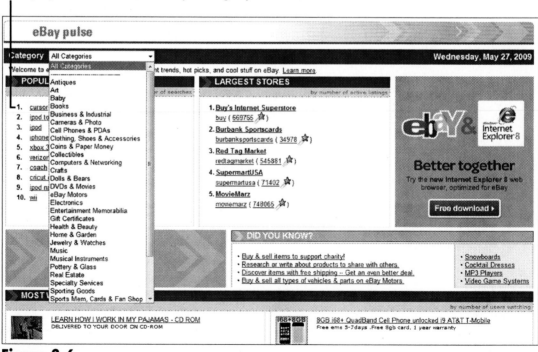

Figure 3-6

- **Seller Tools & eBay Stores:** Here's a quick link to the tools eBay offers, such as Selling Manager. Take my advice and follow my lead in this book; don't subscribe to any of these tools until you're ready. They'll just drain your wallet otherwise.

- **Shipping Center:** This link takes you to eBay's Shipping Center, which is a handy way to get to the Shipping Calculator (and plenty of useful links). And because UPS and the USPS are "partners" with eBay, and business is business, you won't find info on my favorite ground shipper, FedEx Ground. (See Chapter 14 to get the full picture of who you should ship with.)

4. Feel free to check out the drop-down menus for the remaining link boxes on the navigation bar (My eBay, Community, and Help). I don't list all the menu items here, but I do give these eBay areas their own sections later in this chapter.

Search eBay or Browse Beyond

1. Right below the eBay logo on the home page, you see a search box that helps you find items by several methods. You can type in title keywords, use a drop-down list to choose categories to search, and zero in on specific items by clicking a link to eBay's Advanced Search page. (Handy search tricks of the trade are exposed in Chapter 4.)

2. Below the search box, you find more link boxes (similar to those in the navigation bar), including

- **Categories:** Click here for a drop-down tab showing the complete listing of top-level categories.

- **Motors:** Click this direct link to eBay Motors.

- **Stores:** Click here and go directly to eBay Stores.

- **Daily Deal:** Click here to find featured items, fun stuff such as charity auctions, and information about what else is moving on eBay.

3. Along the left of the page, you find an expandable list of links that lead to the most popular auction categories.

4. If you are signed in to your eBay account when you go to the home page, you'll see a different view, as in **Figure 3-7.** eBay presents item views — recommendations of other items you might like — based on your previous searches and items purchased. Crafty isn't it? The way those eBay servers know all about you?

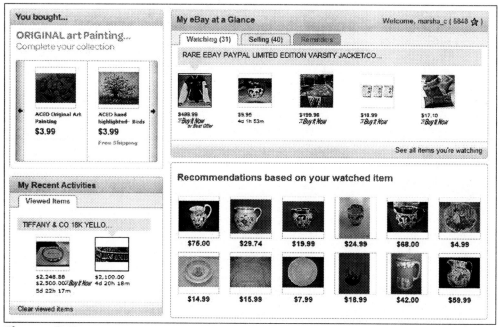

Figure 3-7

5. Near the bottom of the home page, notice the several other links that give you express service to key parts of the site. Here you find links to eBay's international auction sites (a quick and easy way to shop the world), more eBay-owned sites (such as Half.com and Kijiji), eBay service areas (such as the Feedback Forum, or Gift Certificate and Gift Cards), and information and help areas (such as Announcements and the Security Center).

 Why not send someone an eBay gift certificate for any special occasion? You can print it yourself, or eBay will send it to any e-mail address you provide. The gift certificate is good for any item on the site for the value you specify, and you can pay for it immediately with PayPal. If the person you give the gift certificate to bids higher than the value of the gift certificate, he or she can make up the difference using another payment option.

Sign In Before You Look Around

1. You can search for items on eBay without signing in, but what fun is that? If you haven't registered with eBay, you're pretty much out of luck if you find a great deal on a lamp that's just what you've been looking for — and the auction closes in five minutes! See Chapter 2 for the details on registering; then sign in so you don't miss a thing!

2. Click the Sign In link on the home page or at the top of any eBay page. You arrive at the sign-in page, as shown in **Figure 3-8.**

3. Type your user ID and password in the boxes where indicated. And select the Keep Me Signed In for Today check box — as long as you're not at a public computer.

 The Sign In process places a *cookie* (a technical thingy that identifies you to eBay) on your computer. On the Sign In page, click to check the box that says

Keep Me Signed In for Today. When you do, the cookie remains a part of your computer for the rest of the day. If you don't check the box, you stay signed in only while your browser is open. After you close your browser, the cookie expires, and you have to sign in again.

4. Click the Sign In button, and you're signed in to eBay where you can search and transact on the site with ease.

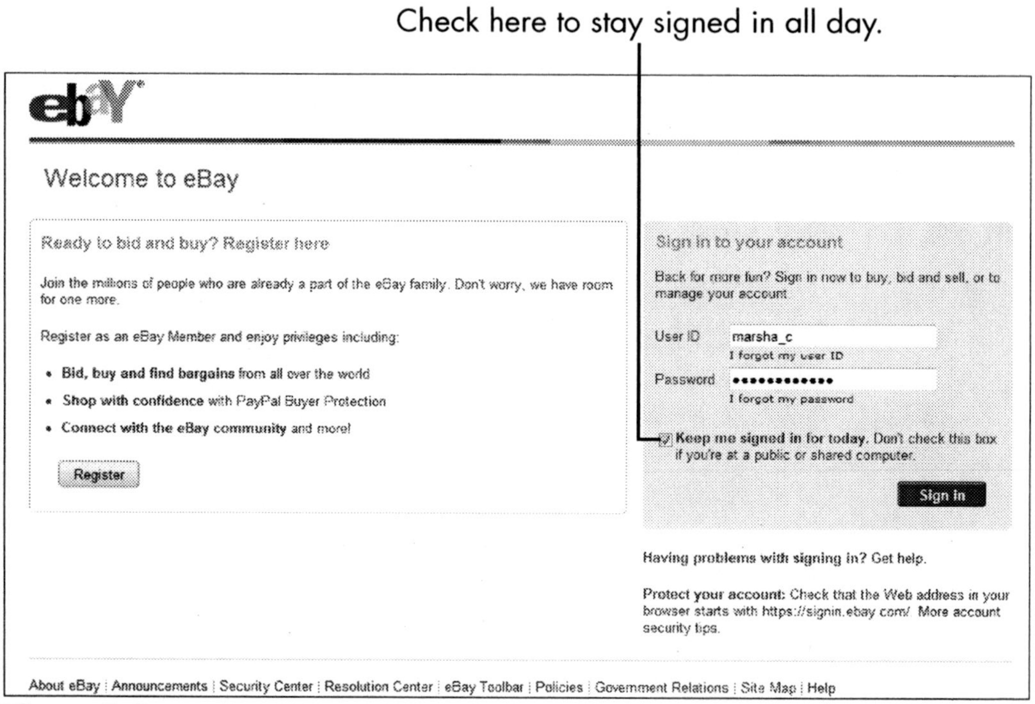

Check here to stay signed in all day.

eBay

Welcome to eBay

Ready to bid and buy? Register here

Join the millions of people who are already a part of the eBay family. Don't worry, we have room for one more.

Register as an eBay Member and enjoy privileges including:

- **Bid, buy and find bargains** from all over the world
- **Shop with confidence** with PayPal Buyer Protection
- **Connect with the eBay community** and more!

[Register]

Sign in to your account

Back for more fun? Sign in now to buy, bid and sell, or to manage your account

User ID   marsha_c
            I forgot my user ID
Password   ●●●●●●●●●●●●
            I forgot my password

☑ Keep me signed in for today. Don't check this box if you're at a public or shared computer.

[Sign in]

Having problems with signing in? Get help.

Protect your account: Check that the Web address in your browser starts with https://signin.ebay.com/ More account security tips.

About eBay | Announcements | Security Center | Resolution Center | eBay Toolbar | Policies | Government Relations | Site Map | Help

Figure 3-8

Take Advantage of the My eBay Page

1. eBay gives all users plenty of personal space; its My eBay page is your space for managing all your activities on eBay. After you register, you get your own My eBay page

that helps you track the items you're watching and bidding on, as well as items you've already bought and sold.
You can access this page at any time by clicking the My
eBay link in the navigation bar at the top of every page. I
think it's the greatest organizational tool around; see my
My eBay page in **Figure 3-9**.

Keep track of all your eBay activities.

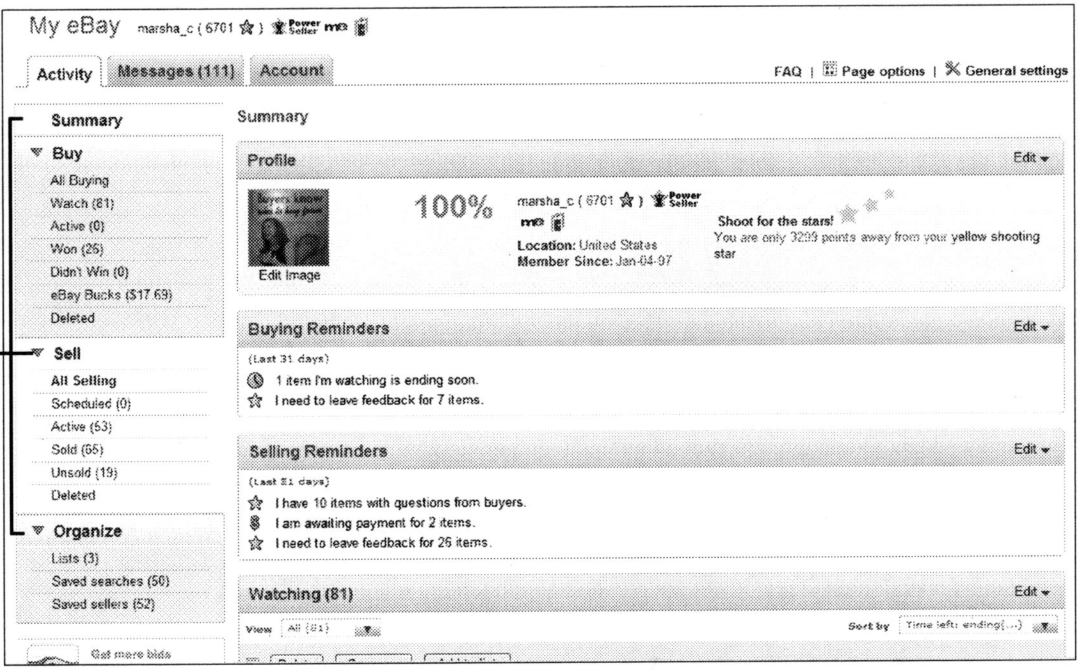

Figure 3-9

2. Check out **Table 3-1** for a quick review of what you can
do on your My eBay page, including how you can track
what you're buying and selling, find out how much
money you've spent, and add categories to your personal-
ized list (so you can get to any favorite eBay place with
just a click of your mouse).

Table 3-1	The Major Links on Your My eBay Page
Click Here	**To See This on Your My eBay Page**
Buy	Every listing that you're currently bidding on, have marked to watch, or made a Best Offer on, and the auction items you won or didn't win.
Sell	Every listing for items you're currently selling. Also, there are links to any listings you've scheduled to start at a later date. Most important, you have links to lists of items you've sold (and not sold).
Messages	This tab links to your My Messages area, eBay's private e-mail service for members. My Messages is the best and safest way to communicate with other eBay members.
Organize	This area links to your collections of Saved Searches, Saved Sellers, and your personally specified lists.
Account	You can use this tab to select activities for which you want eBay to remember your password, which saves you from having to type it every time. (I like to have eBay remember my password when I'm selling, bidding, managing items, and so on.) From here, you can also change your personal information on eBay. You can see what you currently owe eBay, and link to your PayPal and Half.com accounts as well.

3. Your My eBay page has three tabs at the top of the page below the My eBay heading: Activity, Messages, and Account. If you put your mouse pointer over the Account tab, you see a drop-down menu like the one in **Figure 3-10**.

 Clicking Account brings you to the summary page that has snippets of each topic in the My Account section. It's really better to click individual drop-down menu options so you can go directly to the places you want to explore.

4. The options on the Account drop-down menu direct you to areas where you can update your contact information, your preferred payment and shipping addresses, preferences for notifications and other communications, as well as other site preferences. You can also access other areas that interact with your eBay activities, including your PayPal account (for making and accepting payments) and the area showing feedback you received or need to send.

My eBay tabs   Hover mouse for a drop-down menu.

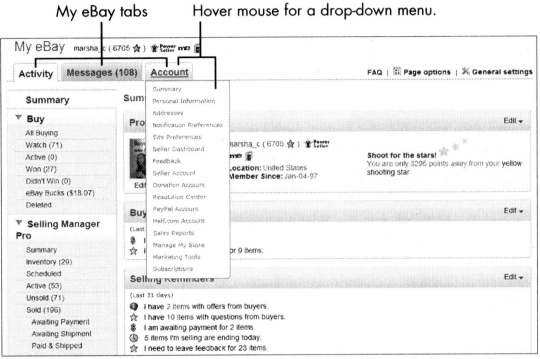

Figure 3-10

 Initially, your contact information comes from your registration. But it's policy on eBay that every user files his or her current contact information — so if you move or change phone numbers, e-mail addresses, or banks, be sure to update that information here.

 When setting your notification preferences, consider carefully how many e-mail messages you want to receive. If you do a lot of buying and selling and you sign up for *all* notifications, you could find yourself with an e-mail deluge. Select wisely — for sanity's sake, narrow your selections to the minimum. And remember, you can always change your choices later.

5. When you finally get your My eBay page set up the way you like it, save yourself a lot of work, keystrokes, and time by setting up a quick way to access the page. Here's how: With your My eBay page showing in your browser, try one of the following:

- Bookmark the page as a favorite by choosing Favorites⇨Add to Favorites in Internet Explorer (or by using the appropriate menu or button for your browser). You can then pick your page from the Favorites list.

- Send a shortcut to your desktop by choosing File⇨ Send⇨Shortcut to Desktop. Then, when you click the shortcut that magically appears on your desktop, your browser opens directly onto your My eBay page.

- As some other eBay members do, make your My eBay page into a browser home page by clicking the down arrow next to the home button (which looks like a little house) and choosing Add or Change Home Page from the drop-down menu that appears. After you finish this setup, your My eBay page appears the minute you log on. That's true dedication. (These instructions are for version 7 of the Internet Explorer browser, but the instructions for other versions should be very similar.)

Organize Your eBay Jaunts

1. Part of the fun of eBay is searching for stuff that other-wise you'd never think of looking for in a million years. Wacky stuff aside, most eBay users spend their time hunting for specific items — say, Barbie dolls, designer dresses, baseball cards, plumbing supplies, or U.S. stamps. That's why eBay came up with the Organize area of your My eBay page (refer to Figure 3-9). Whenever you view your My eBay Organize links, you see a list of your favorite searches and sellers. But because eBay isn't psychic, you have to tell it what you want listed there.

 If you shop eBay the same way I do, you'll look for similar things and sellers over and over. The My eBay Organize area is a place to gather and make note of your favorite searches and sellers. You can perform these searches and visit these stores with a click of your mouse.

2. Save up to 100 favorite searches in the Saved Searches area. To add a search to your favorites, first perform the search. (For details on how to perform a search, see Chapter 4.) When the search appears on your screen, click the Save This Search link, shown at the top of the search results in **Figure 3-11**.

Click here to save a favorite search.

Find	christian louboutin 38	in	All Categories	▼	Search	[Advanced Search]

☐ Include title and description

Related Searches: christian louboutin, jimmy choo 38, manolo blahnik 38, christian louboutin shoes

Refine search

In Women's Shoes

▼ US Size

☐ 6.5 (1)
☐ 7 (4)
☐ 7.5 (22)
☐ 8 (164)
☐ 8.5 (115)
☐ 9 (1)
☐ Not Specified (39)
Choose more...

▼ Style

☐ Heels, Pumps (220)
☐ Sandals (56)
☐ Boots (39)
☐ Platforms, Wedges (18)
☐ Flats (13)
☐ Clogs & Mules (5)
☐ Not Specified (14)
Choose more...

▼ Sub Style

All items | Auctions only | Buy It Now only

347 results found for **christian louboutin 38** [Save this search]

View as [List ▼] [Customize view]   Sort by [Best Match ▼]

Price | Time Left | Shipping to 91325, USA

Featured Items

O-M-G-*CHRISTIAN LOUBOUTIN PINK HYPER PRIVE 38.5 SHOE**
I'M RARELY A FAN OF PINK BUT WHEN I LOVE IT***I LOVE IT!   *Buy It Now* $1,024.74 13h 41m Free
🔍 Enlarge

Optimize your selling success! Find out how to promote your items

NEW CHRISTIAN LOUBOUTIN BROWN LEATHER LOW HEELS 38 7.5   0 Bids $204.99 1h 27m Free
BRAND NEW WITH BAG · FREE SHIPPING AND INSURANCE!

Christian Louboutin ACTIVA heels sandals black 38 8   5 Bids $112.50 20m +$19.00
🔍 Enlarge

Figure 3-11

3. The search is then transported to your My eBay Favorite
Searches area, where it's identified by the name you
provide in the Name This Search box (as shown in
Figure 3-12). In this example, the name of the search
(`christian louboutin 38`) is the same as the
search terms used. If you want to be notified by e-mail
when new items are listed, select the check box and the
time frame in the drop-down menu.

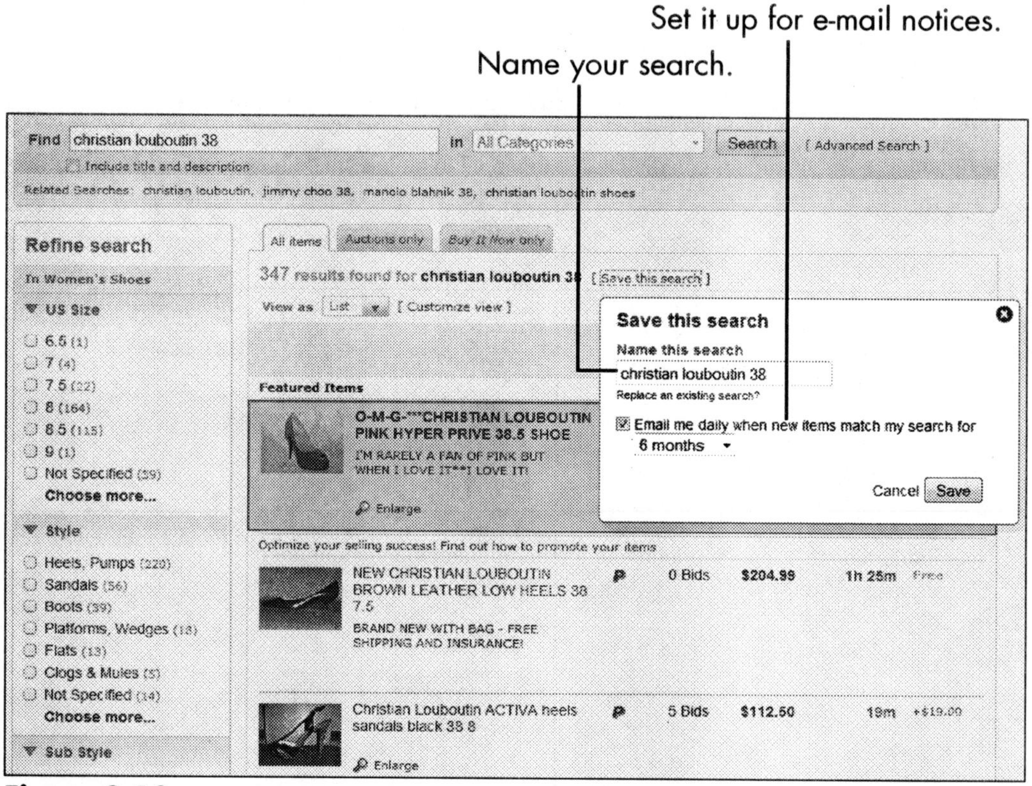

Set it up for e-mail notices.

Name your search.

Figure 3-12

4. When you want to repeat one of these saved searches,
just click the Search name to search for the item. eBay
will even e-mail you up to 20 of your searches when new
items are listed.

5. Similarly, when you find a seller whose merchandise and
prices are right up your alley and you know you'd like to

check out that seller's auctions occasionally, you can list the seller in the Favorite Sellers area:

1. *From one of the seller's item listings, click the link to view the seller's other items.* You see a search page listing all the items for sale by that seller.

2. *Scroll down the list of all items, and on the left side, click the Add to Saved Sellers link.* The seller is saved to your My eBay Saved Sellers (favorites) page.

 If you find sellers whom you'd like to add as favorites while you're browsing or buying in their eBay stores, click the Add to Saved Sellers link at the top of the store's home page.

Ask for Help on eBay

1. Help is available on eBay, but to be fair, the people at eBay Customer Service are pretty busy. They have millions of customers all asking questions at the same time. So before you add your question to the mix, try using the index of this book to help you when you have a question about eBay. Many of the answers are in the book that's in your hands right now.

2. eBay does have chat boards with people willing to be helpful, but as in the real world, people may not be giving out accurate information. They may also have something to sell, so I advise you to stick to the eBay Help area and — in the most extreme cases, such as your pictures not showing up in search — use the Contact Us link on the eBay home page.

3. When you click Contact Us, you land on the Customer Service page, as shown in **Figure 3-13**. Ask your question as follows:

1. *Type your question into the text box provided and then click the Ask button.*

2. *Fill in any other information that eBay asks regarding your question, and then click Submit.*

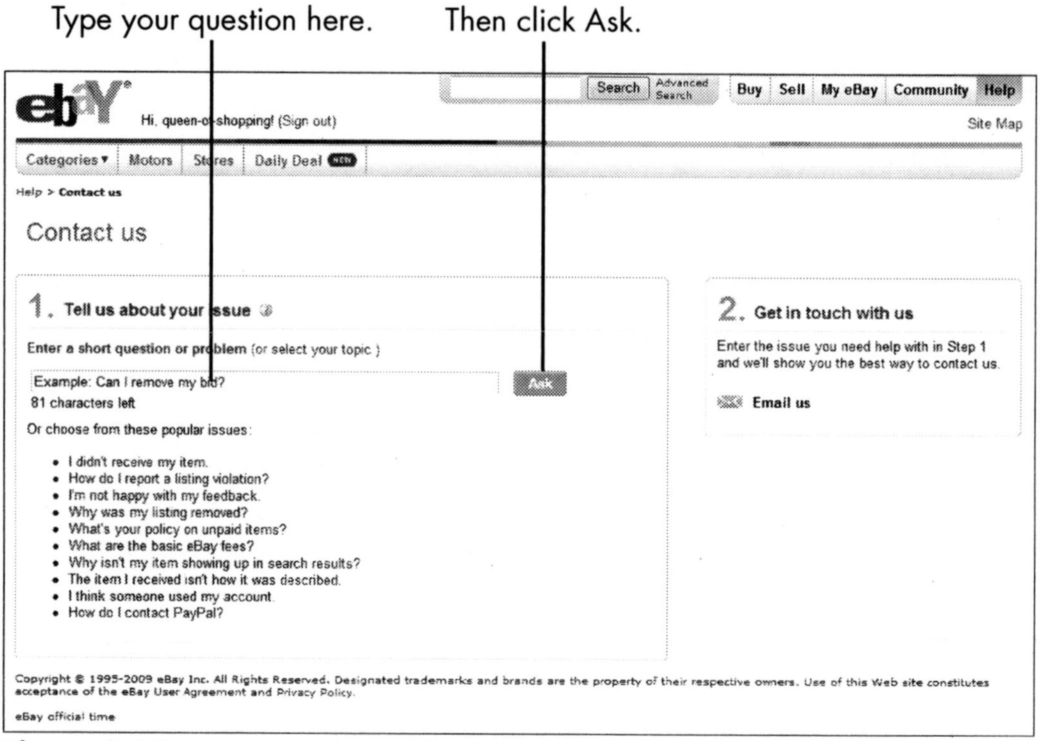

Type your question here.　　　Then click Ask.

Figure 3-13

4. eBay may present an answer to your question, or as shown in **Figure 3-14**, may not have a clue to the answer. You will then be asked to click the Email Us or Chat with Us link to get a real person to answer your questions.

5. Click Chat With Us if you want *immediate* assistance. **Figure 3-15** shows the conversation I had about my question. Seven minutes later, I had my answer (but you know, I would have had an even faster answer by looking in the index of this book).

Click here for immediate help.

Contact us

1. Tell us about your issue ✱

If this answer doesn't help, try rephrasing your question (or select your topic)

How many identical items can I list   [Ask]

75 characters left

⊘ Here's information about: Getting started as a seller on eBay

To start selling on eBay:

1. Create a seller's account. (If you're not an eBay member, you'll need to register first.)

2. Sign up to receive payments through PayPal.

3. Create your listing.

It's a good idea to learn more about the basics of selling successfully on eBay before listing your first item.

Need more help? Contact us directly using the customer support options on the right side of the page.

2. Get in touch with us

We're here to help. Contact us directly for assistance.

✉ **Email us**

💬 **Chat with us**

Figure 3-14

[Print] [Copy All] [Exit]

System	11:12:12 PM
Initial Question/Comment: Listing Your Item

| System | 11:12:18 PM |
Thank you for contacting eBay Live Help!

| System | 11:12:18 PM |
You are successfully connected to eBay Live Help. Please hold for the next available Live Help Agent.

| System | 11:12:53 PM |
Diane T. has joined this session!

| System | 11:12:53 PM |
Connected with Diane T.

| Diane T. | 11:12:58 PM |
Hello, thanks for waiting and welcome to eBay Live Help! My name is Diane. How may I help you?

| queen-of-shopping | 11:13:09 PM |
How many identical items may I list at one time?

| Diane T. | 11:13:23 PM |
I'd be happy to assist with this.

| Diane T. | 11:15:13 PM |
Listing multiple identical items in just one listing has requirements though.

| queen-of-shopping | 11:15:38 PM |
Not in ONE listing. I am asking about MULTIPLE listings for the same item

| Diane T. | 11:17:58 PM |
Oh, sorry I overlooked. Let me make sure of this. One moment please.

| Diane T. | 11:19:24 PM |
Thank you for waiting. There's no limit on how many identical listings you make, but please note that we are continuing to show a maximum of 10 listings per page -- whether Fixed Price or Auction-style -- from any one seller.

| queen-of-shopping | 11:19:34 PM |
Thank you

[Send]

Connected with a Customer Representative   Session ID:17983019

Here's my answer!

Figure 3-15

Part I

Joining the Crowd on eBay

The 5th Wave   By Rich Tennant

"Guess who found a Kiss merchandise blowout on eBay while you were gone?"

Saving Time and Money by Shopping on eBay

Chapter 4

I first discovered eBay because I was busy running a business and bringing up my daughter. I had no time to go from store to store in search of the lowest prices. I was lucky to come across a Web site (eBay) where I could find items I needed and have them delivered to my door.

Fast-forward to today: Prices have gone up, gas prices are sky-high, and time is of the essence. Even when you're retired, there's no joy in going from store to store to store to find the sprinkler part you need. eBay can cut that time into fractions and possibly save you cash at the same time.

Remember these benefits of shopping on eBay:

➡ **eBay's not just for fun stuff** (and you find *plenty* of fun stuff on the site); eBay can save you money by offering items you need at discount prices and delivering them to your door. You also find sellers with retail coupons for everyday items, so if your local paper doesn't have the coupon you need, there may be a seller on eBay selling the coupons at a discount!

➡ **You can sit in your easy chair** (okay, maybe at the kitchen counter) and peruse items for sale from all over the world. If you really always wanted to play with Star Trek's Type 2 phaser (hey, no kids are around to judge you) or you want to repurchase an item you had long ago, eBay's the place. The *only* place (I might add) where you can find the most esoteric and useful items on the planet.

Picture all the stores you've ever seen in your life located in one giant mall. You walk into the mall and try to find the single item you're looking for. That scenario is a bit like your first foray on eBay. Just start surfing around the site, and you instantly understand the size and scope of what's for sale: *everything*. Browsing around the site can be confusing and get you off target. You may feel overwhelmed at first, but I can show you prescribed ways to find exactly what you're looking for. As soon as you figure out how to find the items you want to bid for or buy on eBay, you can jump in and start saving money.

In this chapter, I offer expert tips on finding and buying items at discount. I also give you tips for using the eBay search engine from a buyer's perspective.

Find What You Want with Keywords

1. It doesn't seem like it should be rocket science, but a site the size of eBay can be overwhelming. Here's how to get directly to your item: Search with keywords. Finding items on eBay is all about the keywords. What's a keyword? *Keywords* are usually nouns (plus some adjectives) that you would use to describe your item. Nothing frivolous, please. For an example, suppose you're looking for a sweater; a clear group of (key)words for your search would be

wool sweater large red

You don't need to start your keywords with capital letters because they're not recognized by a search engine — on eBay or anywhere else.

2. At the top of every eBay page, you see a Search box, as in **Figure 4-1**. Type your keywords in that box. Notice that next to it is a link to Advanced Search. *Don't go there.* You don't need the extra options, which can be confusing and unnecessary when you're searching for items to buy! Follow my tips, and you'll find things the easy way.

Top of page Search box

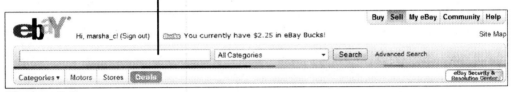

Figure 4-1

3. I typed the words *wool sweater large red* into the Search box and got the results shown in **Figure 4-2**. If I wanted the sweater to be a specific brand or made by a specific company (such as Ralph Lauren or Land's End), I would have included that name as part of my search keywords.

 My search found 98 sweaters. And this is May — the perfect time to get a deal on sweaters for next winter! Keep in mind that eBay operates by supply and demand, just like every other marketplace. If you've just gone through a winter and your sweaters are threadbare, spring and early summer is the best time to buy. If it's the end of summer and the rear of your swim suit is all scratched up from sitting on sand or concrete, look for a new one in fall or winter. Get it? Got it. Good!

Qualifiers to narrow search

Keywords   Search results   Sort found items here.

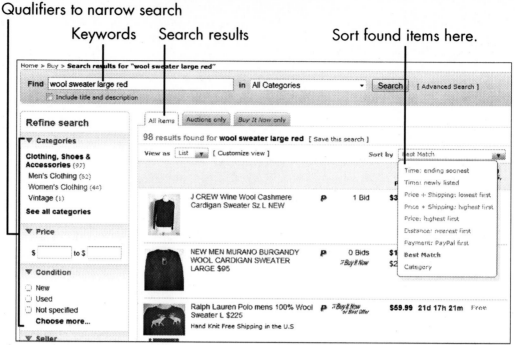

Figure 4-2

4. Refine your results. On the left side of the search-results page, you see a list of qualifiers that help you narrow down the type of items you see in your search results. These qualifiers include

- **Categories:** In this example, if you're looking for a woman's sweater, you could click the link on the left to narrow your search to the category *Women's Clothing*. You can also click a See All Categories link that would open up your search — you could even find dog sweaters. (I found only one, see **Figure 4-3**.)

 It's a lot easier to use the noun *dog* in your search keywords if you want to find a dog sweater. But eBay sellers don't always put words like *women*, *ladies*, *girls*, or *teens* into their titles, so it's best to leave out those very defined keywords and refine your search by category on your own.

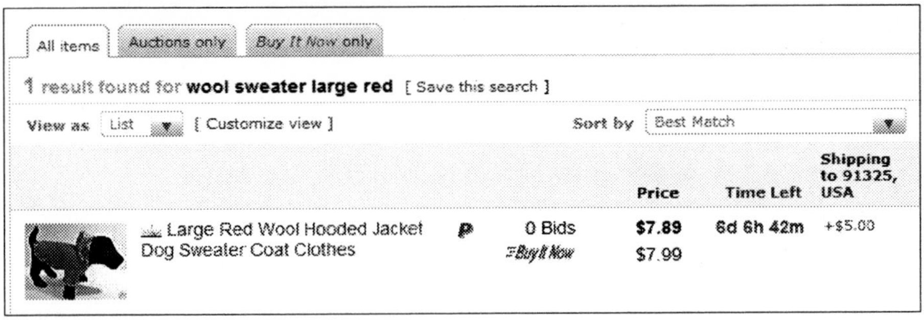

Figure 4-3

- **Price:** I say "Why narrow yourself down to a set price?" If you get a reasonable number of results, just take a gander at everything. Besides, as you can see from the third sweater listed in my search results (refer to Figure 4-2), a seller has chosen to allow buyers to make an offer on the item. I discuss the Best Offer option in Chapter 6, but remember that if I ruled out finding sweaters over $50, I wouldn't have seen this one. And this seller is inviting buyers to make offers — so you *might* be able to buy it for $45.

- **Condition:** New? Used? Especially in these days, there's no shame in buying used, and eBay gives you that option. Clicking *New* or *Used* narrows results to listings in the condition that suits you. (If the sweater is a gift item, you might do best with New . . . some recipients are still pretty traditional about that . . .).

5. Sort your results on tabs. At the top of the search results, you see three tabs that can each help you refine your search in a different way. eBay normally shows you all the items that match your keywords (regardless of the listing type) on the All Items tab. But you can click another tab to view a specific listing type:

   - **Buy It Now Only:** Click this tab to see items that can be bought at a fixed price (or where you can make an offer). By clicking there, you can narrow your search to items available for purchase in an instant with a click of your mouse.

- **Auctions Only:** You might prefer to participate in a traditional eBay auction. That's where the sport of shopping comes in, so click the Auctions Only tab for an adventure! **Figure** 4-4 shows an auction for a lovely sweater starting at 99 cents! In Chapter 6, I show you how to track auctions so you can get the best final sale price — without driving up the bidding.

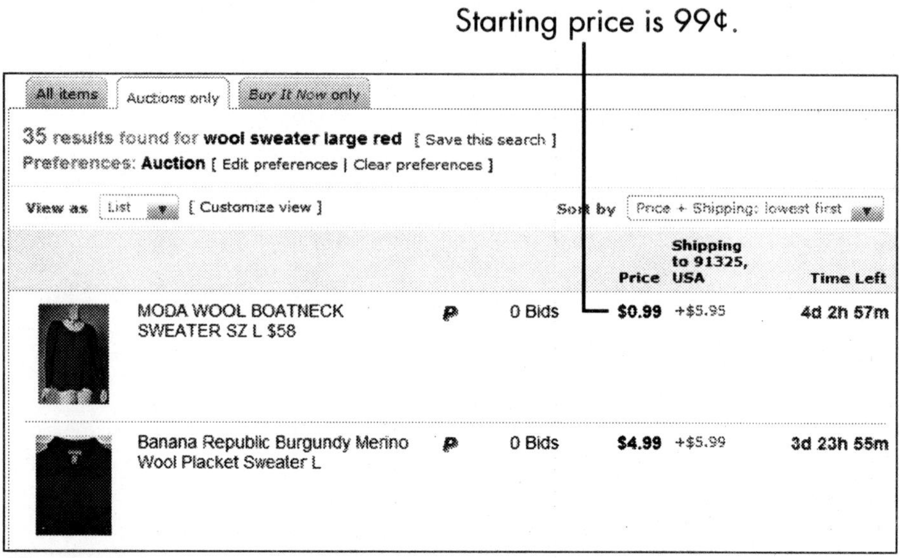

Starting price is 99¢.

Figure 4-4

6. Sort your results with the Sort By menu. At the top of the results listing is a drop-down menu (it's also in Figure 4-2). This menu gives you several options for how you'd like your search to appear. Although eBay has many options in the Sort By drop-down menu, only some of them are really helpful; choose one of the following valuable selections:

- **Best Match:** This is eBay's magical sorting formula that weighs all (ahem) *sorts* of things — including how a seller lists an item, the seller's feedback, and whether eBay feels the shipping costs are appropriate.

Take into consideration that in the shipping-cost arena, eBay's judgment is iffy, at best. Once eBay suggested I charge $5 to ship an item that actually cost $18 to ship because most sellers sold a tiny item — rather than the large version I sold — from the same manufacturer.

- **Time: Ending Soonest:** This selection puts auctions and fixed-price items whose listings are ending immediately on-screen first. This sort order is most beneficial with auctions, because it gives you a chance to swoop in and snap up any undiscovered deals.

- **Time: Newly Listed:** Lists the most recently posted listings first.

- **Distance: Nearest First:** If you're looking for a large piece of furniture for pickup, this is a valuable sort. You don't want to pay shipping on huge items — unless you really, really want to own it.

- **Price: Lowest First:** With this selection, you find items listed in order from the lowest to the highest starting price asked for an item.

- **Price: Highest First:** This sort lists items from highest to lowest asking price. (This is a very useful option when you're searching for a 1967 Mustang and you want to buy a car, not a Hot Wheels toy.)

7. Farther down the page on the left, you find a Completed Item search. This tool is most valuable when you're planning to sell an item — Chapters 12 and 13 show you how. And check out Chapter 11 to see how a Completed Item search helps you see just how much your 1967 Mustang (if you happen to have one) is selling for on eBay.

If you're hunting down a rare or intricately named item, I recommend that you click the Save This Search link at the top of the search-results page (see Figure 4-2). By doing so, you tell eBay to send you an e-mail every time a new item matching your search is listed on the site.

Use Shortcuts in Your Searches

Choosing clear descriptive keywords, as noted in the previous task, is important for finding just what you want on eBay. But you can also use some special tactics with eBay's search engine to give you specific results quicker. **Table 4-1** shows you some of my favorite tricks and shortcuts.

Table 4-1	Shortcuts for Use on the eBay Search Engine	
Symbol	*Effect on Search*	*Example*
Quotes ""	Limits the search to items with the *exact* phrase inside the quotes.	**"Wonder Woman"** returns items about the comic book/TV heroine.
Asterisk *	Serves as a *wild card* (find-everything-like-this) when you're not sure of spelling.	**alumin*** returns items that start with *alumin*, such as *aluminum* (when you're searching for the perfect vintage Christmas tree).
Minus sign –	Excludes results with the word after the –.	Search with **box –lunch**, and you'd better not be hungry because you may find the box, but lunch won't be included.
Minus sign and parentheses	Searches for items with words before the parentheses but excludes words inside the parentheses.	**midge –(skipper,barbie)** means that auctions you find with the Midge doll will not have the other dolls (Skipper and Barbie) offered.
Parentheses	Searches for both versions of the word in parentheses.	**political (pin,pins)** searches for both *political pin* and *political pins*.

Here are additional tips to help you streamline any eBay search:

➠ **Don't use *and, a, an, or,* or *the*:** Called *noise words* in search lingo, these words are interpreted as part of your search but don't help it. So if you want to find something from *The Sound of Music* and you type **the sound of music**, you may not get any results. Many sellers drop noise words from the beginning of an item title when they list it, just as libraries drop noise words when they alphabetize books. So, instead, type **sound music** — and to be even more precise, type **"sound of music"** (in quotes) to search for that exact phrase.

➠ **Use the asterisk symbol often to locate misspellings.** I've snagged some great deals by finding items incorrectly posted by the sellers. Here are a few examples:

- *Rodri**: In this search, I look for items by the famous Cajun artist *George Rodrigue.* His Blue Dog paintings are world-renowned and very valuable. By using this search, I managed to purchase a signed Blue Dog lithograph for under $200 (because the seller had misspelled the artist's name). (I resold it on eBay later that year for $900, with Rodrigue spelled correctly!)

- *Alumi* tree*: Remember the old aluminum Christmas trees from the '60s? They've had quite a resurgence in popularity these days. You can buy these "antiques" in stores for hundreds of dollars . . . or you can buy one on eBay for half the price. You can find them even cheaper if the seller can't spell *aluminum* or uses the British spelling (*aluminium*).

- *Cemet* plot*: If you're looking for that final place to retire, eBay has some great deals. Unfortunately, sellers haven't narrowed down whether they want to spell it *cemetery* or *cemetary*. This search will find both.

After you study these examples, I'm sure you can think of many more ways that using asterisks can help you find the deals. Be sure to e-mail me and let me know when you find something special in this way!

Expand or Shrink a Search

1. Scrolling down a search results page can open up even more options — called Preferences — for finding just what you want on eBay. Some options are there to narrow down your search, and others will open it up. **Figure 4-5** shows the most important choices you have.

2. Using the Buying Formats preferences is similar to the tabs at the top of your search results (see the task, "Find What You Want with Keywords," earlier in the chapter), but with one important addition: eBay hides store listings unless the core search comes up with 30 or fewer auction-style and fixed-price items. You can click the Include Store Inventory option to open up your search to every item on the site.

3. Use the Show Only preferences if you want to narrow your search. You can set these preferences:

- **Completed listings.** This is an important choice when you want to find out what the item you're seeking sold for in the past. After you click this preference to see only completed listings, you can sort the Completed results by price to determine the previous high and low selling prices.

- **Free shipping.** At first glance, looking for items with free shipping seems to be a good idea, but what if another seller has the item for sale for less (including shipping)? If cost-saving is what you seek, go back to the top of the search-results page and use the Sort By drop-down menu. Set your search to sort by *Price + Shipping: Lowest First.*

Set preferences to control your search.

Preferences					
	Parure/Bracelet/Necklace/ERs				
▼ Buying formats	Vintage Signed Schiaparelli Pearl Necklace,Ears & Pin	℗ *Buy It Now or Best Offer*		$795.00	24d 14h 56m	Free
☐ Auction						
☐ Buy It Now						
☐ Include Store inventory						
Choose more...	Unique Vintage Pin Brooch / Pendant Schiaparelli ?	℗	3 Bids	$29.98	14h 37m	+$5.55
▼ Show only						
☐ Completed listings	Schiaparelli Milk Glass and Emerald Green Pat.#2563980	℗	1 Bid	$9.99	21h 4m	+$5.00
☐ Free shipping						
Choose more...						
▼ Location	Vintage Schiaparelli Watermelon Brooch L@@K!!!!!!!!!	℗	4 Bids	$33.00	1d 0h 55m	+$4.95
☐ US Only						
☐ North America						
☐ Worldwide						
Choose more...	Schiaparelli Purple Pink Kite Shape Necklace Earrings	℗ *Buy It Now or Best Offer*		$1,200.00	23h 13m	Free
▶ Distance	Layaway available for this rare find!					
Customize preferences						
🖫 **Matching eBay Stores**	Unusual & Rare Vintage Schiaparelli Watermelon Earrings	℗	2 Bids	$27.00	1d 1h 33m	+$4.95
Celebrity Owned (1)						
Boji Jewels and More (1)						
Solid Copper Cookie Cutters Pl. (1)						

Figure 4-5

4. Choosing to search with a preference for the Location of searched-for items is valuable when many of your search results are in countries outside the United States. You may prefer, especially when you're first starting out, to purchase items from North America only. Even though it's very cool to get a package of Egyptian cotton shirts from Egypt, shipping can take a very long time.

 So what about the Choose More links you see in the search preferences? You can click a Choose More link and get a dialog box with extra choices, but hold on a sec. The purpose of this book is to simplify the eBay experience, so I'd suggest that here's another place you don't need to go. In the 12 years I've been shopping on eBay, I've never had to use the Choose More options. Keep it simple. *Don't go there.*

Narrow Your Search in a Category

1. In this chapter's first task, I mention that when you click a category listed under Refine Search, you'll get closer to what you're looking for. In that section's *wool sweater large red* search, clicking the Women's Clothing Category opens up a much easier way to find your item.

2. By choosing a category like Women's Clothing, you get appropriate options for narrowing your search. As **Figure 4-6** shows, eBay allows you to refine your search by Style, Condition, and Brand. Very cool, eh? Depending on what you're looking for, eBay's category refinements can make your search run a good deal smoother! This works with many types of searches.

3. This same idea works in any category. Suppose you have a hankering to watch the old classic BBC television program, *Absolutely Fabulous.* And you want it on DVD because you're cool that way. Simply search for the keywords *Absolutely Fabulous* and then select the category of DVD to pare down the many results, as shown in **Figure** 4-7.

Choose Style, Condition, and Brand.

Refine search	All items	Auctions only	Buy It Now only

12 results found for wool sweater large red [Save this search]
Preferences: **Auction** [Edit preferences : Clear preferences]

Refine search		Price	Shipping to 91325, USA	Time Left
Categories	MODA WOOL BOATNECK SWEATER SZ L $58	$0.99	+$5.95	4d 0h 19m
Women's Clothing				
Sweaters (11)	LADIE'S RED 100% WOOL SWEATER,SIZE (L)	$0.99	+$12.38	5d 22h 32m
Shirts, Tops (1)				
In Women's Sweaters	EILEEN FISHER STUNNING WOOL OPEN CARDIGAN SWEATER SZ L FREE SHIPPING FREE SHIPPING FREE SHIPPING FREE SHIPPING	$15.95	Free	1d 0h 57m
Style				
Cardigan (4)				
Pullover (4)	NIKE GOLF Burgundy V Neck Wool Sweater Large LG 12 14	$9.99	+$8.95	6d 0h 38m
V-Neck (3)				
Boat, Cowl (1)	The J Peterman Company Red Wool Sweater Cardigan Size L	$9.98	+$10.10	3d 1h 34m
Turtleneck, Mock (1)				
Not Specified (2)				
Choose more...				

View as List [Customize view]   Sort by Price + Shipping: lowest first

Condition
New: With Tags (3)
New: Without Tags (1)
Pre-Owned (6)
Not Specified (2)
Choose more...

Brand
BCBG Max Azria (1)
Coldwater Creek (1)
Eileen Fisher (1)
Iceberg (1)
J. Peterman (1)

Figure 4-6

If you put into practice all the search techniques presented in the chapter so far, you type *"Absolutely Fabulous"* DVD into the Search box. What you type includes the identifying keywords for your item, quotation marks to get the exact phrase, and the additional keyword *DVD* to identify the media format.

You go directly (do not pass Go, do not collect $200) to the DVD version of the TV program. Bingo! Yahtzee! You get the results you're looking for without traversing all those link-clicking steps.

You have 255 total results.

Only 28 are in the DVD category.

Figure 4-7

Understand eBay Acronyms

When you shop on eBay, you're going to come across some acronyms in item titles. Knowing what these acronyms stand for ahead of time (so you don't have to click every item) will help you quickly figure out what you're looking at. **Table 4-2** shows you a list of some of the more common abbreviations used on the site.

Table 4-2		A Quick List of eBay Abbreviations
eBay Slang	**What It Abbreviates**	**What It Means**
MIB	Mint in Box	The item is in the original box, in great shape, and just the way you'd expect to find it in a store.
MOC	Mint on Card	The item is mounted on its original display card, in store-new condition.
NRFB	Never Removed from Box	Just what it says, as in "bought but never opened."
COA	Certificate of Authenticity	Documentation that vouches for the genuineness of an item, such as an autograph or painting.
MINT	Mint	A never-used item or collectible in perfect condition
OOAK	One of a Kind	You are looking at the only one in existence!
NR	No Reserve Price	A reserve price is the price set by a seller when he or she begins an auction. If bids don't meet the reserve, the seller doesn't have to sell the item.
HTF, OOP	Hard to Find, Out of Print	Out of print, only a few ever made. (HTF means scarce; it doesn't mean you spent a week looking for it in the attic.)

Get In on eBay's Daily Deals

1. I love to shop. But I can't stand to pay full retail for anything. So if your shopping patterns mirror mine, you might like to receive a daily e-mail from eBay called the *Daily Deal*. Each day, eBay works with sellers to select four very popular items and offer them for sale at very low prices — with free shipping! (Now, that's what I call a deal.) Best of all, getting on this wonderful mailing list is simple.

2. Go to the eBay Home page at www.ebay.com. You see a button that says *Daily Deal* under the top-of-page Search box. Click it. You arrive at the page that shows the day's four deals. On the top right is the picture of a little envelope. Click it.

3. Next you see a page where you confirm your e-mail address. Type it in and agree to receiving the e-mails. Click Submit. That's it! You're now on the list to receive the Daily Deal e-mail, as shown in **Figure 4-8**. Happy shopping!

Figure 4-8

Checking Out the Sales and Sellers

Chapter 5

When you're shopping on eBay, you're faced with hundreds of items — perhaps even hundreds of listings for the *same* item. Even if you know exactly what you want to buy, you find not one but many auctions and fixed-price listings with that same item for sale. How do you decide where to place your order or your bid?

In this situation, you need to understand the ins and outs of sales and sellers; that's exactly what I help you with in this chapter. I show you the tools on eBay that guide you to a safe and positive transaction. Specifically, you need to know

➠ **The different eBay sales formats.** Here's where you find out how to read and evaluate an item page to get the edge and spend your money the safest way.

➠ **Where to look for information about the sellers.** Sellers can look all the same on the surface, so I lead you to the most important seller information and show you where to go to ask the seller questions before you put your money on the line.

Check Out the Listing Page

1. All item pages on eBay — whether auctions, fixed-price items, or Buy It Now items — look about the same. **Figure 5-1** shows a full-width, conventional auction-item page. At the top left of the page, you see the item picture; the top middle shows the item title. (*Note*: In this figure, I'm including the *Seller info* box — which I explain more about in the later task, "Examine the Seller and Item Info.") When you view an auction page like this one, you scroll down to see a complete description of the item, along with shipping information and return policy.

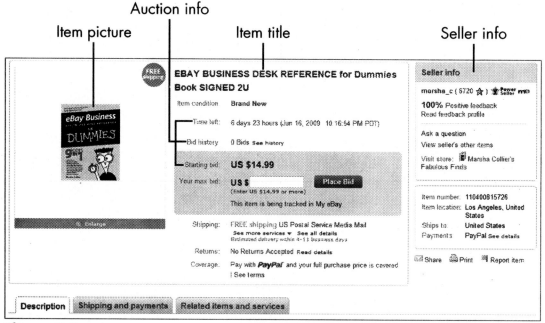

Figure 5-1

2. Try viewing several eBay auction listings and observe the subtle differences. For example, you may see the words *Financing Available* or auctions with preset item specifics that appear above the description that the seller wrote. If you're looking at an item in a fixed-price sale, you see the words *Buy It Now*, as shown in **Figure 5-2**.

Click to buy a fixed-price item.

Figure 5-2

3. You'll also see the words *Buy It Now* on some auction (rather than fixed-price) listings. I know it's confusing, but eBay has a special option for auctions that allows you to purchase an item on the spot, as shown in **Figure 5-3**.

Place a bid or buy outright.

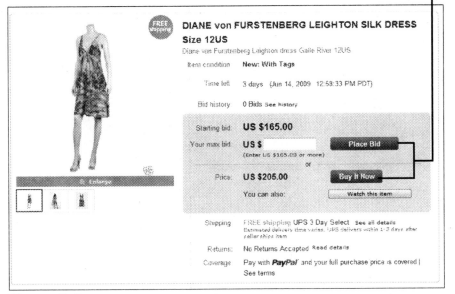

Figure 5-3

4. One more option you should know about is *Best Offer*. That's what the option is called when you see it in a search (see **Figure** 5-4), but on the item page, this option is called *Make Offer*, as shown in **Figure** 5-5.

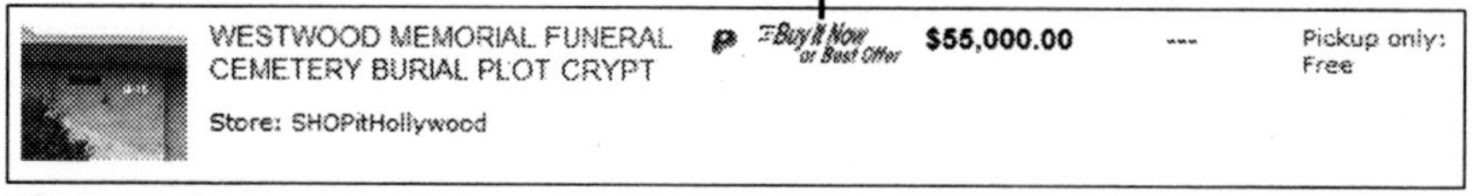

Best Offer appears here.

WESTWOOD MEMORIAL FUNERAL CEMETERY BURIAL PLOT CRYPT

Buy It Now or Best Offer $55,000.00   ---   Pickup only: Free

Store: SHOPitHollywood

Figure 5-4

In the best-offer process, you have the opportunity to make an offer for the item at a lower price. In Chapter 6, I give you strategies for making an offer that has the best chance of being graciously accepted by the seller.

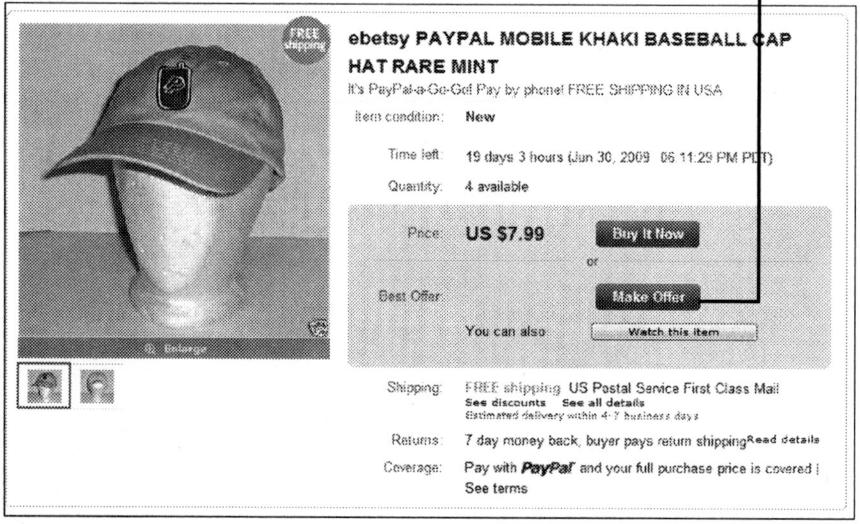

Click to make your best offer.

ebetsy PAYPAL MOBILE KHAKI BASEBALL CAP HAT RARE MINT

It's PayPal-a-Go-Go! Pay by phone! FREE SHIPPING IN USA

Item condition: New

Time left: 19 days 3 hours (Jun 30, 2009 06:11:29 PM PDT)

Quantity: 4 available

Price: **US $7.99**   Buy It Now

or

Best Offer: Make Offer

You can also: Watch this item

Shipping: FREE shipping US Postal Service First Class Mail
See discounts   See all details
Estimated delivery within 4-7 business days

Returns: 7 day money back, buyer pays return shipping Read details

Coverage: Pay with **PayPal** and your full purchase price is covered !
See terms

Figure 5-5

5. Scroll down a typical auction listing to get familiar with the information included; here's some of the stuff you'll see:

- **Item category:** Located just above the item title bar. You can click the category listing and browse to do some comparison shopping.

- **Item title:** Identifies the item. Also, notice that some sellers (refer to **Figures** 5-3 and 5-5) also use subtitles to pass on more information about their items.

 If you're interested in a particular type of item, take note of the keywords used in the title (you're likely to see them again in future titles). Doing so helps you narrow down your searches.

- **Watch this item:** Click this button to add the item to the Watching area of your My eBay All Buying page. From there you can keep an eye on the progress of the auction — without actually bidding.

- **Starting bid, Current bid, or Price:** This is the dollar amount that the bidding has reached. This amount changes throughout the auction as people place bids. If no bids have been placed on the item, it will read *Starting bid*. A fixed-price listing will show the asking price.

 Sometimes, next to the current dollar amount, you see *Reserve not met* or *Reserve met*. This means the seller has set a *reserve price* for the item — a secret price that must be reached before the seller will sell the item. The majority of auctions do not have reserve prices.

- **Buy It Now price:** If you want an item immediately and the price listed in this area is okay with you, click Buy It Now. You're taken to a page where you can complete your purchase. Buy It Now is an option and does not appear in all listings.

- **Time Left:** Appears for auctions only and shows how many days, hours, and (eventually) minutes are left until the auction is over. A date and time that the listing will close will also be posted. When the item gets down to the last hour of the auction, you'll see the time expressed in minutes and seconds. You'll also see the current date and time.

 Sometimes an item has no bids because everyone is waiting until the last minute. Then you see a flurry of activity as bidders try to outbid each other (a bidding strategy called *sniping,* which Chapter 6 explains). It's all part of the fun of the auction.

- **Quantity:** Appears only when multiple items are available. If it's a multiple-item, fixed-price sale, you have no opportunity to bid — you simply use Buy It Now to purchase whatever quantity of the item you want. You'll be prompted for a quantity when you buy.

- **Shipping costs:** If the seller offers free shipping — or is willing to ship the item anywhere in the country for a flat rate — you'll see that here. This area links to eBay's shipping calculator if the seller customizes the shipping expense according to weight and distance.

- **Return Policy.** Shows you the terms of your sale, including whether the seller accepts returns and offers merchandise credit or money back for returned items.

- **Coverage:** Depending on what kinds of payment the seller accepts, you will see the level of PayPal buyer protection on the transaction.

- **High bidder:** In an auction, this field shows you a shortened version of the high bidder's user ID (to protect the innocent, of course — and their privacy) and the feedback rating of the current high bidder (who could be you if you've placed a bid!).

When you're bidding, eBay hides your bidder ID by using anonymous names such as a***k. Your actual user ID is shown only to the item's seller.

Get to the Heart of the Listing

1. When you've made it through the top of an item listing, be sure you scroll farther down. When you do, you see three tabs (shown in **Figure 5-6**) that take you to the heart of the listing.

| Description | Shipping and payments | Related items and services |

Figure 5-6

2. Click the Description tab — and behold the most important part of the page! Read all the information about the item carefully before buying or bidding. Look at the Description tab for more photos of the item. The folks at eBay would like you to believe that you can see all the photos you need in the photo box at the top of the page; it gets such prominent placement because they charge the seller $.15 per picture! Savvy, experienced sellers (the pros!) use the same information I give you in Chapter 13 to insert photos into their descriptions, as shown in **Figure 5-7**.

3. Click the Shipping and Payments tab to see the details on shipping. As **Figure 5-8** shows, you see the following information:

- Whether the seller is charging a flat shipping fee or is offering more than one shipping option through a shipping calculator.

- A drop-down menu for selecting a country if you're having the item shipped to another country. Changing the country also changes the rate displayed.

- Who pays for the shipping (usually the buyer).

- Whether insurance is offered.

- Which states have to pay sales tax (if any) and the sales tax rate.

- Whether the seller is willing to ship to your area. (Sometimes sellers won't ship internationally, and they'll let you know that here.)

- The terms of the seller's Return Policy. For example, whether buyers have to pay for return shipping.

Pictures enhance item descriptions.

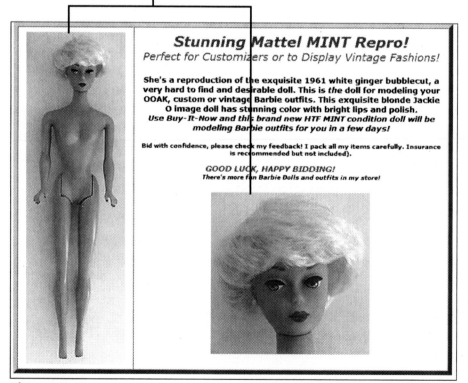

Figure 5-7

Not all sellers accept returns, and that's not always a bad thing. Don't penalize a seller who doesn't accept returns; small sellers may not have the luxury of being able to return opened items to the manufacturer for a refund. Be sure also to check the item description for other shipping information and terms of sale.

- Payment methods that the seller accepts, for example, credit cards or PayPal. Often this section tells you to read the item description for more details.

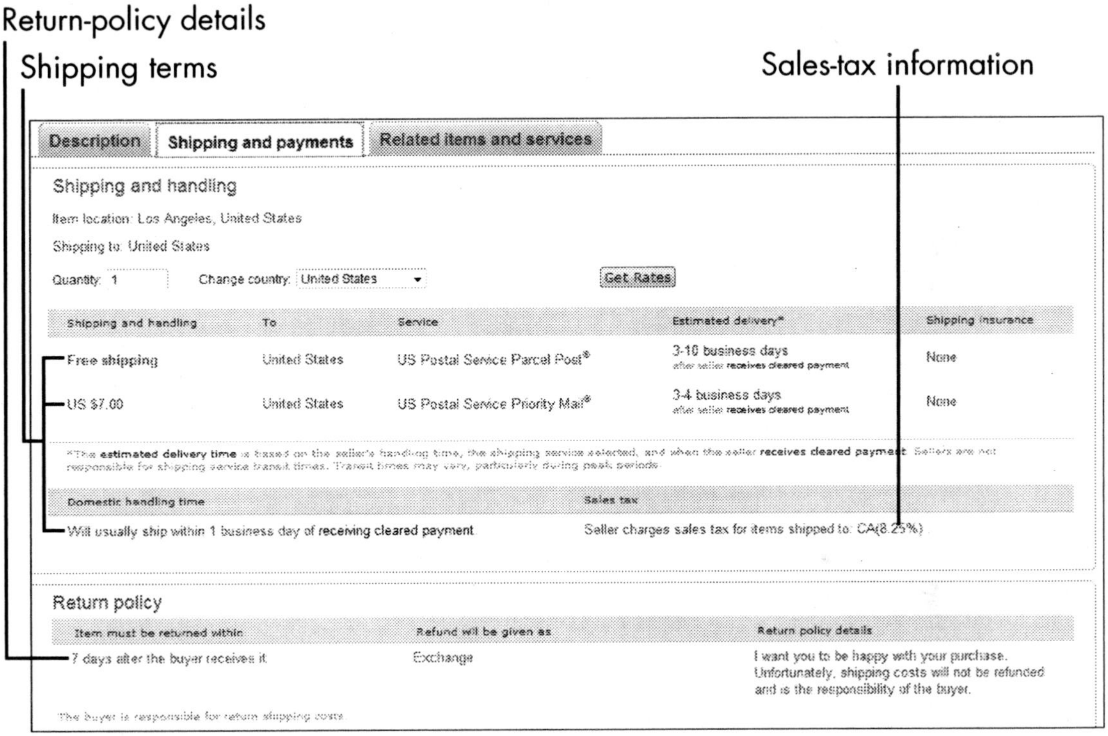

Return-policy details

Shipping terms

Sales-tax information

Figure 5-8

Note: For security's sake, it's against eBay policy for sellers to say that they take money orders or checks. If you wish to pay in either manner, click the Ask a Question link in the Seller Info area to e-mail the seller with your request. Many sellers still welcome good old money orders.

4. Click the Related Items and Services tab to see where eBay (to the consternation of many sellers) puts links to similar (and competing) items that you may be interested in. There is also some sort of eBay promotion shown in **Figure 5-9**.

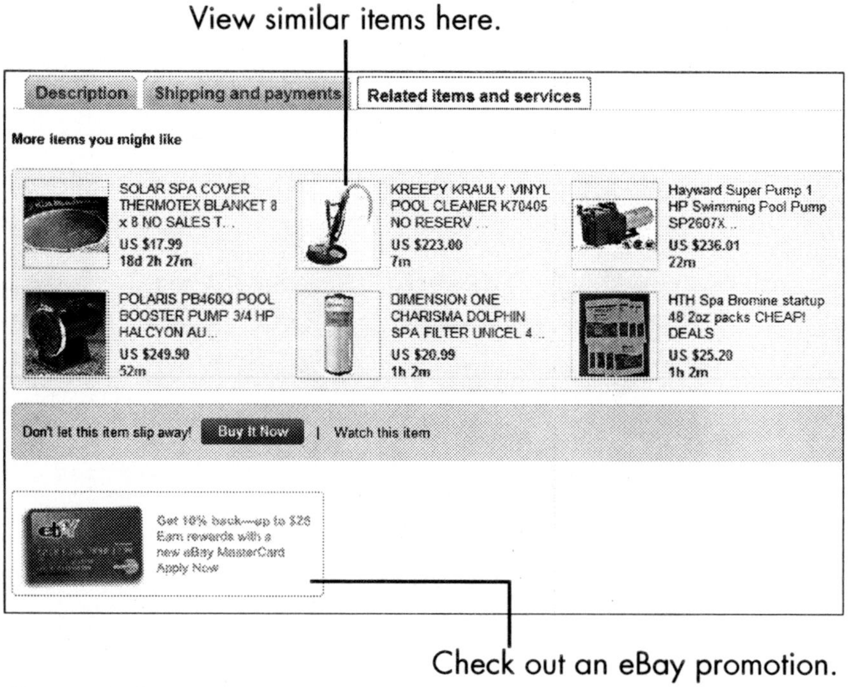

View similar items here.

Check out an eBay promotion.

Figure 5-9

Examine the Seller and Item Info

1. On the right side of a listing page, you see two stacked boxes similar to those shown in **Figure 5-10**. The top box is the Seller Info box where you find valuable information about (guess what?) the seller. Below it is an item information box, which offers you some handy details about the listed item.

Seller status and feedback info   Examine this feedback carefully.

Extra item information

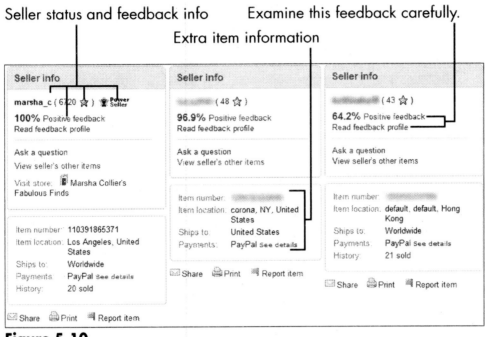

Figure 5-10

2. As with any community, eBay has its share of good folks and not-so-good folks. Your best defense against the not-so-good variety is to read the seller's feedback. Know thy seller ranks right after caveat emptor as a phrase that pays at eBay. As I tell you nearly a million times in this book, read the feedback profile! You see a link for just that purpose, as well as several other handy bits of information, in the Seller Info box:

- **Seller icons:** Show the status of the seller. A varied-color star reflects the feedback level of the seller (the color of the star changes with amount of positive feedback the seller attains). If the seller is a Top-rated seller (which means upholding the highest standards of customer satisfaction based on the DSRs awarded by customers), you see the Top-rated seller badge. A blue and red ME icon will point you to the seller's About Me page.

- **Feedback score:** This number is also to the right of the seller's name in parentheses. Click the number next to the seller's ID to view his or her eBay ID card and entire feedback history. Read, read, and reread all the feedback to make sure you feel comfortable doing business with this person.

- **Positive feedback percentage:** The eBay computers calculate this figure. It's derived from all the positive and negative feedback that a user receives.

- **Ask a Question:** Clicking this link hooks you up with eBay's e-mail system so you can ask the seller a question regarding the item.

- **Visit seller's other items or store:** This link takes you to a page that lists all the seller's current auctions and fixed-price sales. If the seller has an eBay store, a link to it appears here as well.

 Consider a quick glance at the Seller Info box as the "lightweight" version of feedback investigation. A perfunctory glance at this box might be okay if you're purchasing an item that's worth a few dollars to you — and if the seller's info box shows you 99% to 100% positive feedback. However, if the Seller Info box looks closer to the second or third example, and you're looking at a pricier item, it's time for a more thorough analysis. Further on, I show you how.

3. Below the Seller Info box is another box with important details about the listed item:

- **Item number.** A very important number for eBay buyers and sellers. Use it to cross-reference to your PayPal transaction and, if you're the seller, also to your eBay invoice.

 You can type the item number into any search box (without the title) to find a listing . . . but it's so much easier to click the Watch This Item link above the Seller Info box to keep track of a listing's progress.

- **Item location:** Tells you (at the very least) the country where the seller is located. You may also see more specific info, such as the seller's city and geographic area. (What you see depends on how detailed the seller chooses to be.) The item location is handy if you'd like to go pick up the item — but e-mail the seller first to see whether he or she would be willing to meet you at (say) a local Starbucks to complete the transaction.

- **Ships to:** If the seller ships to only the United States, you see that here. If the seller ships to any other countries, this is where you find them listed.

- **Payments:** See the type of payments accepted, such as PayPal.

- **History:** Tells you how many bids have been placed or how many items in a multiple price listing have sold. When the listing is live, you can click the number of bids to find out who is bidding and when bids were placed. You can click the number of bids to see how the bidding action is going, but you won't be able to see the high bidder's proxy bid. (In some circumstances, only the seller and buyer can access this data, so don't worry if you can't seem to get through to the history.)

4. Don't forget to look below the information boxes for three important links. Click these to

- **Share.** Ever come across an item that would be perfect for a friend? Click here and you can send them a link to the listing by e-mail. It's also handy if you want to send the link to yourself.

- **Print.** The Print link is pretty lame. If you click it, a quasi-version of the page comes up — without the seller's description! Fail.

- **Report Item.** Very important! Once you become familiar with eBay's rules, you get to be part of the community, and sometimes that means helping police the site. If you feel there is a violation in the listing you're viewing ($10 shipping for a 2-ounce item? Or an electronic copy of this book?) you can click here to report it to eBay.

Conduct the Full-Scale Seller Investigation

1. When you consider buying a more expensive item, be sure to click the seller's feedback number (beside the seller's user ID in the Seller Info box) when you visit the auction listing. Clicking the number takes you to the member's *Feedback Profile*, as shown in **Figure 5-11**. At the top of the profile, you get a lot of info, including

- **User ID:** The eBay member's nickname appears, followed by a number in parentheses — the net number of the positive feedback comments the person has received, minus any negative feedback comments. Next to the user ID, you see icons similar to those that show up in the Seller Info box on the item page.

These icons link to the seller's store and About Me page. You'll also see the seller's star rating and Top-rated seller designation (if applicable).

- **Seller data:** The important piece of data here is the date the person signed up as a member of the eBay community. Also you'll see the country from which the seller is registered.

Follow these links for lots more info.

See recent feedback totals.　Get more detailed ratings.

Feedback Profile

marsha_c (6724 ☆) 🏆 Power Seller me 📷
Positive Feedback (last 12 months): 100% [How is Feedback Percentage calculated?]

Member since: Jan-04-97 in United States

Recent Feedback Ratings (last 12 months)

	1 month	6 months	12 months
Positive	54	515	781
Neutral	0	0	0
Negative	0	0	0

Detailed Seller Ratings (last 12 months)

Criteria	Average rating	Number of ratings
Item as described	★★★★★	496
Communication	★★★★★	497
Shipping time	★★★★★	498
Shipping and handling charges	★★★★★	495

Member Quick Links

Contact member
View items for sale
View seller's Store
View more options ▾

| Feedback as a seller | Feedback as a buyer | All Feedback | Feedback left for others |

7,549 Feedback received (viewing 1-25)　　　　Revised Feedback: 0

Feedback	From / Price	Date / Time
Beautiful doll Well pkgd & Super Fast Shipping Great EBay Experience A++++!!!!!!	Buyer: marthahughes51 (158 ☆)	Jun-11-09 13:12
Barbie Vintage Repro PLATINUM BLOND BUBBLE CUT Doll (#110399635782)	US $19.99	View item

Figure 5-11

2. After you click the feedback number, you should examine some important details if you want to be a savvy, security-minded shopper. On the left side of the page you see the totals for Recent Feedback Ratings — and next to those, on the right, the Detailed Seller Ratings. You will see the

counts of feedback comments divided up by time: 1 month, 6 months, and 12 months. Note the following significant entries:

- **Positive comments:** You may notice that the *actual* number of positive comments (in Figure 5-11, 7,549 versus 6,724) is higher than the positive figure. This is because any feedback from one member to another posted within a seven day period only counts as ONE feedback rating. (The net rating was previously based on comments from *unique* users.)

- **Neutral comments:** Neutral comments are usually left when a party wasn't overjoyed with the transaction but nothing happened that was bad enough to leave a dreaded, reputation-ruining, negative comment.

- **Negative comments:** The number of negative comments may vary, just as the positives do, and for the same reasons.

 This time-based data is useful because often the last couple of months' transactions tell the tale. If a previously reliable eBay seller has decided to join the Dark Side, here is where the evidence will show up first. A number of new negative comments from different buyers constitute a definite danger sign (even if the seller has an overall high rating)!

3. To the right of the Recent Feedback Ratings, you can peruse the Detailed Seller Ratings. This box is where all those little feedback stars you place get to shine. (See Chapter 8 for the details of leaving feedback.) You'll be able to see how many ratings have been left — for each category — and where the Average Rating lies.

4. Don't forget to look to the far right of all the fancy feed-back data for the Member Quick Links box, which contains these handy links:

- **Contact Member.** Click here and you'll be taken to an e-mail form that allows you to send an e-mail to the seller through eBay's message system. You'll never see the member's e-mail address, because eBay keeps it private.

- **View Items for Sale.** Click here to see the current listings for this eBay seller.

- **View Seller's Store** (if the seller has one, of course), his or her other auctions (where you can see whether the seller is experienced in selling the type of item you're looking to buy).

5. The last link at the far right is View More Options. Clicking here shows you a drop-down menu with even more ways to get the scoop on the seller, as shown in **Figure 5-12.**

Get more seller insights here.

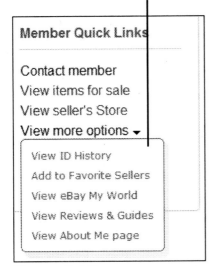

Figure 5-12

- **View ID History.** If the seller has made any changes to his or her user ID, you'll be able to see the IDs previously used on eBay here.

- **Add to Favorite Sellers.** This will add the seller (if you're so inclined) to your Favorite Sellers portion of your My eBay page. Chapter 3 has the scoop on what-all you can do with your My eBay page.

- **View eBay My World.** The My World page is a fun one where you can get a good look at the person's life on eBay.

- **View Reviews & Guides.** If the seller has reviewed products or written a guide (if you have a special area of interest check out the guides — with the caveat that eBay does not edit these for accuracy).

- **View About Me page.** The About Me page is where members talk about themselves, their businesses, and their collections. For example, you can find my About Me page at `http://members.ebay.com/about me/marsha_c`. If a new seller (without a lot of feedback) does the smart thing — puts up an About Me page and talks about his or her eBay goals and business — then you may feel more comfortable about doing business with that person.

 If you visit Chapter 9, I show you how to set up your own My World and About Me pages.

Read the Feedback Comments

1. Go to the seller's Feedback Profile by clicking the feedback number (beside the seller's user ID in the Seller Info box) when you visit an auction/item page. Below the

Recent Feedback Ratings, Detailed Seller Ratings, and Member Quick Links, are tabs that you click to see (and read) the actual feedback comments. By default, you see the All Feedback tab selected. You may use the other tabs to sort the comments for review as follows:

- **Feedback as a Seller:** These are comments from people who bought something from this seller.

- **Feedback as a Buyer:** When you buy and play by the rules, you get some positive feedback that shows up here.

- **All Feedback:** A conglomeration of all feedback left for the particular member, regardless of whether that person was a buyer or a seller in a transaction. You can tell which party left the feedback because the words *Seller* or *Buyer* appear on the right of each comment.

- **Feedback Left for Others:** Checking the type of feedback that a seller leaves about others can give you an insight into his or her personality.

2. Click the Feedback As a Seller tab and begin perusing the feedback entries for the seller you're investigating. By scrolling down the feedback history page, you'll be able to read the actual reviews left by other eBay members. In **Figure 5-13**, you can see a sample of my current feedback. On the Feedback as a Seller tab, you see each member's user ID, along with his or her feedback rating and comments. You also see the date when feedback was left, along with the transaction number. If the transaction is 90 days old or fewer, you can click the View Item link to see the transaction.

Feedback as a seller	Feedback as a buyer	All Feedback	Feedback left for others

5,226 Feedback received (viewing 1-25) Revised Feedback: 0

Feedback	From Buyer / Price	Date / Time
Beautiful doll Well pkgd & Super Fast Shipping Great EBay Experience A++++!!!!!! Barbie Vintage Repro PLATINUM BLOND BUBBLE CUT Doll (#110399835782)	madhatughosu51 (158 ⭐) US $19.99	Jun-11-09 13:12 View Item
Beautiful doll Well pkgd & Super Fast Shipping Great EBay Experience A++++!!!!!! VINTAGE #1 Blond Ponytail Repro Barbie DOLL w/ EARRINGS (#110399838797)	madhatughosu51 (158 ⭐) US $20.99	Jun-11-09 13:12 View Item
quick transaction...quality material ...excellent dealer Museum Putty QUAKE HOLD Wax Quakehold Earthquake LARGE (#110391865371)	verifeelx (615 ⭐) US $7.90	May-28-09 09:47 View Item
wonderful experience. truthfully fast,smooth. A+++++ Amiga 2009 EBAY BUSINESS All-in-One Reference For Dummies 2nd (#350203719495)	zzmmm (12 ⭐) US $24.49	May-27-09 19:06 View Item
Excellent seller. Fast ship. AAA+++ Museum Putty QUAKE HOLD Wax Quakehold Earthquake LARGE (#110379891869)	spacel707 (562 ⭐) US $7.97	May-27-09 18:06 View Item
fast shipping...thanks Museum Putty QUAKE HOLD Wax Quakehold Earthquake LARGE (#110379891869)	mmmtan (298 ⭐) US $7.97	May-27-09 16:30 View Item
Love It...Love It...Love It! Awesome piece, awesome service, awesome price! Portable PHOTO WINGS Lighting Diffuse Soft Box Umbrella (#120148378419)	kmmpbe (501 ⭐) US $28.99	May-27-09 09:25 View Item

Figure 5-13

 When buying from a seller who sells the same item repeatedly, use the clickable View Item links to past transactions to see whether *other* buyers of the same item were pleased with their purchases.

Evaluate Nuances of Feedback

1. Many independent eBay sellers are experienced buyers as well as sellers — they have an excellent grasp of how eBay feels from a customer's point of view, and they know how to handle any of your concerns. Keep in mind that the feedback system relies on the expectation that members give each other the benefit of the doubt. And so, the system allows for response to feedback that can help explain any concerns — and their resolutions.

2. When you come across negative (or neutral) feedback about a seller, look specifically for the seller's response; see whether (and how) the problem was resolved before you make your final judgment. You may even see a follow-up feedback comment from the buyer, saying that everything has been settled. A seller or a buyer may respond to the feedback by clicking the Reply to Feedback Received link at the bottom of the feedback page. (See Chapter 8 for more about leaving and responding to feedback.)

When I'm considering making a big purchase, I always check the Feedback Left for Others tab; it helps me know the type of person I'm dealing with. When you read feedback that makes nasty slams at the other person, or if the person uses rude words or phrases when leaving feedback, it's a clue that you may be dealing with a loose cannon.

Bidding and Buying on eBay

Chapter 6

*B*uying on eBay is actually very easy and involves two basic steps:

➡ **Finding an item you want to buy:** eBay items have an item description that tells you the details about the item. It gives you a clear idea about whether this is an item you want to buy.

➡ **Selecting the type of transaction you wish to participate in:** eBay listings appear in a number of ways. You can participate in an old-fashioned auction or you can Buy It Now. You can even make an offer on an item. (Be sure to check out Chapter 5 to see what the different sales pages look like.)

In this chapter, I explain exactly what to look for in the item. The different buying options will also be covered in depth. Once you have this information down pat, you should easily be able to purchase an item without unpleasant surprises.

Get Key Info from the Item Description

1. All eBay listings include an *item description*, which lists details about the item being sold. This description (as shown in **Figure 6-1**) is the most critical item on the item page. Read it carefully; pay very close attention to what is, and *isn't*, written.

Carefully read everything about the item.

Figure 6-1

2. Read the item description for clues about how the seller does business. You can often judge a seller by his or her item description:

- Well-crafted, succinct, and grammatically correct descriptions generally mean a seller is someone who planned and executed the listing with care. It takes time and effort to post a good listing.

- If the description has huge lapses in grammar, convoluted sentences, and misspellings, *you may get burnt!* There are those sellers who aren't serious about selling and may be out to sell junk for a quick buck. Before you deal with this seller, make sure that you feel comfortable that he or she is selling on eBay for the long term.

3. Read the item description carefully. A detailed item description should provide answers to general questions such as the following. (See Chapter 5 for tips on how to assess what you're buying.)

- Is the item new or used? Is it a first edition or a reprint? An original or a reissue?

- What condition is it in? Is it broken, scratched, flawed, or mint?

 Most experienced eBay buyers know that, depending on the item, a tiny scratch here or there may be worth the risk of making a bid. But a scratch or two may affect your bidding price.

- Is the item in its original packaging? Does it still have the original tags?

- Is the item under warranty?

- Are delays in delivery likely? If so, what sort and how long?

- Does the seller guarantee you a refund if the item is broken or doesn't work upon delivery?

- Is this item the genuine article or a reproduction — and if it's the real deal, does the seller have papers or labels certifying its authenticity? (Look at Chapter 5 for more advice for buying collectibles.)

- Who pays the shipping costs — you or the seller? While some sellers provide free shipping, most expect the buyer to pay for shipping. Be sure you factor in the cost of shipping when you consider how much you're willing to bid.

- How large is the item and how much does it weigh? This information is important, not only because that life-size fiberglass whale may not *fit* in your garage, but because size affects shipping costs. (It's a pretty safe bet that a baby grand piano sent from Anchorage to your home in Florida will cost a lot to ship.)

4. The best eBay sellers show several photos of their items, as in **Figure 6-2**. If additional pictures are available further down the page, take a good look. If a picture is available, is it clear enough that you can see any flaws? You can always ask the seller to e-mail you a picture taken from another angle.

Figure 6-2

Make the Tough Bid-or-Buy Choice

1. A particularly quirky situation can arise when an auction has some characteristics of a fixed-price sale. In this case, you see the Place Bid button along with the Buy It Now button.

2. If you like the item so much that you don't want to chance losing it (and you're willing to pay the listed price), click the Buy It Now button.

3. If you'd like to take your chances on winning the item at a lower price than the Buy It Now price on the listing, you can place a bid on the item. Just click the Place Bid button and go for it.

4. After a bid is placed (by you or someone else), the Buy It Now option disappears ... *unless* the seller has put a reserve price on the listing. If the seller has done that, the option to Buy It Now won't disappear until a bid meets the reserve price.

5. When the Buy It Now button is gone, the listing becomes a standard auction, and the item will be sold to the highest bidder. If you're still bidding, be sure to keep an eye on the listing by looking in the Bidding area of your My eBay page each day until the auction is over.

Ask the Seller a Question

1. The seller is obligated to describe the item honestly and in detail, so if your questions aren't answered in the item description or in the pictures provided, then for goodness' sake, e-mail the seller for the facts.

2. To ask a seller a question, click the Ask a Question link in the Seller Info box. You'll be taken to a page that has links to common questions (see **Figure 6-3**); click one that matches your query and see if your question is answered. If not, click the Contact Seller link.

3. **Figure 6-4** shows the form that appears. Select the type of question you have and then write your questions in the message area. When you're finished, click Send.

Click a link for
related common
questions.

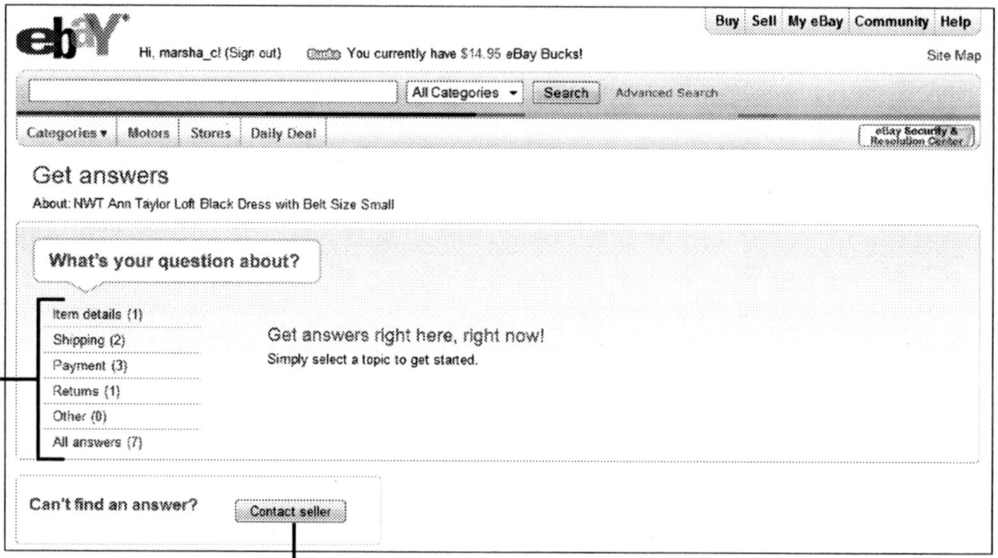

eb Y®
Buy | Sell | My eBay | Community | Help

Hi, marsha_c! (Sign out)   You currently have $14.95 eBay Bucks!   Site Map

[ ] All Categories ▾ | Search | Advanced Search

Categories ▾ | Motors | Stores | Daily Deal   eBay Security & Resolution Center

Get answers
About: NWT Ann Taylor Loft Black Dress with Belt Size Small

What's your question about?

Item details (1)
Shipping (2)   **Get answers right here, right now!**
Payment (3)   Simply select a topic to get started.
Returns (1)
Other (0)
All answers (7)

Can't find an answer?   [Contact seller]

Or contact the
seller for special
questions.

Figure 6-3

4. Expect to hear back from the seller within a day. If it
takes the seller more than a day or two to respond
(unless it's over the weekend — eBay sellers are entitled
to a little rest), and you get no explanation for the delay,
think twice before shelling out your cash.

Be sure to ask any questions you have *before* you bid.
If you wait to ask questions until after you've won
the item, you may get stuck with something you
don't want. Double-checking can save you woe and
hassle later. If you make a purchase and find out that
the seller misrepresented the item in the description,
you have the right to request to return the item or get
a refund from PayPal.

Type specifics
of your question here.

Choose your type
of question here.

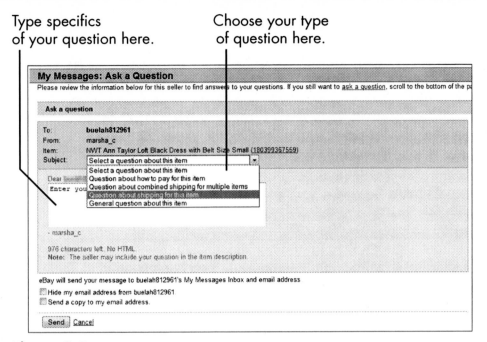

My Messages: Ask a Question
Please review the information below for this seller to find answers to your questions. If you still want to ask a question, scroll to the bottom of the p

Ask a question

To:	buelah812961
From:	marsha_c
Item:	NWT Ann Taylor Loft Black Dress with Belt Size Small (180399367559)
Subject:	Select a question about this item

Select a question about this item
Question about how to pay for this item
Question about combined shipping for multiple items
Question about shipping for this item
General question about this item

Dear

Enter you

- marsha_c

976 characters left. No HTML.
Note: The seller may include your question in the item description.

eBay will send your message to buelah812961's My Messages Inbox and email address

☐ Hide my email address from buelah812961
☐ Send a copy to my email address.

[Send] Cancel

Figure 6-4

5. If you buy the item and discover that *you* overlooked a detail in the description, then the seller isn't obligated to take the item back. If it is the seller's error and the seller won't take back the item, you may be able to apply for a refund through PayPal's Buyer Protection.

You'll often come across auctions that have the words *Reserve not met* next to the bid amount. By placing a reserve on the auction, the seller ensures that the item doesn't sell until the bidding reaches the mysterious reserve figure. The point of the reserve is to protect the seller's investment and get qualified bidders, not to waste your time. If you're bidding on a reserve-price auction, don't be afraid to e-mail the seller and ask what the reserve is. Yeah, reserves are mostly kept secret, but there's no harm in asking — and many sellers are glad to tell you.

Factor in Shipping Costs

1. Before you think about placing a bid on an item, keep in mind that the maximum bid you place won't be the only money you spend on an item. You need to also factor in the shipping costs, and, if applicable, sales tax. So make sure that the amount you're willing to spend includes these. If you have only $50 to spend, for example, don't place a $50 bid on a fragile item that has to be shipped a long distance because, as the buyer, you're the one who probably has to pay for shipping and insurance (insurance is included in the seller's shipping charges).

2. Don't abandon the sale just because you have to pay shipping. Sellers try to make shipping as affordable as possible to build sales.

- If the item is not an odd shape, excessively large, or fragile, experienced sellers base the shipping charge on rates at the U.S. Postal Service, which is the unofficial eBay standard. Expect to pay about $5.00 for the first pound.

- Some sellers (smartly) use First Class Mail for items that weigh less than 13 ounces after they're packed — and sellers of media often use the slower-delivery Media Mail for their items. These shipping techniques can save you big bucks!

- It's routine for the seller to add a dollar or so for packing materials such as paper, bubble wrap, tape, and such. This is a fair and reasonable handling charge because the cost of these items can add up over time.

 You may come across sellers trying to nickel-and-dime their way to a fortune by jacking up the prices on shipping to ridiculous proportions. If you have a question about shipping costs, ask before you bid on the item.

3. Before bidding on big stuff, such as a barber's chair or a sofa, check for a statement like this one in the item description: "Buyer Pays Actual Shipping Charges." When you see that, e-mail the seller before you bid to find out what those shipping charges would be to your home. On larger items, you may need to factor in packing and crating charges, as well. The seller may also suggest a specific shipping company.

4. As the bumper sticker says, *stuff* happens — sometimes to the stuff you buy. For that reason, you might want to make sure that the seller plans on insuring your eBay purchase. eBay transactions sometimes involve two types of insurance, each of which costs money to the seller:

- **Shipping insurance:** This insurance covers your item as it travels through the U.S. Postal Service, UPS, FedEx, or any of the other carriers.

 Some experienced sellers insure all their packages by buying annual policies with a company called Package In-Transit Coverage (U-PIC at www.u-pic.com). Such a policy offers convenience to the seller — who doesn't have to stand in line at the post office to get an insurance stamp. Instead, he or she simply logs the packages and reports on them monthly. A seller who uses this service will let you know when the item ships.

- **Buyer protection:** Paying through PayPal, eBay's electronic payment provider, (see Chapter 2 for information on getting a PayPal account), provides excellent protection against all kinds of seller shenanigans. Generally your items are covered for the full purchase price.

Bid on an Auction

1. You've found the perfect item (say, a really classy Elvis Presley wristwatch), it's in your price range, and you're ready to bid. What do you do? Well, first make sure you're registered. (For help in registering, see Chapter 2.) Then you find the bidding form (shown in **Figure 6-5**) at the top of the auction listing, or you can click the Place Bid button at the bottom of that page. If the item includes a Buy It Now option, you see that below the bid form.

Place a bid here.　　　Or buy the item immediately.

Figure 6-5

2. To fill out the bidding form and place a bid, sign in to your eBay account when you log onto the site. (You won't be able to do anything as the login page will pop up automatically.)

3. Scroll to the bid form on your selected item's page and enter your maximum bid in the appropriate box. The bid must be higher than the current minimum bid. You don't need to type in the dollar sign with your bid, but you do need to use a decimal point — unless you really *want* to pay $1049.00 instead of $10.49. If you make a mistake with an incorrect decimal point, you can retract your bid (see "Retract Your Bid in an Emergency," at the end of this chapter).

4. Click Place Bid (or Buy It Now if you're making a direct purchase). The Review and Confirm Bid page, as shown in **Figure 6-6,** appears on your screen, showing you all the costs involved in purchasing the item and explaining the terms of the purchase.

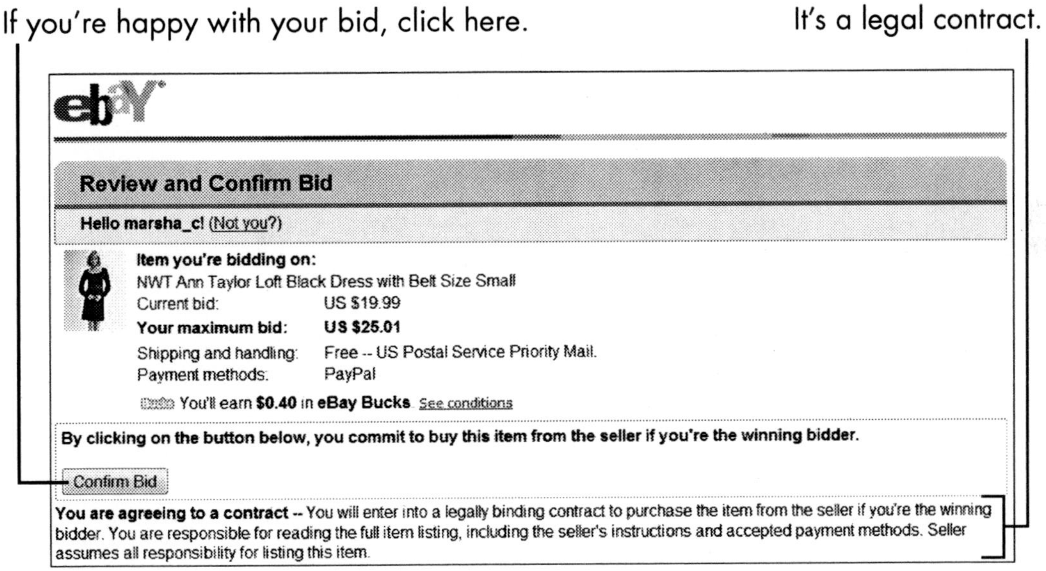

If you're happy with your bid, click here.   It's a legal contract.

ebaY

Review and Confirm Bid

Hello marsha_c! (Not you?)

Item you're bidding on:
NWT Ann Taylor Loft Black Dress with Belt Size Small
Current bid: US $19.99
Your maximum bid: **US $25.01**
Shipping and handling: Free -- US Postal Service Priority Mail.
Payment methods: PayPal

You'll earn **$0.40** in eBay Bucks. See conditions

By clicking on the button below, you commit to buy this item from the seller if you're the winning bidder.

[Confirm Bid]

You are agreeing to a contract -- You will enter into a legally binding contract to purchase the item from the seller if you're the winning bidder. You are responsible for reading the full item listing, including the seller's instructions and accepted payment methods. Seller assumes all responsibility for listing this item.

Figure 6-6

 This is your moment of truth: If you're not sure that you really want the item or you don't intend to buy it: *do not bid!* eBay considers a bid on an item to be a binding contract. You can save yourself a lot of heartache if you promise *to never bid on an item you don't*

intend to buy. Don't make spurious bids on the silly assumption that because you're new to eBay, you can't win; believe me, you can. Therefore, *before* you confirm your bid, be sure that you're in this auction for the long haul.

5. If you agree to the terms, click Confirm Bid. *Remember:* By agreeing to the terms, you "are agreeing to a contract . . . [and] will enter into a legally binding contract to purchase the item from the seller." In other words, if you bid on it and you win, you buy it. After you agree to the terms, the Bid Confirmation screen appears.

After you click Confirm bid, you'll see a page which will let you know the status of your bid. As you can see by **Figure 6-7**, I was outbid (so sad). You can keep track of any listing you're bidding or have indicated to watch on your My eBay Buying page.

Bid Confirmation	Item number: 180399367559

You are signed in

✗ **You've just been outbid. Do you want to bid again?**
- Another bidder placed a higher maximum bid or placed the same maximum bid before you did.
- Increase your maximum bid to have a chance to win this item.

Item you've bid on:
NWT Ann Taylor Loft Black Dress with Belt Size Small

Time left:	4 hours 46 mins [Aug-28-09 17:58:25 PDT]
History:	3 bids
Current bid:	US $25.57
Your maximum bid:	US $25.01

You'll earn **$0.51** in **eBay Bucks**.
See conditions

- How can you increase your chances of winning? See strategies
- How can you be notified when you are outbid? Get SMS alerts.

Increase your maximum bid: US $ [   ]   (Enter US $26.57 **or more**)

Bid Again >   or View seller's other items

Reminder: Even if you don't bid again, you could still end up as the winning bidder if higher bids are retracted or canceled. Continue to check the status of this item until it ends.

Click here to bid higher.

Figure 6-7

Bid to the Max by Proxy

1. To bid on eBay, you don't have to sit in on an auction 24 hours a day, 7 days a week, manually upping your bid every time someone bids against you. (You mean you have a life?) So you would like to place your high bid, but you don't want the other bidders to know how high you're willing to go. When you make your maximum bid on the bidding form, you actually make several small bids — again and again — until the bidding reaches the maximum you specified.

 If the current bid is up to $19.99, for example, and you put in a maximum of $45.02, your bid automatically increases incrementally so that you stay ahead of the competition — at least until someone else's maximum bid exceeds yours. Basically, you bid by *proxy*, which means the automatic-bid feature stands in for you so your bid rises incrementally in response to other bidders' bids. No one else knows for sure whether you're bidding automatically, and no one knows how high your maximum bid is.

2. The *bid increment* is the amount of money by which a bid is raised. As a buyer (or seller), you have no control over the bid increments. The current maximum bid can jump up a nickel or a quarter or even an Andrew Jackson, but there is a method to the madness, even though you may not think so.

3. To determine how much to increase the bid increment, eBay uses a *bid-increment formula* that's based on the current high bid. **Table 6-1** lists the bidding increments. Here's an example:

- A 5-quart bottle of cold cream has a current high bid of $14.95. The bid increment is $0.50 — meaning that if you bid by proxy, your automatic bid will be $15.45.

- A 5-ounce can of top-notch caviar has a high bid of $200. The bid increment is $2.50. If you choose to bid by proxy, your bid will be $202.50.

 When you place an automatic bid (a proxy bid) on eBay, eBay's bidding engine places only enough of your bid to outbid the previous bidder. If there are no previous bidders and the seller hasn't entered a reserve price, your bid appears as the minimum auction bid until someone bids against you. Your bid increases incrementally in response to other bids against yours.

Table 6-1	eBay's Bidding Increments
Current High Bid ($)	*Next Bid Increased By ($)*
0.01–0.99	0.05
1.00–4.99	0.25
5.00–24.99	0.50
25.00–99.99	1.00
100.00–249.99	2.50
250.00–499.99	5.00
500.00–999.99	10.00
1000.00–2499.99	25.00
2500.00–4999.99	50.00
5000.00 and up	100.00

4. To place a proxy bid in an auction, type your maximum bid in the appropriate box, or click the Place Bid button. A confirmation page appears, as shown in **Figure 6-8**, and you have one last chance to back out.

Confirm that this bid is what you want.

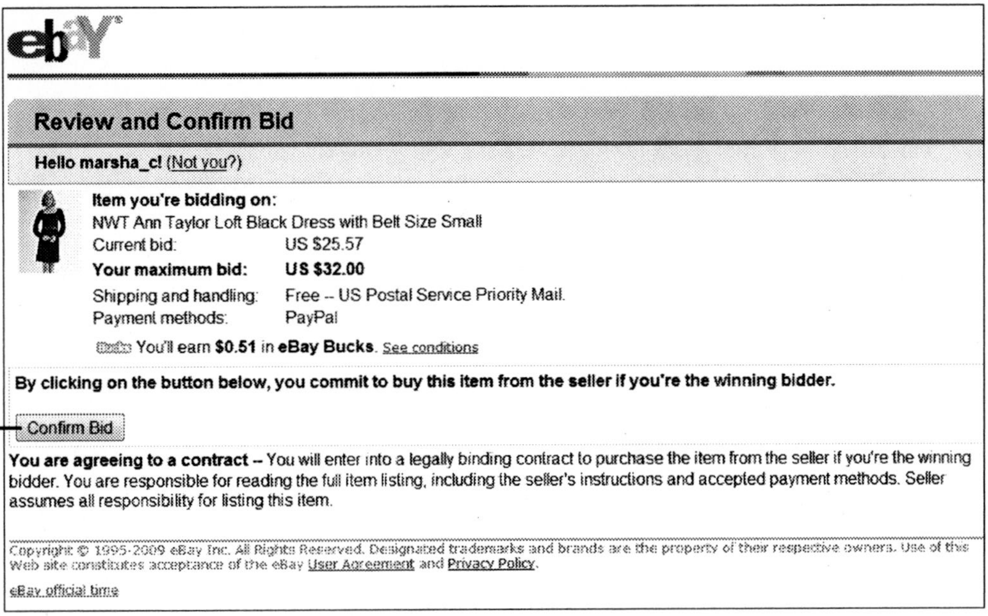

Figure 6-8

Before placing your proxy bid, give serious thought to how much you want to pay for the item. Be sure to take into account any other costs (like shipping and tax) you're expected to pay.

5. If everything is in order, click Confirm Bid. Or, if you get cold feet, click Back to Item. After you've placed your bid, the acknowledgment page lets you know whether you're the high bidder.

6. If you're not the high bidder in an auction, just scroll down the acknowledgment page to the rebidding area and place another bid, as explained in Step 4.

Synchronize Your Clock with eBay's

1. A bricks-and-mortar auction, such as those held by Sotheby's or Christie's, ends when the bidding ends. No auctioneer is going to cut off the feverish bidding for that one-of-a-kind Van Gogh, right? As long as someone is bidding, all systems are go. The last bidder standing wins. Auctions on eBay, however, close at a prescribed time. So you need to do some special work to make sure that you can make the most strategically timed bid possible.

2. To find out what time an auction ends, simply look at the auction page. Note that eBay runs on Pacific Time and uses a 24-hour clock (00:00 to 24:00 versus the more familiar 12:00 to 12:00).

3. To get the serious deals, synchronize your computer's clock with eBay's. Open your Internet browser and visit `http://viv.ebay.com/ws/eBayISAPI.dll?EbayTime`. The official clock at the eBay mothership appears, in the form of the Official Time page. Keep the browser open.

4. Right-click at the right end of your computer's taskbar and choose Adjust Date/Time from the resulting menu. The Date/Time Properties window appears, as shown in **Figure 6-9.**

5. Click the Internet browser to activate it, and then click the browser's Refresh button. After the page refreshes, immediately type the official eBay time into your computer's clock, and then click OK.

 If your computer is running the Windows XP or Vista operating systems, the box that appears when you right-click the taskbar has a third option: Internet Time. In this window you can synchronize your computer's clock to the Microsoft time server or the

National Institute of Standards and Technology's atomic clock.

Click here to change the time on your computer.

Date and Time	Additional Clocks	Internet Time

Date:
Friday, August 28, 2009

Time:
1:17:45 PM

Change date and time...

Time zone

(GMT-08:00) Pacific Time (US & Canada)

Change time zone...

Daylight Saving Time ends on Sunday, November 01, 2009 at 2:00 AM. The clock is set to go back 1 hour at this time.

☑ Remind me one week before this change occurs

How do I set the clock and time zone?

OK	Cancel	Apply

Figure 6-9

Bid from a Mellow Place

1. Sometimes the best strategy at the beginning of an auction is to do nothing at all. That's right; relax, take off your shoes, and loaf. I generally take this attitude through the first six days of a week-long auction I want to bid on, and it works pretty well. During this time mark the page to watch in your My eBay area and check in every day to keep tabs on the items you're watching and revise your strategy (or maximum bid) as the auction proceeds.

 You may want to make a *token bid* (the very lowest you are allowed). Why? Because if an auction has received no bids, the seller has the right to up the

minimum bid up to 12 hours before the auction
ends. A seller may choose to up the minimum bid to
protect his or her sale. By placing a minimum token
bid when you first see the auction, you can foil a Buy
It Now from another bidder (because Buy It Now is
disabled after a bid is in place) or prevent the seller
from upping the minimum.

2. As you check back each day, take a look at the other bids
and the high bidder. Is someone starting a bidding war?
Look at the time when the competition is bidding and
note any patterns, such as lunchtime bidding. If you
know what time your major competition is bidding, you
can bid after he or she does (preferably when your foe is
stuck in rush-hour traffic).

3. During the final 24 hours of the auction, rev up your bidding strategy and decide, once and for all, whether you
really *have* to have the item you've been eyeing. Maybe
you put in a maximum bid of $45.02 earlier in the week.
Now's the time to decide whether you're willing to go as
high as $50.02. Maybe $56.03?

No one wants to spend the day in front of the computer (ask almost anyone who does). Just place a
sticky note where you're likely to see it (or set up an
alarm on your cell phone), reminding you of the
exact time the auction ends. If you're not going to be
near a computer when the auction closes, you can
also use an automatic bidding software program to
bid for you; see "Outbid the Competition at the Last
Minute," later in this chapter, for details.

4. When only half an hour is left before the auction ends,
head for the computer and dig in for the last battle of the
bidding war. The last thing you want is to get caught in
Internet gridlock and not get access to the eBay Web site.

5. Log on to eBay about 15 minutes before the auction ends. Go to the items you're watching and click the auction title. If the auction is seeing a lot of action, when it has about 10 minutes to go, click the Refresh button on the listing page every 30 seconds to get the most current info on how many people are bidding. Once you place your bid, **Figure 6-10** shows the confirmation (I did this with only 32 seconds to go)!

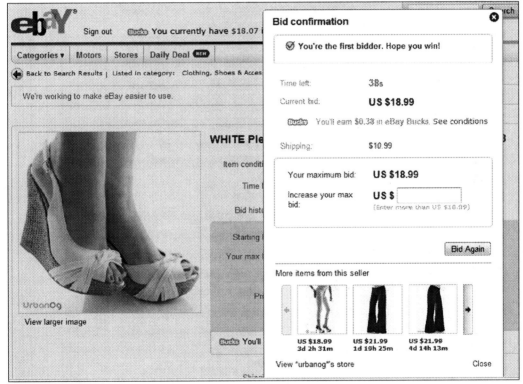

Figure 6-10

Outbid the Competition at the Last Minute

1. *Sniping* is the fine art of outbidding your competition in the very last seconds of the auction — without leaving them enough time to place a defensive bid. If you're going to snipe, assume that the current high bidder has a *very* high-dollar proxy bid in the works.

When I first touted this method in 1999, it was a fairly new idea. Now everyone knows about sniping, and it's pretty much an accepted bidding method. Some bidders, however, whine and moan when they lose to a sniper, but the fact is, the high bidder wins in any auction, whether you're sniping or using the automatic bid system. Some eBay members consider the practice of sniping unseemly and uncivilized— like when dozens of parents used to mob the department-store clerks to get to the handful of Cabbage Patch dolls that were just delivered. Of course, sometimes a little uncivilized behavior can be a hoot.

2. Sniping is my number one favorite way to win an auction on eBay. Sniping is an addictive, fun part of life on eBay. I recommend that you try it. You're likely to benefit from the results and enjoy your eBay experience even more — especially if you're an adrenaline junkie. Here are things to keep in mind when you get ready to place your snipe bid:

- **Know how high you're willing to go.** If you know you're facing a lot of competition, figure out your highest bid to the penny. You should have already researched the item and figured out its value. Raise your bid only to the level where you're sure you're getting a good return on your investment; don't go overboard. Certainly, if the item has some emotional value and you just have to have it, bid as high as you want. But remember, you'll have to pay the piper later. You win it, you own it!

- **Know how fast (or slow) your Internet connection is.** Before you start sniping, figure out how long it takes to get your bid confirmed on eBay. Test it a few times until you know how many seconds you have to spare when placing a bid.

If your Internet connection is slow, make your bid within the final two minutes before the auction ends. Adjust the amount of the bid as high as you feel comfortable so you can beat out the competition. If you *can* make the highest bid with just 20 seconds left, most likely you'll win. With many bids coming in the final seconds, your bid might be the last one eBay records.

3. Don't lose heart if you lose the auction. Remember, sniping is a game. This stuff is supposed to be fun. If you can't afford an item, don't get caught up in a bidding war. If you're losing sleep, barking at your cat, or biting your nails over an item, rethink what you're doing. If it's taking up too much of your life or an item costs too much, be willing to walk away — or log off — and return to bid another day.

Automate Your Snipe Bids

1. When it comes to eBay bidding and winning, a bunch of software programs and Web sites can help automate your shopping and feedback process. I like that my bids are placed for me — whether I'm near a computer or sleeping peacefully. One service that I have used successfully is BidRobot (see **Figure 6-11**). BidRobot deftly places sniping bids for you from its servers. It's won many an auction for me while I've been on the road or busy writing. The service is one of the least expensive out there, charging a low flat rate. Get a three-week free trial (all you can snipe for three weeks!) at www.bidrobot.com/cool.

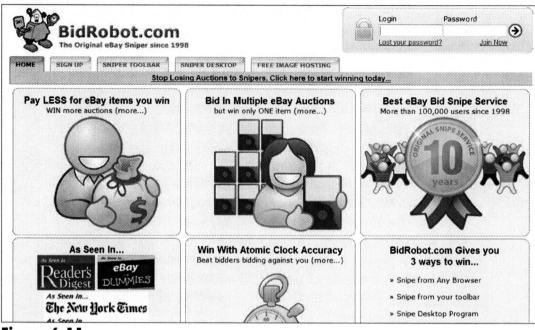

Figure 6-11

2. BidRobot also has a BidGroup feature you can use if you're bound and determined to get the lowest price for an item. This is accomplished by planning a bidding schedule at a set price. The bidding continues until you win your item (or not). To use BidGroup, search for your specific item on eBay. You may find a large number of eBay auctions that offer your item.

3. Select the auctions you'd like to bid on. Review the listings (checking the seller's feedback, description and PayPal Buyer Protection availability) and select six different listings.

4. Create your first snipe by typing your first snipe bid in the pale yellow Bid section at the very top of the BidRobot bid screen. Click as prompted on-screen to indicate that you want to create a group of bids with the other five auctions.

5. Group the other auctions. To bid on other seller's auctions, scroll down until you find the Pending Bid Group that contains your first item bid. Then use the form in that BidGroup area to add more snipe bids for other auctions in that specific BidGroup. You may add bids for as many additional auctions to this group as you like.

 If you win any one of the auctions in your BidGroup, the remaining bids in that specific group aren't placed. This is automatic.

Follow Strategies for Successful Bidding

Here are a few short tips that I know really work. Follow them and you should be able to increase your number of successful bids, but you'll also get better deals:

→ **Shop eBay.ca, eh!** That's right. If you're in the U.S., why not bid on auctions on the eBay Canada Web site? In fact, if you're an international bidder and are willing to pay shipping from the U.S., you'll have no problem handling Canadian shipping charges. From the eBay home page, scroll down the left side of the page and click the Canada link. Or you can visit www.eBay.ca.

If you're an American resident, all you have to do is think about the conversion between the U.S. and Canadian dollars — oh yes, there are bargains to be had. Be sure the seller has reasonable shipping to the United States *before* you bid.

→ **Place your bids in odd figures.** Many eBay bidders place their bids in the round numbers that match eBay's proxy system. You can win by a few cents if you place your bids in odd numbers like $10.97 or $103.01.

➡ **Don't get carried away in a bidding war.** Unless the item is rare, odds are that a similar item will show up on eBay again someday soon. Don't let your ego get in the way of smart bidding. Let your opposition pay too much!

➡ **Don't freak out if you find yourself in a bidding war.** Don't keel over if, at the split-second you're convinced that you're the high bidder with your $45.02, someone beats you out at $45.50.

➡ **Watch for item relistings.** If you see an item that you want but that has too high an opening bid (or too high a reserve), there's a good chance that no one else will bid on the item, either. Put that auction into your Watch area of My eBay. Then, after the auction ends, double-check the seller's auctions every so often to see whether the item has been relisted with a lower starting bid and a lower (or no) reserve.

➡ **Combine shipping when possible.** When you purchase an item, check the seller's other auctions to see whether you're interested in making a second purchase. If you see something else that appeals to you, e-mail the seller to see whether he or she will combine the items in shipping. That way, you can make two purchases for a smaller single shipping bill.

➡ **Don't bid early, but if you do, bid high.** The only time this bidding-early business works is if no one else is interested in the auction. Usually, though, the tactic gears up another eBay user to outbid you because suddenly the item is valuable to at least one person. If you *must* bid before the auction's close, bid high. As a matter of fact, bid a couple of dollars more than you want to pay. (I mean literally a couple, not a couple hundred.)

➠ **Try for a Second Chance offer:** If you get outbid and miss the chance to increase your bid on an auction item, why not e-mail the seller and ask whether he or she has any more of the item. You may get lucky, and the seller can send you a Second Chance offer for your high bid. Sellers may send Second Chance offers to underbidders in an auction under three circumstances:

> When the winner doesn't go through with the winning bid.

> When the reserve price wasn't met.

> When the seller has more than one of the sold item.

Any purchase you make in this manner is covered under PayPal's Buyer Protection Program, and you have the opportunity to leave feedback.

➠ **Bid during off-hours.** Between the hours of 23:00 (that's 11:00 p.m. Pacific Standard Time) and 03:00 (that's 3:00 a.m. Pacific Standard Time), things run a bit slowly on eBay. If you're online at that time, you may be able to take advantage of some very serious bargains. So swallow a shot of espresso and have fun if you're a night owl. To view the auctions that are going to end in the next few hours, use the Search Options on the left side of the page. Here you can cruise the auctions closing while the world is asleep, and bid to your heart's content to get some great bargains.

➠ **Check out eBay stores.** Before buying any item from a listing on eBay, check to see whether the seller has a red store icon along with the other seller information, as shown in **Figure 6-12**. If so, be sure to click the icon *before* you bid on the item. Most sellers run auctions for items to draw people into their eBay stores, where you may be able to find more interesting merchandise you can buy, have the seller put it in the same box along with your auction item, and save on shipping. For more on eBay stores, see the next section.

Click the store icon to see
what's offered there.

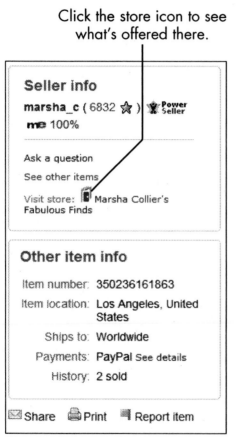

Figure 6-12

Buy an Item Outright

1. Although eBay's success was built on auctions, eBay also allows sellers to handle outright sales. You can make a direct purchase in any of the following ways:

- **By using the Buy It Now feature in an eBay auction:** You may have already looked at auctions and seen a

Buy It Now price located below the minimum or starting bid amount. That little indicator means that if you want the item badly enough, and the Buy It Now price is within your budget, you can end the auction right then and there by buying the item for the stated amount.

 You can still place a bid on an auction that has a Buy It Now option. When you do, the option to buy disappears and the item goes into auction mode. If the item has a reserve, the Buy It Now option doesn't disappear until the bidding surpasses the reserve amount.

- **In a fixed-price sale:** eBay also offers items for sale without the option to bid. These fixed-price listings may be for a single item or for multiple items. When multiple items are offered (see **Figure 6-13**), you can buy as many as you like.

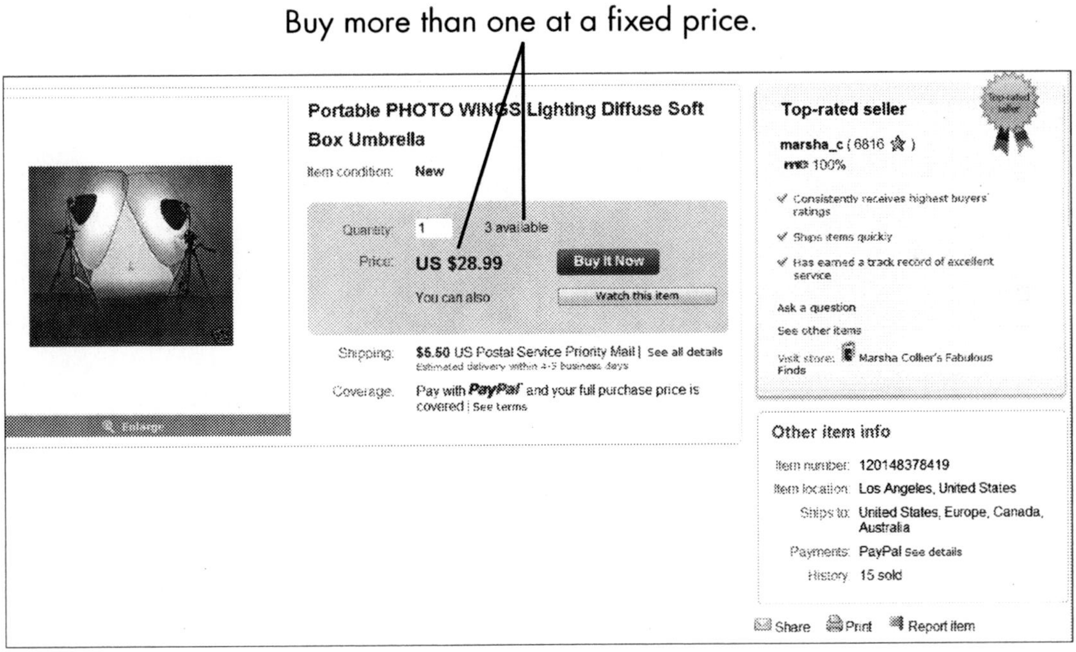

Buy more than one at a fixed price.

Portable PHOTO WINGS Lighting Diffuse Soft Box Umbrella

Item condition: New

Quantity: 1   3 available

Price: **US $28.99**   **Buy It Now**

You can also   **Watch this item**

Shipping: **$6.50** US Postal Service Priority Mail | See all details
Estimated delivery within 4-5 business days

Coverage: Pay with **PayPal** and your full purchase price is covered | See terms

Top-rated seller

marsha_c (6816 ☆)

100%

✓ Consistently receives highest buyers' ratings
✓ Ships items quickly
✓ Has earned a track record of excellent service

Ask a question
See other items

Visit store: 🏪 Marsha Collier's Fabulous Finds

Other item info

Item number: 120148378419
Item location: Los Angeles, United States
Ships to: United States, Europe, Canada, Australia
Payments: PayPal See details
History: 15 sold

✉ Share   🖶 Print   ⚑ Report item

Figure 6-13

- **In one of eBay's stores:** eBay stores are the secret weapon for knowledgeable eBay shoppers because you can consistently find great deals there. Sellers can list items in their eBay stores for even lower fees, passing their savings on to you, the savvy bargain hunter.

2. You can get to the eBay Stores hub from the eBay home page by clicking the eBay Stores link under the search in the top bar or by typing the following Web address:

   www.ebaystores.com

At the center of the eBay Stores hub page, as shown in **Figure 6-14**, you see a small group of store logos. These logos change every few minutes as eBay rotates its *Anchor Stores* through the area. Store owners pay a considerable amount to have their stores listed as Anchor Stores.

These stores are featured.   These are the Anchor Stores.

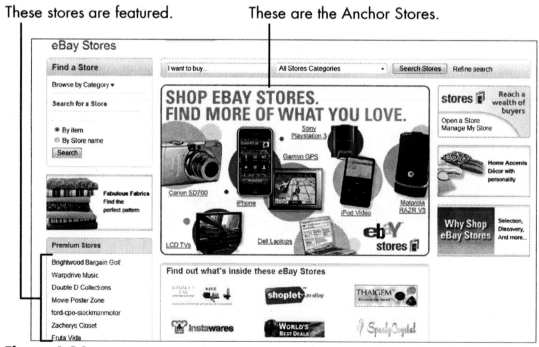

Figure 6-14

3. To the left of the store logos is a list of clickable links to stores. These are *Premium Stores.* You can find more stores, including the smallest ones — the cottage industry sellers — by clicking one of the category links on the left side of the page.

Retract Your Bid in an Emergency

1. As a buyer, you may, under certain circumstances, retract your bid. Just note that each time you retract your bid from an auction, the retraction shows up above the Feedback comments. Sellers often check this area to determine a bidder's reliability. (A history of bidding on items and then changing one's mind is a danger signal for sellers.) Here are the circumstances in which it's okay to retract a bid:

- **You accidentally typed the wrong bid amount:** Say you typed $900 but you meant $9.00. Oops. When you retract a bid because of a bidding error, you wipe out any of your previous bids in the auction. In a case like this, you can retract the bid, but you'd better rebid the proper amount (that original $9.00) immediately, or you may be in violation of eBay's policies.

- **The seller has added information to the item description that changes the value of the item considerably:** The bull that was let loose in the seller's shop has changed the mint condition of the Ming vase you just bid on? No problem.

- **You can't reach the seller through eBay's e-mail or through the telephone number you got from eBay's find members area.** Has the seller gone AWOL and you have a question about an item you've bid on? eBay can help get you in touch, as follows:

1. *Use eBay's e-mail system by clicking the Ask a Question link in the Seller Info box on the auction page.*

2. *Or to get the seller's telephone number, click the Advanced Search link (at the top-right corner of most eBay pages) and then click the Find a Member link (on the left side of the page).*

3. *Next, input your transaction number and the seller's user ID.* After checking to make sure that you've begun a transaction with this person (in this case, you placed a bid), the good people at eBay will send the seller's telephone number in an e-mail message to your registered e-mail address. Your phone number will also be e-mailed to the seller.

- **You placed more than one bid on the same auction, and one of those bids was during the auction's last 12 hours.** If you did so, you can retract the last bid within one hour of placing it. In this case, only that last bid is retracted; any other bid placed before the last 12 hours of the listing remains valid.

 If you have to retract your bid within the last 12 hours of the auction, you must send an e-mail to the seller asking him or her to cancel your bid. It is up to the seller whether to cancel your bid. A bid retraction isn't a guarantee that you will get out of purchasing the item. Sometimes sellers simply don't have the opportunity or time to cancel a bid. If that happens to you, you have to buy the item.

2. To retract your bid (or find more information), go to

```
http://offer.ebay.com/ws/eBayISAPI.
dll?RetractBidShow
```

You can also find your way to the Bid Retraction form, shown in **Figure 6-15**, by clicking the Buying Related links on your My eBay Buying page.

Fill in the item number...   ...And a good reason for retracting here.

Bid Retractions

Before bidding on an item on eBay, be sure to read the item description and check the seller's feedback. If you have any questions about the listing, contact the seller by going to the View Item page and clicking on either the seller's User ID or on the Ask Seller a Question link.

Please remember that every bid on eBay is binding (unless the item is listed in a category under the Non-Binding Bid Policy or the transaction is prohibited by law or by eBay's User Agreement). Bidding on multiple identical items should be done only if you intend to buy all of the items.

It is ONLY OK to retract a bid if...

- You accidentally enter a wrong bid amount (for example, you bid $99.50 instead of $9.95). If this occurs, re-enter the correct bid amount immediately.
- The description of an item you have bid on has changed significantly.
- You cannot reach the seller. This means that you have tried calling the seller and the seller's phone number doesn't work, or you have tried emailing the seller and it comes back undeliverable.

Before you retract your bid, please read complete information on bid retractions including the Special Retraction Rules.

Item number of auction in question:

Your explanation of the retraction:
Choose one

If you have a valid reason not listed above, you can:
Contact the seller and ask the seller to cancel the bid, or contact Rules & Safety

Retract bid

Figure 6-15

3. After you make sure your reason for wanting to retract is valid, fill in the item number, choose Your Explanation of the Retraction from the drop-down list, and click Retract Bid.

Be careful when you retract a bid. All bids on eBay are binding, but under what eBay calls exceptional circumstances, you may retract bids — I encourage that you do so sparingly. eBay vigorously investigates members who abuse bid retractions. Too many bid retractions and you may find yourself suspended.

Paying For and Receiving Your Merchandise

Chapter 7

After the auction ends, there's no marching band, no visit from a D-List celebrity (with camera crew), no armful of roses, and no oversized check to duck behind. In fact, if you've won the auction, you're most likely to find it out from either the seller or the *Won* section of your My eBay page; as a rule, you won't hear about it right away from eBay. eBay tries to get its End of Sale e-mails out pronto, but sometimes there's a bit of lag time. So, if you think you may have won the auction and don't want to wait around for eBay to contact you, follow the advice in the first section of this chapter and find out for yourself.

Whether you win an auction or are simply buying an item outright, your next task is to pay for the item. When you buy something in a bricks-and-mortar store, you need to check out to pay. eBay isn't much different. This chapter shows you the ins and outs of using eBay's Checkout, which is a convenient way to pay for your completed auctions, fixed-price sales, and Buy it Now sales with a credit card or eCheck through PayPal (see Chapter 2 for how to set up a PayPal account).

After you pay and receive the package from the seller, open and inspect your item right away. The vast majority of eBay transactions go without a hitch. You win, you send your payment, you get the item, you check it out, and you're happy. If that's the case — a happy result for your auction — be sure to leave some positive feedback for the seller! (Find out how to leave feedback in Chapter 8.)

A snag in the transaction is annoying, but don't get steamed right away. Contact the seller and see whether you can work things out. Keep the conversation civilized. The majority of sellers want a clean track record and good feedback, so they'll respond to your concerns and make things right. Assume the best about the seller's honesty, unless you have a real reason to suspect foul play. Remember, you take some risks whenever you buy something that you can't touch before you pay. If the item has a slight problem that you can live with, leave it alone and don't go to the trouble of leaving negative feedback about an otherwise pleasant, honest eBay seller.

Find Out Whether You Won the Auction

1. The Buy section of your My eBay summary page shows you all your bidding, watching, and buying action on the site. Click the My eBay link in the navigation bar at the top of the page to get to your summary page.

2. Click the Won link in the Buy summary area at the left of the page (as pictured in **Figure 7-1**). You'll see that eBay highlights the titles of auctions you've won and indicates the amount of each winning bid.

Click Won. Items you've won Winning bids

Activity	Messages (63)	Account			✗ General settings

Summary

▽ **Buy**
All Buying
Watch (60)
Active (0)
Won (9)
Didn't Win (0)
eBay Bucks
Deleted

▽ **Selling Manager Pro**
Summary
Inventory (29)
Scheduled
Active (47)
Unsold (64)
Sold (158)
  Awaiting Payment
  Awaiting Shipment
  Paid & Shipped
Archived (9)
Reporting
Picture Manager
Automation Preferences

Buying Reminders Edit ▾

{Last 31 days}
☆ I need to leave feedback for 4 items

Won (9) Edit ▾

View [All (9) ▾]   Period [Last 60 days ▾]   Sort by [Time ended: re(...) ▾]

		Price	Shipping	$ ▣ ☆ ★	
	BNWT Diane von Furstenberg Heron in GUAVA sz.8 ___ (94 ★) 100.0% Sale date: 06/24/09 Tracking number: ···	$66.00	$3.75	$ ▣ ☆ ★	Leave ▾ feedback
	Cosequin for Cats & Small Dogs 90 Capsules- 11308 ___ (2093 ★) 99.9% Sale date: 06/22/09 Tracking number: ···	$25.97 ⚡Buy It Now	$4.95	$ ▣ ☆ ★	Leave ▾ feedback
	Brand New Canon PowerShot SD1100IS 8 MP Digital Camera ___ (760 ★) 99.7% Sale date: 06/17/09 Tracking number: 9102128882300747890221	$174.99 ⚡Buy It Now	Free	$ ▣ ☆ ★	Leave ▾ feedback
	NEW DIANE von FURSTENBERG UNIQUE JERSEY SPRING DRESS, S ___ (4088 ★) 99.7% Sale date: ···	$45.00	$5.95	$ ▣ ☆ ★	Leave ▾ feedback

Figure 7-1

 Throughout the bidding process, dollar amounts of items that you're winning appear in green on your My eBay Active page. If you've been outbid, those amounts appear in red and you'll see a red bar that reads *OUTBID*, as in **Figure 7-2**.

3. If you find that you're the winner, proceed as soon as possible to Checkout and pay for your item. An easy way to get to Checkout is to go to the listing and click the Pay Now link you will find there.

Click Active.   You're outbid here.

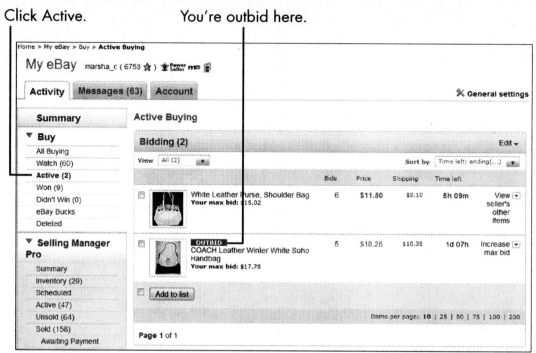

Figure 7-2

Save Your Winning Information

1. PCs were supposed to create a paperless society, but we're not there yet. (Cars were supposed to fly by the year 2000, too . . . maybe it's just as well that some predictions don't come true — think about how some folks steer shopping carts.) Many people feel more comfortable keeping their receipts and filing them in real manila folders. If that describes you, print out copies of your eBay purchase records to help keep your transactions straight.

2. The item page shows the amount of your winning bid, the item's description, and other relevant information. The second you find out you've won the item, look for the Print link at the bottom of the Seller Info box.

3. Click the Print link to bring up a page for printing.
It resembles an item page, but when you scroll, notice
the description is missing. At the top of the page (see
Figure 7-3) is a bar with a couple of links. Click Seller's
Description, and you will get a page that has only the
description — so you can print that, too.

Click here to print the item description.

Figure 7-3

 eBay displays completed listings in search results for
only 30 days, so don't put off printing out that final
item page for your records. If you save your End of
Sale e-mails that you get from eBay, you can access
the listing for up to 90 days by using the link in the
e-mail.

4. Many sellers have multiple listings going at the same
time, so the more organized you are, the more likely you
will receive the correct item from the seller. Here's a list
of the documentation you might feel more comfortable
printing for safekeeping in your "Item Purchases" file:

- A copy of your winning e-mail from eBay. *Don't* delete the e-mail — at least not until you print a copy and keep it for your records. You may need to refer to the e-mail later, and there's no way to get another copy.

- Printed copies of any e-mail correspondence between you and the seller that details specific information about the item or special payment and shipping arrangements.

- A printed copy of the final auction page.

Make Your Payment Immediately

1. eBay's Checkout is integrated directly onto the item page so you can win an auction *and* pay for an item in less than a minute. (Some sellers indicate, in the item description, that they will send you a link to their private checkout page.) When the sale is over, the item page will have checkout information, as shown in **Figure 7-4**.

Click here to start Checkout.

Figure 7-4

2. Keep in mind that you can make your payment in one of three ways:

- **Credit Card:** You can use your American Express, Discover, Visa, or MasterCard to make your payment through PayPal. The cost of the item is charged to your card, and your statement will reflect a PayPal payment with the seller's ID.

- **eCheck:** Sending money with an eCheck is easy. It debits your checking account just like a paper check. It does not clear immediately, and the seller probably won't ship until PayPal tells him or her that the eCheck has cleared your bank.

- **Instant Transfer:** An instant transfer is just like an eCheck, except it clears immediately and the money is directly posted to the seller's account. To send an instant transfer, you must have a credit card on file with PayPal as a backup (in case your bank denies payment).

 PayPal is my favorite payment service — for its convenience and for another reason: its buyer-protection program, which covers your purchases against fraud or gives you the option to return your item if it arrives not as described.

3. Click the Pay Now button on the item page or the Pay For It button in the winning e-mail that you get from eBay (as in **Figure 7-5**), and you're taken step-by-step through the checkout process. You pay for the item, the seller is notified, and you get an e-mail confirming your payment, along with the seller's e-mail address.

Item and seller information.

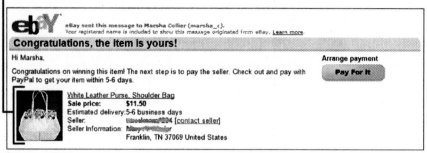

Figure 7-5

4. If you're dealing with a Buy It Now or fixed-price listing, you don't have to wait and go back to the listing once you've purchased the item. After you confirm to eBay that you want to make a purchase, you're taken immediately to a page with a Pay Now button, as shown in **Figure** 7-6.

Just click here to pay.

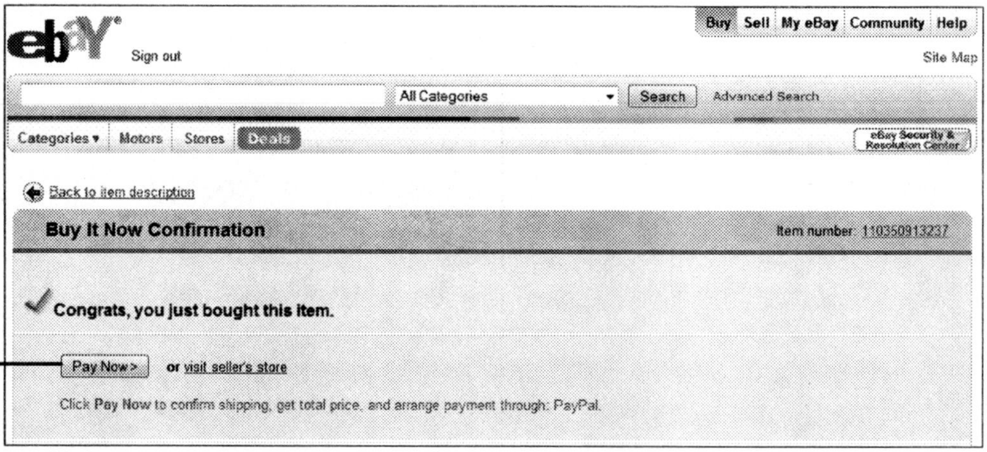

Figure 7-6

5. After you click the magic Pay Now button, you're whisked to a page where you can review your purchase, as shown in **Figure 7-7**. Below the Order Details section, you find a link you can click if you want to type a message to the seller. Click Add Message and type away, perhaps something like *"Please mark package to leave on porch."*

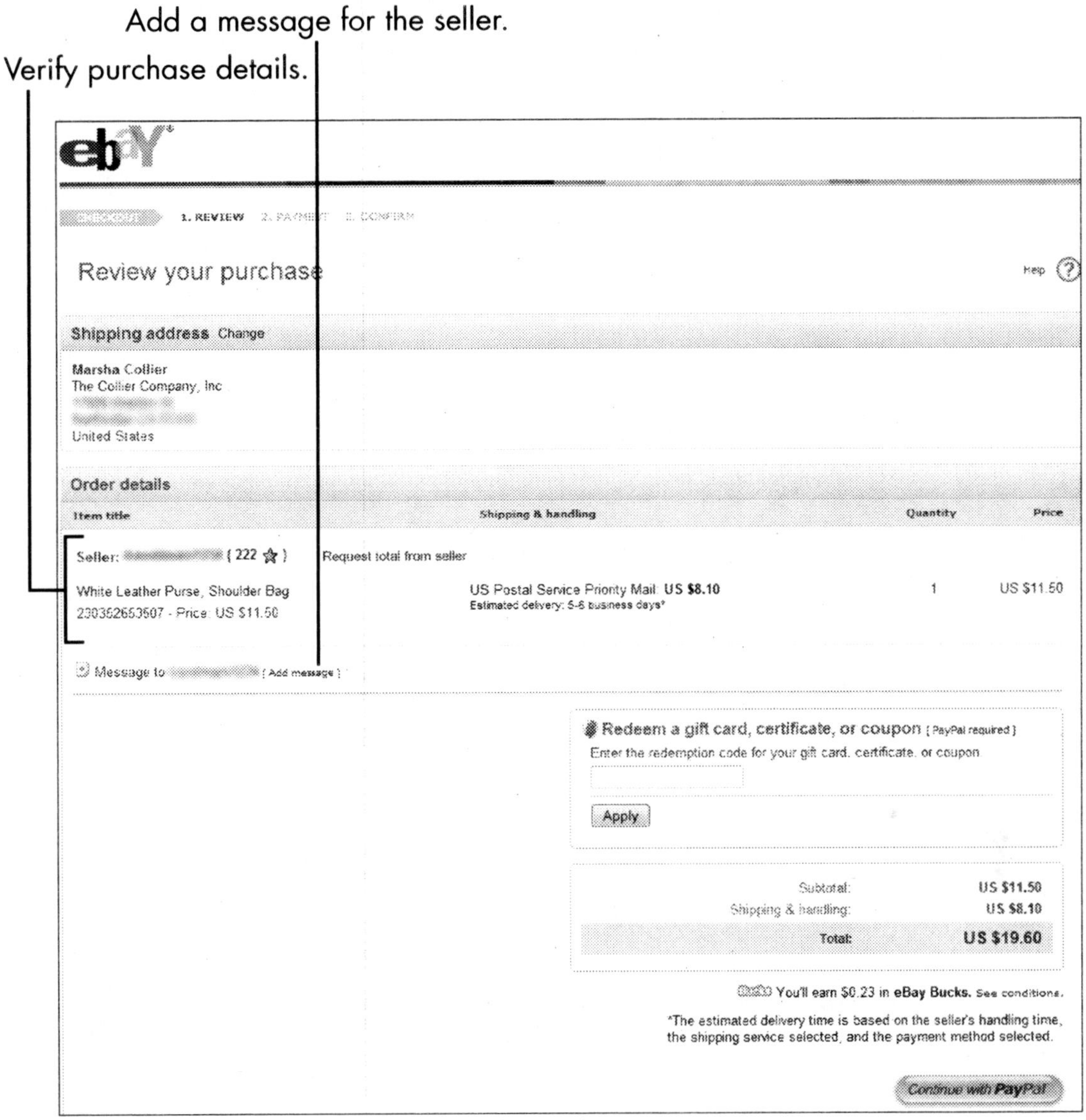

Add a message for the seller.

Verify purchase details.

Figure 7-7

6. If you're satisfied that the order details are correct, scroll to the bottom and click the Continue with PayPal button.

7. The next page is the sign in page for PayPal (see **Figure 7-8**). Your e-mail address (assuming you have a PayPal account) will already be filled in; just type in your password and click the Log In button — don't worry, it's safe.

Type your password and click Log In.

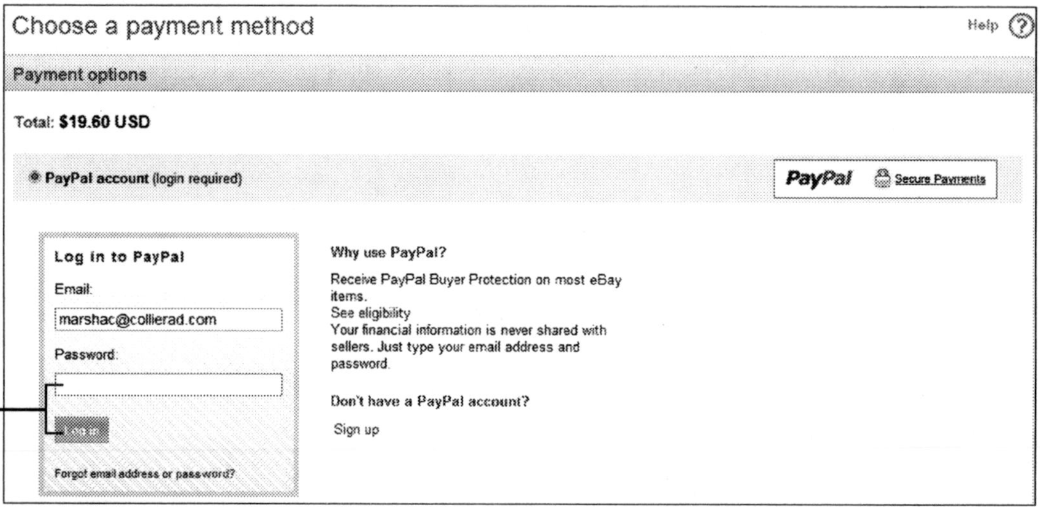

Choose a payment method   Help ⑦

Payment options

Total: **$19.60 USD**

◉ PayPal account (login required)   *PayPal* 🔒 Secure Payments

Log in to PayPal

Email:

marshac@collierad.com

Password:

Log In

Forgot email address or password?

Why use PayPal?

Receive PayPal Buyer Protection on most eBay items.
See eligibility
Your financial information is never shared with sellers. Just type your email address and password.

Don't have a PayPal account?

Sign up

Figure 7-8

8. The next page (see **Figure 7-9**) is your last chance to confirm everything, so take a special look at the Payment Method box. If you have money in your PayPal account from a previous payment deposited in your account), PayPal will use that money to make the payment. If there's not enough in your account (or no cash at all in the account), PayPal will take payment in one of two ways:

Check the payment info and make a change here.

Confirm your payment

Shipping address Change

Marsha Collier
The Collier Company, Inc

United States

Payment method

Withdrawals from your PayPal account

PayPal 🔒 Secure Payments

$19.60 USD from bank account   [More funding options]

*PayPal will use your credit card Mastercard   if your bank does not have enough funds to complete this transaction

Visit Funding Sources to learn more about PayPal policies and your payment source rights and remedies.

Confirm payment

Order details Change

Item title	Shipping & handling	Quantity	Price
Seller: (222 ⭐)			
White Leather Purse, Shoulder Bag	US Postal Service Priority Mail: **US $8.10**	1	US $11.50
230352653507 · Price: US $11.50	Estimated delivery: 5-8 business days*		

Subtotal		US $11.50
Shipping & handling		US $8.10
Total:		**US $19.60**

Figure 7-9

- **Direct from your bank account.** This will withdraw the payment directly from the bank account you registered with PayPal. If you have more than one registered bank account, and want to use one that's different from the one shown, read on.

- **From your credit card.** I always use my credit card for all online purchases. (Hey, it's one way to get frequent-flyer miles.)

9. You can change the default (of bank withdrawal) by clicking the More Funding Options link. If you don't click here to make a change, the money will be withdrawn from your bank account for payment when you click Confirm Payment.

Figure 7-10 shows you the Funding Options page. Note that each line has a drop-down menu. Click the option button next to the payment method you want to use. Then click the down arrow; when another list of your registered payment options appears, select a bank account or credit card you've registered with PayPal.

Click an option.   And choose from its drop-down list.

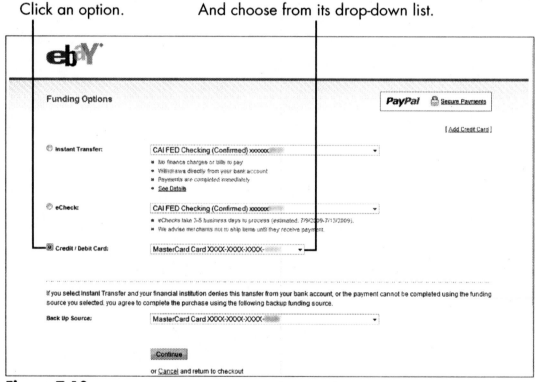

Figure 7-10

10. After you make your payment choice, click Continue and then (finally) confirm your payment. When you check on the item on your My eBay Won page, you'll see a bold dollar sign ($) on that item's line, as shown in **Figure 7-11**. It indicates that you've paid. (The same information will appear on the seller's My eBay Sold page.)

The bold symbol shows you paid.

Figure 7-11

If, for some reason, you're sending the seller a check or money order (which you can do only if you pre-arrange it with the seller), be sure to include a document that identifies you to the seller. Buyers routinely send out payments *without* name, address, or any clue as to what they've purchased. (Big oops.) No matter how you pay, be sure to include a copy of the eBay confirmation letter, a printout of the auction page, or a copy of the e-mail the seller sent you.

Inspect Your Item Immediately

1. As soon as you receive the package containing the item you won (or bought) on eBay, open and inspect it immediately. If you're not happy with the item you receive, the seller may have some 'splaining to do. E-mail or call the seller immediately and (politely) ask for an explanation if the item isn't as described. Some indications of a foul-up are pretty obvious:

- The item's color, shape, or size doesn't match the description.

- The item is scratched, broken, or dented in ways that don't match the description (the description said the doll was new, but the box is tattered and the doll has seen more than its share of action).

- You won an auction for a set of candlesticks and received a vase instead.

2. Of course, while I can give you advice on what you *deserve* from a seller, you're the one who has to live with the item. If you and the seller can't reach a compromise and you really think you deserve a refund, ask for one.

 If an insured item arrives at your home pretty well pulverized, call the seller to alert him or her about the problem. Find out the details of the insurance purchased by the seller. After you have all the details, follow the seller's instructions on how to make a claim. If the item was shipped through the post office, take the whole mangled shebang back to the post office and talk to the good folks there about filing a claim.

Make a Claim if the Item's Not Right

1. PayPal's protection program covers fraud. As a buyer who pays for eBay items through PayPal, you can be covered against fraud for the full purchase price of your item. Before you make a claim to PayPal, make sure that you exhaust your options for dealing directly with the seller (see the previous section) and that you also understand what PayPal means by "fraud."

 Fraud is loosely defined as nondelivery of an item or receipt of an item that's *significantly* different from the way it was described. Sorry — this doesn't cover your disappointment when you open the box and just don't like the item. Oh yes, remember that it also won't cover downloadable software or digital items — even if you buy them on eBay.

2. Remember the following few rules for using PayPal's buyer-protection system and making claims:

- **Number of claims:** You may make only one claim per PayPal payment.

- **Timing:** Your claim must be made within 45 days of your PayPal payment.

- **Participation:** You must be ready and willing to provide information and documentation to PayPal's buyer-protection team during the claims process.

3. Gather your information about the transaction-gone-wrong (see the earlier task "Save Your Winning Information"), and start your claim with PayPal by clicking the Resolve a Problem link from the drop-down menu next to the item in your My eBay Won area. Then follow the directions you find; it's a simple and clear process. eBay does want to have happy buyers!

Part II

Shopping at the eBay Marketplace

The 5th Wave · By Rich Tennant

"Oh, that there's just something I picked up as a grab bag special from the 'Everything Else' category."

Giving (and Getting) Essential Feedback

Chapter 8

You know how they say you are what you eat? On eBay, you are only as good as your feedback says you are. Your feedback is made up of comments — good, bad, or neutral — that people leave about you (and you leave about others). In effect, people are commenting on the overall professionalism of the buyers and sellers they meet on eBay.

Even if you're just on eBay for fun, a little businesslike courtesy can ease your transactions with everyone. Feedback comments are the basis of your eBay reputation.

Feedback serves two purposes:

➡ Good sellers can be rewarded with praise when they earn it.

➡ Potential buyers can find out about sellers' good (or not-so-good) practices.

Get ready to...

That's why no eBay transaction is complete until the buyer fills out the feedback form. Writing feedback well takes some practice. It isn't a matter of just saying things; it's a matter of saying *only the appropriate things*. Think carefully about what you want to say — because once you submit feedback, it stays with the person for the duration of his or her eBay career.

So in this chapter, I give you the information you need to embrace the feedback concept, as well as how-to instructions for leaving constructive feedback.

 Before leaving any feedback, though, always remember that occasionally no one's at fault when transactions get fouled up; communication meltdowns, shipping mix-ups, or misplaced packages can happen to anyone.

Embrace the Importance of Feedback

1. Starting with your first feedback comment, the number that appears next to your user ID is your feedback rating. Every time you get a positive comment from a user who hasn't commented on you within the past week, you get a point that raises your total rating number. Every time you get a negative rating, this negative cancels out one of your positives and your number goes down. Neutral comments rate a 0 — they have no impact either way.

2. Understand that your feedback rating follows you everywhere you go at eBay, even if you change your user ID or e-mail address. It sticks to you like glue, and you'll see it on your My eBay summary page every time you sign in. **Figure 8-1** shows the feedback rating I see on my own summary page.

See your feedback rating.

Home > My eBay > **Summary**

My eBay   marsha_c (6674 ☆) 🏆 Power Seller me 📷

| Activity | Messages (152) | Account |

FAQ | 🖵 Page options | ✕ General settings

| Summary | Summary |

▼ **Buy**

All Buying

Watch (82)

Active (0)

Won (28)

Didn't Win (11)

eBay Bucks ($13.08)

Profile   Edit ▾

100%   marsha_c (6674 ☆)
🏆 Power Seller me 📷

Location: United States
            Member Since:
Jan-04-97

Edit Image

Shoot for the stars!
You are only 3326 points away from your
yellow shooting star

Figure 8-1

3. Click the number next to any user ID and get a complete look at the user's feedback profile — which compiles three types of feedback — as shown in **Figure 8-2**:

- **Positive feedback:** Some wise person once said, "All you have is your reputation." Reputation is what makes eBay function. If the transaction works well, you get positive feedback; whenever it's warranted, you should give it right back.

 The thinking behind the feedback concept is that you wouldn't be caught dead in a store that has a lousy reputation, so why on earth would you want to do business on the Internet with someone who has a lousy reputation?

- **Negative feedback:** If there's a glitch in your eBay transaction (for instance, it takes six months to get your *Charlie's Angels* lunchbox, or the seller substitutes a rusty thermos for the one you bid on, or you never get the item), you have the right — some would say *obligation* — to leave negative feedback.

- **Neutral feedback:** You can leave neutral feedback if you feel so-so about a specific transaction. It's the middle-of-the-road comment. Say you bought an item that had a little more wear and tear on it than the seller indicated, but you still like it and want to keep it. Neutral feedback is okay in such a case.

Three types of feedback comments

Feedback Profile

marsha_c (6674 ☆) 🏆 Power Seller me 🗐

Positive Feedback (last 12 months): 100% [How is Feedback Percentage calculated?]

Member since: Jan-04-97 in United States

Recent Feedback Ratings (last 12 months)				Detailed Seller Ratings (last 12 months)			Member Quick Links
	1 month	6 months	12 months	Criteria	Average rating	Number of ratings	Contact member
Positive	74	566	756	Item as described	★★★★★	476	View items for sale
Neutral	0	0	0	Communication	★★★★★	475	View seller's Store
Negative	0	0	0	Shipping time	★★★★★	476	View more options ▾
				Shipping and handling charges	★★★★★	473	

Figure 8-2

4. Along with the feedback rating, you also see a star next to user's IDs; that's an eBay star. You'll notice stars of many colors — even shooting stars! What do they mean? **Figure 8-3** shows eBay's Star Chart, which rewards eBay members with new, ever-more-impressive stars as their feedback ratings grow.

Anyone with a –4 rating has his or her eBay membership terminated. Remember, just because an eBay member may have a 750 feedback rating, it doesn't hurt to click the number after the user ID to double-check the person's eBay feedback profile. Even if someone has a total of 1,000 feedback comments, 250 of them *could* be negative.

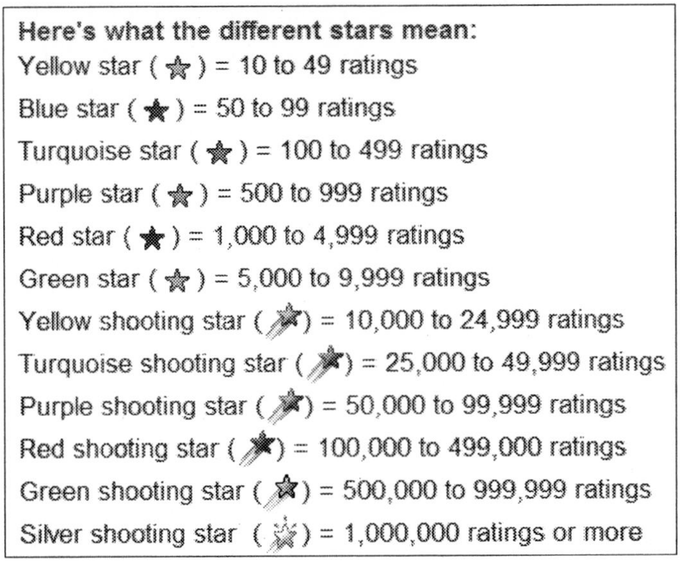

Here's what the different stars mean:

Yellow star (☆) = 10 to 49 ratings

Blue star (★) = 50 to 99 ratings

Turquoise star (☆) = 100 to 499 ratings

Purple star (☆) = 500 to 999 ratings

Red star (★) = 1,000 to 4,999 ratings

Green star (☆) = 5,000 to 9,999 ratings

Yellow shooting star (🌠) = 10,000 to 24,999 ratings

Turquoise shooting star (🌠) = 25,000 to 49,999 ratings

Purple shooting star (🌠) = 50,000 to 99,999 ratings

Red shooting star (🌠) = 100,000 to 499,000 ratings

Green shooting star (🌠) = 500,000 to 999,999 ratings

Silver shooting star (🌠) = 1,000,000 ratings or more

Figure 8-3

Examine the Feedback Profile

1. When you click the feedback number next to a member's user ID, you see all the tools you need to gauge that member's reputation. Think of members' feedback profiles as their eBay "report cards." First, check out the Recent Feedback Ratings and Detailed Seller Ratings (DSR) areas. Looking at the number of positive ratings and the average star ratings (DSRs) gives you a pretty good idea of a member's performance in eBay transactions.

I outline what the DSRs mean in the later task, "Leave Feedback and the Detailed Seller Ratings (DSRs)." As an eBay member, your goal is to get straight *As* on your report card — in this case, as much positive feedback as humanly possible. (Unlike a real report card, you don't have to bring it home to be signed.)

2. You can get to your personal feedback profile page right
from your My eBay page by clicking the number next
to your user ID. The profile will look something like
Figure 8-4. Below the Recent Feedback Ratings and
Detailed Seller Ratings are the tabs that you click to see
the actual feedback comments. You can choose to view
All Feedback, Feedback as a Seller, Feedback as a Buyer,
or Feedback Left for Others.

Click the tabs to see feedback comments.

Feedback Profile

marsha_c (6674 ☆) 👤 Power Seller 📷
Positive Feedback (last 12 months): 100% [How is Feedback Percentage calculated?]

Member since: Jan-04-97 in United States

Recent Feedback Ratings (last 12 months)				**Detailed Seller Ratings** (last 12 months)			
	1 month	6 months	12 months	Criteria	Average rating	Number of ratings	
➕ Positive	74	566	756	Item as described	★★★★★	476	
◯ Neutral	0	0	0	Communication	★★★★★	475	
➖ Negative	0	0	0	Shipping time	★★★★★	476	
				Shipping and handling charges	★★★★★	473	

Member Quick Links

Contact member
View items for sale
View seller's Store
View more options ▾

Feedback as a seller	Feedback as a buyer	**All Feedback**	Feedback left for others

7,495 Feedback received (viewing 1-25)   **Revised Feedback: 0** 🔖

Feedback	**From / Price**	**Date / Time**
➕ Fast payment, Great Ebayer, Thank You from Designerathletic	Seller: ▨▨▨c (293367 ⭐)	May-13-09 11:52
-- (#300313281400)	--	View Item
➕ Exactly as described. Great seller. Thank you!!!!	Buyer: ▨▨▨ (258 ☆)	May-13-09 09:04
Museum Putty QUAKE HOLD Wax Quakehold Earthquake LARGE (#110379891560)	US $7.97	View Item
➕ Very quick shipping.	Buyer: ▨▨▨ (2)	May-12-09 14:38
PBS TV Marsha Collier MAKING YOUR FORTUNE ONLINE eBay (#350108514161)	US $24.95	View Item

Figure 8-4

Each feedback entry, as shown in **Figure 8-5,** contains
these reputation-building (or reputation-trashing)
ingredients:

- **The user ID** of the person who sent the feedback. The
  number in parentheses next to the person's name is
  his or her own feedback rating.

- **The date and time** the feedback was posted.

- **The item number** of the transaction that the feedback refers to. If the item has closed in the past 30 days, you can click the transaction number to see what the buyer purchased.

- **Seller or Buyer** — indicating whether you were the seller or the buyer in the transaction.

- **Feedback bullets** come in different colors: praise (in green with a plus mark), negative (in red with a minus mark), or neutral (in grey with a white dot).

- **The feedback comment** the person left about you.

Positive bullet   Comment   Who left feedback   When it was posted

Feedback as a seller	Feedback as a buyer	All Feedback	Feedback left for others

662 Feedback received (viewing 1-25)   Revised Feedback: 1 ⊛

Feedback	From / Price	Date / Time
⊗ Item arrived quickly and exactly as described. Excellent seller. Thank you!	Buyer: marsha_c (6674 ⭐)	May-13-09 19.13
1996 BARBIE REPRODUCTION OF 1960 WEDDING DAY BARBIE NIB (#360119469208)	US $5.99	View Item

Figure 8-5

 Sellers are allowed to leave only positive feedback for buyers — I know this may not make sense, but that's the way it is. You can leave a "positive" while still being honest about your transaction, in your own words. eBay made this rule so sellers wouldn't leave retaliatory feedback to buyers who left them negative feedback.

3. A feedback profile also contains a positive feedback percentage that appears on the line under the member's user ID. Of course, having a high percentage here is good. Click the How is Feedback Percentage Calculated link if you want the gory details about how eBay does its math.

Get the Kind of Feedback You Want

1. If you're selling on eBay, getting positive feedback establishes your good-seller reputation. Here's how to get a good reputation:

- Establish contact with the buyer (pronto!) after the listing ends (see Chapter 14).

- After you've received payment, send the item quickly (see Chapter 14).

- Make sure that your item is exactly the way you described it (see Chapter 12).

- Package the item well and ship it with care (see Chapter 14).

- React quickly and appropriately to problems — for example, the item's lost or damaged in the mail, or the buyer is slow in paying (see Chapter 14).

2. If you're buying on eBay, try these good-rep strategies:

- Send your payment fast.

- Keep in touch through e-mail with the seller.

- Work with the seller to resolve any problems in a courteous manner.

3. If you're selling on eBay, here are some practices to avoid so you can *also* avoid tarnishing your name big-time:

- Telling a major fib in the item description. (Defend truth, justice, and legitimate creative writing — see Chapter 13.)

- Taking the money but "forgetting" to ship the item. (See Chapter 14.)

- Packaging the item poorly so it ends up smashed, squashed, or vaporized during shipping. (To avoid this pathetic fate, see Chapter 14.)

4. If you're buying, you can't get official negative feedback, but the seller still has their "say." Here's how to make your feedback comments a serious mess:

- Bid on an item, win the auction, and never respond to the seller.

- Send a personal check that bounces and never make good on the payment.

- Ask the seller for a refund because you just don't like the item.

Know When and Where to Leave Feedback

1. You should leave feedback on eBay as soon as a transaction is completed. For buyers, that means as soon as they receive their items and check them out. For sellers, timing is up for grabs. I don't leave feedback for buyers until I know they are happy with their item. Even though a seller can't leave a negative, I don't want to leave a spurious positive for a difficult buyer.

2. When multiple items are purchased in a transaction, a feedback entry is left for each item. Rather than leaving feedback for all items at once, if a buyer or seller leaves feedback stretched out over several weeks (only one item per week), the person on the other end of the transaction gets a single feedback point each time a positive entry occurs. Leaving feedback in this way results in a greater increase in a seller's feedback rating. It's a courteous gesture that breeds good eBay karma.

 Try to think of the feedback process from the receiver's perspective. If you leave feedback for all items at once, that transaction — even though multiple items are involved — counts as only a +1 for the receiver's feedback rating.

3. Several ways are available to leave feedback comments:

- If you're on the user's Feedback page, click the Leave Feedback link; the Leave Feedback page appears.

- In the Won area of your My eBay page, click the Leave Feedback link next to the listing.

- Go to your auction and click the Leave Feedback icon.

- In the Feedback Forum, click the Leave Feedback link to see a list of all your completed auctions and won items from the last 90 days for which you haven't yet left feedback.

Leave Feedback and the Detailed Seller Ratings (DSRs)

1. You're not required to leave feedback, but because it's the benchmark by which all eBay users are judged, whether you're buying or selling, I recommend that you *always* leave feedback comments.

 Get in the frame of mind that every time you complete a transaction — the minute the package arrives safely and you've taken the time to check the item — you should go to eBay and post your feedback.

2. To start the feedback process, first find the item you purchased on your My eBay Won page. Click the Leave Feedback link next to the item, and you arrive at the Leave Feedback form.

3. On the form, click the Positive, Negative, or Neutral radio button — whichever applies — as in **Figure 8-6**.

Add your comment.

Click a feedback option.

Leave Feedback

Your Feedback counts – share your trading experience with the eBay Community. Other members learn from your overall ratings, and buyers can leave specific Feedback about the item description, the seller's communication, and shipping. **Learn more**

| Show Items: | **All** | | **Bought** | | **Sold** | | Find a transaction | Enter a User ID or item # | [Search] |

Leave Feedback for 1 (viewing 1-1)

1996 BARBIE REPRODUCTION OF 1960 WEDDING DAY BARBIE NIB - [View item summary]   Item # 380119469208

Seller: ▬▬▬▬ (553 ⭐) 🌟 **Power Seller** 🔳

Ended: Apr-29-09 12:46:20 PDT

Rate this transaction. This Feedback helps other buyers and sellers. 🔘

● Positive   ○ Neutral   ○ Negative   ○ I will leave Feedback later

Please explain: Item arrived quickly and exactly as described. Thank you!   23 characters left

Click on the stars to rate more details of the transaction. These ratings will not be seen by the seller. 🔘

How accurate was the item description?   ★ ★ ★ ★ ★ · Very accurate
How satisfied were you with the seller's communication?   ★ ★ ★ ★ ★ · Very satisfied
How quickly did the seller ship the item?   ★ ★ ★ ★ ★ · Very quickly
How reasonable were the shipping and handling charges?   ★ ★ ★ ★ ★ · Very reasonable

[Leave Feedback]   Cancel

Once you leave Feedback, you can't edit it or take it back.

Click a star rating in each detail area.

Figure 8-6

4. Type your feedback comment in the Please Explain text box. (See the task "Leave Feedback with Style," later in this chapter, for suggestions on keeping your comments brief, accurate, and professional.)

5. In addition to a feedback comment and rating (Positive, Negative, or Neutral), buyers can — and, I think, should — leave Detailed Seller Ratings as well. The DSR part of the feedback system asks you to rate sellers by clicking one to five stars, which indicate how well you think a seller fulfills four different selling criteria. Here are some other considerations to keep in mind when you're deciding what level of Detailed Seller Ratings to leave for a seller:

- **Shipping takes time:** Ground shipping can take up to 10 days, which isn't the seller's fault. So before you specify a rating, be sure to check the postmark or the date on the shipping label.

- **Shipping costs money:** Sellers have to add a little to cover the costs of tape, boxes, and packing materials. If you're unfamiliar with postage rates, you should also know that a package costs a lot more to ship across the country than to ship to the next state. So do a little homework and evaluate shipping costs *before* you buy. If the shipping is too high, go to another seller.

 A 5-star rating doesn't cost you anything as a buyer, and if the seller is a PowerSeller, it can affect a discount they receive on their eBay fees. Being a good seller (with high DSRs) can save a PowerSeller as much as 20 percent on Final Values Fees, so your rating is a very serious matter. **Table 8-1** outlines what the stars mean to me when I leave a rating.

6. After you click to indicate your star ratings, click the Leave Feedback button, and you're done.

Table 8-1	What the DSR Stars Mean	
Rating Question	**# of Stars = Meaning**	**In the Real World**
How accurate was the item's description?	1 = Very inaccurate 2 = Inaccurate 3 = Neither inaccurate nor accurate 4 = Accurate 5 = Very accurate	In Marsha's world, the item was either described right or wrong — to me, there is no in-between. So when I rate a seller, either the item is as advertised or it isn't.
How satisfied were you with the seller's communication?	1 = Very unsatisfied 2 = Unsatisfied 3 = Neither unsatisfied nor satisfied 4 = Satisfied 5 = Very satisfied	As I buyer, I lean more with being *very* satisfied that I got enough communication from the seller . . . or not. If I get one e-mail, I'm usually satisfied. But if I haven't heard from a seller until the item reaches my door, I'm definitely rating in the 2-star range.
How quickly did the seller ship the item?	1 = Very slowly 2 = Slowly 3 = Neither slowly nor quickly 4 = Quickly 5 = Very quickly	Now, here I have another issue: As a buyer, you need to check the postmark on the package you receive. If the seller ships the next day — or the day after that — you have to click 5 (Very Quickly), no matter how long the postal service or shipper took to get the item to you.
How reasonable were the shipping and handling charges?	1 = Very unreasonable 2 = Unreasonable 3 = Neither unreasonable nor reasonable 4 = Reasonable 5 = Very reasonable	When I purchase an item, I know what the shipping cost will be. The only surprise here is when you get an item in a small envelope and you've paid $9.00 for shipping — or if you paid for Priority Mail and it comes in another class of service. This issue is, to me, pretty black-and-white: The shipping and handling charges are either reasonable or unreasonable.

Leave Feedback for a Buyer

1. As a seller, you can also leave feedback for a buyer. Click the Leave Feedback link on the completed item page and enter the required information. Note that your item number is usually filled in, but if you're placing feedback from the user's Feedback page, you need to have the number at hand.

2. Type in your comment (only positive feedback can be left for a buyer, so choose your words carefully).

3. Click the Leave Feedback button.

Respond to Feedback

1. After reading feedback you've received from others, you may feel compelled to respond. If the feedback is negative, you may want to defend yourself. If it's positive, you may want to thank the person who left it. To respond to feedback, click the Feedback link in the drop-down menu under the Account tab on your My eBay page, and then click the Go to Feedback Forum link at the top of the page.

2. You're transported to the Feedback Forum (see **Figure 8-7**), where you can reply to feedback comments left for you. Click the Reply to Feedback Received link on the right side of the page in the Feedback Tools box.

3. On the Reply to Feedback page, find the feedback you want to respond to and click the Reply link.

Find all the Feedback Tools here.

Feedback Forum

Find a member   Enter User ID or email address   [Search]

Each time you buy or sell something, you have an opportunity to leave Feedback about your experience. That Feedback is an essential part of what makes eBay a successful community.

Feedback consists of a positive, negative, or neutral rating, along with a short comment. Buyers and sellers build reputations that are based on all the Feedback ratings and comments left by their trading partners.

This information is available in each member's Feedback Profile, and helps prospective trading partners buy and sell with confidence.

More fast facts about Feedback:

- Along with an overall rating, buyers can also rate sellers on the details of the purchase. These detailed seller ratings are anonymous, and don't count toward the overall Feedback Score.

- Since Feedback becomes a permanent part of your record, buyers are encouraged to contact sellers to try to resolve any issues before leaving neutral or negative Feedback.

- Buyers can revise Feedback they've left for sellers in the case of a mistake.

- Sellers can leave only positive ratings for buyers. That means buyers should feel free to leave honest Feedback without fear of retaliation. We also have safeguards in place to protect sellers against unfair negative or neutral Feedback.

Feedback basics

All about Feedback
Frequently asked questions
Feedback policies
Detailed seller rating tips for sellers
Protecting the seller's reputation
Take a tutorial on Feedback

Feedback tools

Leave Feedback
View a Feedback Profile
Reply to Feedback received
Follow up to Feedback left
Request Feedback revision
Make Feedback public or private

Read a note from eBay's founder, Pierre Omidyar, outlining the philosophy, values, and benefits of the Feedback Forum.

Figure 8-7

4. Type your response and click Leave Reply.

If you want to follow up to a feedback you've already left for someone, follow the preceding steps, but in Step 2, click the Follow Up to Feedback Left link on the Feedback Forum page.

Do not confuse *replying* to feedback with *leaving* feedback. Replying does not change the other user's feedback rating; it merely adds a line below the feedback with your response. Replying is optional and courteous; leaving rated feedback is vital.

Leave Feedback with Style

1. eBay says to make feedback "factual and emotionless." You won't go wrong if you comment on the details (either good or bad) of the transaction. If you have any questions about what eBay says about feedback, click the Feedback link under the Account tab on your My eBay page. On the resulting page, click the Go to Feedback Forum link.

 I think you should always leave feedback, especially at the end of a transaction, although doing so isn't mandatory. Think of leaving feedback as voting in an election: If you don't leave feedback, then you can't complain if the service was lousy.

2. In the Feedback Forum, you can perform six feedback-related tasks:

- Read feedback about an eBay user.

- Leave feedback for many transactions at once. Here you see all pending feedback for all transactions within the past 90 days. You're presented with a page of all your transactions for which you haven't left feedback. Fill them in, one at a time, and with one click you can leave as many as 25 feedback comments at once.

- Review and respond to existing feedback about you.

- Review the feedback you have left for others. Here you may also leave follow-up feedback (after the initial feedback) if the situation changes.

- Make your feedback profile public or private. Remember, if you make your feedback profile private, you may hinder your future business on eBay.

- Check the Feedback FAQ to review any changes in the feedback system.

3. eBay likes to keep feedback comments simple. If you want to compliment, complain, or take the middle road, you have to do it in 80 characters or less. That means your comments have to be short and sweet (or short and sour if it's negative, or sweet and sour if you're mixing drinks or ordering Chinese food). If you have a lot to say but you're stumped about how to say it, **Table 8-2** has a few examples for any occasion. String them together or mix and match!

Table 8-2	Appropriate Feedback Phrases	
Positive Phrases	*Negative Phrases*	*Neutral Phrases*
Very professional	Beware track record	Slow to ship but item as described
Quick e-mail response	Never responded	Poor communication but item came OK
Exactly as described	Not as described	Item not as described but seller made good
Fast service	Desperately slow shipping	
A+++	Never sent item	
Good communication		
Highly recommended		
Smooth transaction		
Would deal with again		
An asset to eBay		
I'll be back!		

4. In the real world (at least in the modern American version), anybody can sue anybody else for slander or libel; it's the same situation on the Internet. Be careful not to make any comments that could be libelous or slanderous. eBay is not responsible for your actions, so if you're sued because of negative feedback (or anything else you've written), you're on your own. The best way to keep yourself safe is to stick to the facts and don't get personal.

 If you're angry, take a breather *before* you type your complaints and click the Leave Feedback button. If you're convinced that negative feedback is necessary, try a cooling-off period before you send a comment. The seller may come through and make good. Nasty feedback based on emotion can make you look vindictive (even if what you're saying is true). If you do leave a negative comment that you later regret, you can't remove it. You can go back to follow up and leave an explanation or a more positive comment (but it won't change the initial feedback or rating), so think twice before you blast.

5. And speaking of safety features you should know about feedback, you may want to study up on these:

- Remember that feedback, whether good or bad, is *sticky.* eBay won't remove your feedback comment if you change your mind later. Be sure of your facts and carefully consider what you want to say.

- Before you leave feedback, see what other people had to say about that person. Is your thinking in line with the comments others have left?

- Your feedback comment can be left as long as the transaction remains on the eBay server. This is usually within 90 days of the end of the listing. After 90 days have passed, you must have the transaction number to leave feedback.

- Your comment can be a maximum of only 80 letters long, which is really short when you have a lot to say. Before you start typing, organize your thoughts and use common abbreviations to save precious space.

- Before posting negative feedback, try to resolve the problem by e-mail or telephone. You may discover that your reaction to the transaction is based on a misunderstanding that can be easily resolved.

- eBay users generally want to make each other happy, so use negative feedback *only as a last resort*. See Chapter 10 for more details on how to avoid negative feedback.

Setting Up Your About Me and My World Pages

*e*Bay is more than just a Web site for buying and selling stuff. Today — with *social marketing* as the guiding buzzword — eBay wants the world to know that it has created (and works hard to maintain) a community. eBay is about people connecting with people. And prime real estate in *this* community (your About Me and My World pages) costs nothing! In this chapter, find out how to claim your own section of prime online real estate and give it some curb appeal.

In real-life communities, you participate as much as works for you. You can get involved in all sorts of neighborhood activities, or you can just sit back, mind your own business, and watch the world go by. The My World page is a great hub for interacting with your eBay neighbors, but anyone who's serious about participating in the commerce on eBay *needs* an About Me page. It's an entrée into eBay's social network, and it serves to

➡ **Establish identity:** Checking out the About Me page of people you encounter on eBay gives you an opportunity to get to know them.

> ➡ **Authenticate sellers:** Because eBay is a cyberspace market, sellers have no other way to let prospective bidders know that they're real people. (Don't you shop at some stores because you like the owners or people who work there?)
>
> ➡ **Lay a professional base:** The About Me page takes a first step toward establishing a professional and trusted reputation at eBay.

Feel Comfortable Making Your Online Home on eBay

1. Want to know more about the people behind those user IDs? Thousands of eBay members have created personal Web pages on eBay — their About Me pages. Look for eBay users with active About Me pages — they have a Me icon (with a blue lowercase *m* and a red lowercase *e*) next to their user IDs. Click the Me icon to see what's on any member's About Me page.

2. The About Me page enables you to personalize yourself as a bidder to sellers — and as a business to prospective bidders. Sellers usually like to know about their bidders to build confidence in their trading partners. (See my About Me page in **Figure 9-1** for an example.) Your About Me page also becomes your About the Seller page if you have an eBay store.

The About Me page can also be a deal-maker or a deal-breaker. Once I was looking around eBay for some extra-long printer cables and found several sellers selling them. One lower-priced seller had a low feedback rating because he was new on eBay — but he had an About Me page, so I clicked: He turned out to be a computer technician. He and his son made computer cables together at home in the evening, as a family business, to pay for father-son trips to see their favorite baseball team play — and he guaranteed the cables. So I bought 'em. And we *both* got positive feedback.

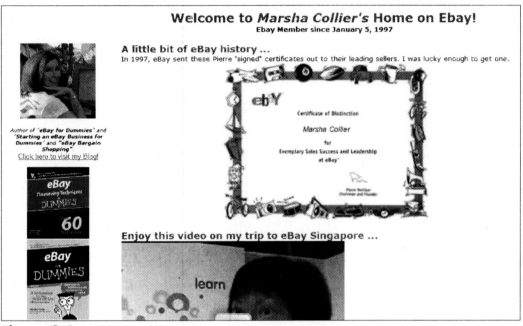

Figure 9-1

3. If you don't have an About Me page, I encourage you to plan for and set up one immediately. It doesn't have to be a work of art; just get something up there to tell the rest of the community who you are. You can always go back later and redesign it. As you plan your About Me page, put some thought into the information you want to share, including

- Who you are and where you live.

- Your hobbies. If you collect things, here's where to let the world know.

- Whether you run your eBay business full-time or part-time, and whether you have another career. This is more integral information about you; let the world know.

 When you begin to sell on eBay, your About Me page is an important sales tool — so take some time when you create your page. A well-thought-out About Me page improves your sales because people who come across your auctions and check out your About Me page can tell that you're serious about your eBay activities.

- The type of merchandise that your business revolves around. Promote it here; tell the reader why your merchandise and service are the best!

- Your most recent feedback and a list of your current auctions.

Prepare Your Greeting and Other Page Elements

1. You can prepare several elements for your About Me page even before you start the page-building process. It's a smart move. Think about how to present yourself through the following elements:

- **Title:** Come up with a title for your page. It should be as simple as a welcome or greeting.

- **Subtitle:** This consists of a few words below your page title that elaborate on your page theme.

- **Introductory paragraph:** This paragraph can tell a little about you and your hobbies or interests. You can also talk about the items you sell on eBay, but most of all, it should reflect your personality.

- **Second subtitle and paragraph:** Here you can elaborate on your interests and business on eBay. Add more information. Pictures are good, too!

 In the paragraphs of the About Me page, you can use HTML, a markup language used on the Web, to add images or fancy text. (To find out more about HTML, see the later task, "Try a Little HTML.") The titles, however, are standard and won't permit HTML coding.

- **eBay activity:** Decide what you'd like to show on the page — how many of your most recent feedback comments to display, and whether you'd like to show your current listings on the page.

 Don't get carried away by showing your last 100 feedback messages; doing so takes up too much space. Display either 10 or 25 and leave it at that. If visitors want to know more about your feedback rating, they can click your feedback number. (After all, they clicked your Me icon to get here, and that's right next to your feedback number.)

- **Links:** Formerly, you could link to your own e-commerce Web site from your About Me page. eBay's put the kibosh on that now. There are strict policies governing the use of links these days; you are not allowed to link to any site that offers to trade, sell, or purchase goods or services outside of eBay.

2. If you've been an advanced user on eBay for a while, you may want a more elaborate page. **Figure 9-2** shows an excellent example of a business-like About Me page.

Add selling information.

Add your logo.

Figure 9-2

Consider adding the following elements to your existing page:

- **Your logo:** If you've designed a logo for your eBay business, be sure to put it on the page.

- **Returns policy:** Outline your standard returns policy for your customers.

- **Shipping policy:** Explain how you ship and when you ship. Offer discounts on shipping for multiple purchases through your eBay store.

- **Searchable index to your eBay store:** Let your customers search your store by apparel size, brand name, or item. You can accomplish this with HTML coding.

- **Payment methods:** Let your customers know what payment methods you accept.

3. Before you move on to actually create your About Me page, I suggest that you look at what other users have done. eBay members often include pictures, links to other Web sites (including their personal or photo pages), and links to just about any Web location that reflects their personalities.

 Extra links and photos are great, but if your purpose is to generate more business, I recommend that you keep your About Me page focused on your auction listings, with a link to your personal, non e-commerce Web site.

Build Your About Me Page

1. You have several ways to get to the spot on eBay where you can create your About Me page, but I think the simplest way is to click the Site Map link at the upper right of any eBay page. You see the Site Map page as shown in **Figure 9-3.**

2. In the Connect area, click the About Me link. If you haven't signed in, type your user ID and password in the appropriate boxes. You're taken to the About Me page, as shown in **Figure 9-4.**

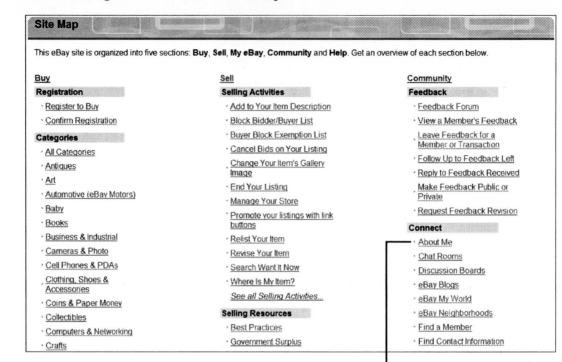

Click here to get to About Me.

Figure 9-3

Click here to get started building your page.

Figure 9-4

3. Click the Click Here button and decide whether you want to use eBay's easy step-by-step process or enter your own HTML code, and then click Continue.

> Your About Me page can be as simple or as complex as you want. You may use one of eBay's templates as presented or gussy up the page with lots of pictures and varied text using HTML. Because entering HTML code assumes you really know what you're doing, you might want to choose the step-by-step process to start out. You can always go back and try your hand at getting fancy with HTML some other time (see the later task, "Try a Little HTML").

4. Enter the following information in the About Me: Enter Page Content form:

- **Page title:** Type the title of your About Me page (for example, *Welcome to Larry Lunch's Lunchbox Place*).

- **Welcome paragraph:** On the Paragraph 1 Standard tab, type a personal, attention-grabbing bit of text that greets your visitors (something like *Hey, I like lunchboxes a lot* — only more exciting). You have the option of typing in your own HTML coding or using the buttons at the top of the box to change the font, color, size, and attributes (see **Figure 9-5**). The HTML generator is similar to the Sell an Item page — and works a lot like most word-processing programs.

  You can preview your paragraph at any time by clicking Preview Paragraph at the bottom of the text-entry area. If you don't like what you see, close the Preview window and continue to edit your masterpiece.

- **Another paragraph:** Type text for the second paragraph of the page, such as *Vintage, Modern, Ancient,* or *I Collect All Kinds of Lunchboxes*. Then maybe talk about yourself or your collection (such as, *I used to stare at lunchboxes in the school cafeteria . . . only more, you know, normal*).

- **Picture:** If you're adding a picture, type a sentence describing it, for example: *This is my wife Loretta with our lunchbox collection.*

- **Picture URL:** Type the Web site address (URL) where people can find your picture.

Click these buttons to format your text.

About Me: Enter Page Content

1. Choose Page Creation Option   ② **Enter Page Content**   3. Preview and Submit

Fill out this form with the information that you want on your About Me page. When you're ready, you can preview your page by clicking the **Continue** button below. Read tips on creating a good About Me page.

Add Text and a Picture

Make your About Me page appealing with creative use of a page title and text. You can also add a picture with a description.

Page Title:

Welcome to Susan's home on eBay!

Example: Adventures with Antiques, Bob's Books and Comics, etc.

Paragraph 1:

| Standard | Enter your own HTML |

Font Name ▼ | Size ▼ | Color ▼ | **B** | *I* | U | ≡ ≡ ≡ | ≣ ≣ ≣ ≣

I enjoy buying fun items on eBay - but I'm beginning to get the hang of selling too. I sell things that I like and that I know are of good quality. Please visit my auctions. Some of the things I like to sell are:

- Disney memorabilia
- Barbie Fashions
- Unique Fabrics

Preview Paragraph 1

Type your text here.

Figure 9-5

- **Feedback:** Select how many of your feedback postings you want to appear on your About Me page. (You can opt not to show any feedback, but I think you should

put in a few comments, especially if they're compli-
mentary, as in, "Larry sent my lunchbox promptly, and
it makes lunchtime a blast! Everybody stares at it. . . .")

- **Items for Sale:** Select how many of your current auctions you want to appear on your About Me page. If
you don't have any auctions running at the moment,
you can select the Show No Items option.

- **Favorite Links:** Type the names and URLs of any Web
links you want visitors to see, for example, a Web site
that appraises lunchboxes ("It's in excellent condition
except for that petrified ham sandwich. . . .").

5. After you've finished entering this information (and are
happy with how it looks), click Continue at the bottom
of the page.

 Don't worry if you're not absolutely wild about your
page on the first pass. The important part is to get it
published. You can go back and make changes as
often as you want.

6. On the About Me Preview and Submit page, you are presented with three layout options, as shown in **Figure 9-6**.
Click the button that corresponds to the layout option
you want. Scroll down the page and check out what your
About Me page will look like. If you don't like your current layout choice, go back up the page and change the
layout option.

7. Give your page another look, and if you don't like what
you see (or read), click the Back button and do some
more editing. When you're happy with your masterpiece,
click the Submit button — and you've done it. Now anyone with Internet access can find your personal About
Me page on eBay.

You can link to your About Me page from your Web site or from your e-mail because every About Me page has its own personal *URL* (Uniform Resource Locator — that is, address on the Internet). You can find your own About Me page by typing members. ebay.com/aboutme/ followed by your user ID. For example, here's the URL for my page:

members.eBay.com/aboutme/marsha_c

Click a button to choose that layout.

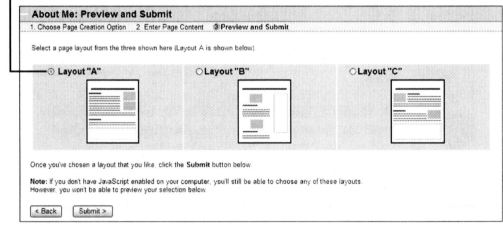

Figure 9-6

Try a Little HTML

It's not highly publicized, but you can use some unique-to-eBay HTML codes to give your About Me page a custom look. Some of these codes can be combined with others (such as those for bold and color). Play around with them and see what you come up with! **Table 9-1** gives you the secret codes (sorry, no decoder ring) that you can type into the HTML portion of your text entry.

Table 9-1	eBay Centric HTML Codes
Code You Enter	**What It Displays**
`<eBayUserID>`	Displays your user ID and real-time feedback rating.
`<eBayUserID BOLD>`	Displays your user ID and feedback rating in boldface.
`<eBayUserID NOLINK>`	Displays your user ID with no clickable link (useful if you plan to change your ID soon).
`<eBayUserID NOFEEDBACK>`	Displays your user ID with no feedback number after it.
`<eBayUserID BOLD NOFEEDBACK>`	Combines two of the previous tags into one.
`<eBayFeedback>`	Shows your up-to-the-minute feedback comments in real time.
`<eBayFeedback COLOR="red">`	Changes the color of the second line on your feedback comment table to red.
`<eBayFeedback TABLEWIDTH="75%">`	Changes the width of your feedback comment table as a percentage of the allowed space (the default value is 90%).
`<eBayItemList>`	Inserts a list of the items you currently have up for sale.
`<eBayItemList BIDS>`	Displays everything you're currently bidding on.
`<eBayTime>`	Inserts the official eBay time into your text.
`<eBayMemberSince>`	Inputs the date and time of your initial eBay registration.

Reach the World through Your My World Page

1. If *blogging* (online journaling — the hot trend these days) is the key to the new Web, then your My World page is the hub of your eBay user interaction. Your About Me page is there for customers, and the My World page is mostly used by the eBay community. People like to know about other people, and the My World page shows your world, your way.

2. To visit the hub, just go to

```
http://myworld.ebay.com/
```

You arrive at the My World hub, as shown in **Figure** 9-7. Click the View My World button on the left, and after you click through, you'll arrive at your personal My World space — ready to edit.

Click here to start your My World space.

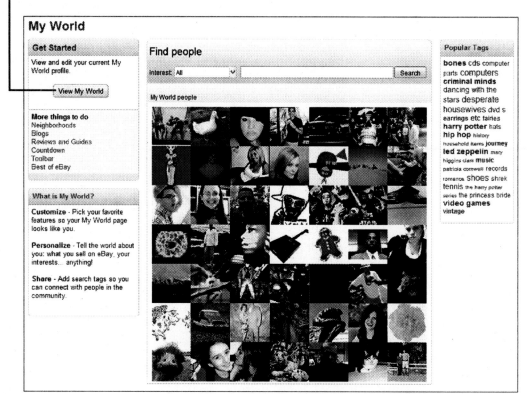

Figure 9-7

3. Setting up your My World page is all too simple. Click your user ID on your My eBay page (or any page for that matter) and you'll arrive at your own (ready-to-fill-out) My World page.

4. Here's the lowdown on what you can do with your My World page:

- **Edit Image.** By clicking here, you come to a page that allows you to upload a picture from your computer automatically, or use one of the handy (but unexciting) eBay-supplied avatars to appear on your My World page.

- **Items for Sale.** Here you can choose which and how many of the items you have for sale to show on your page.

- **Add Content.** Here you can add things about your eBay life that you'd like everyone to see, including your favorite searches and sellers, a simple biography of yourself, any eBay neighborhoods you've joined, and any reviews and guides you've written.

- **Guest Book**. Use this feature to enable people to leave messages on your page. Visit my My World page at

  ```
  http://myworld.ebay.com/marsha_c
  ```

  to view some of the comments left by other eBay users, as pictured in **Figure 9-8**.

- **Change Theme.** Don't like eBay's default peach color? Click here to select a color that's a little more you.

- **Change layout.** After you've put in your content, this link allows you to move things around on the page, or even change the number of columns.

5. When you're finished crafting your My World page, click
Save to make it an active part of eBay's My World area.

Add a guest book for your visitors.

Figure 9-8

Enhancing Your Presence and Following the Rules

There's a whole lot more to eBay than just buying and selling. There are rewards to reap (once you become a PowerSeller), recognition to receive as a Top-rated seller, online stores to create, and a fun community to connect with.

In this chapter, find out the requirements for Top-rated and PowerSeller status. eBay really does watch over the many transactions that take place daily, evaluates the proceedings, and acts accordingly. This chapter gives you some insight into the rules and regulations that eBay enforces, as well as the rewards and benefits it makes available to buyers and sellers. For example . . .

➠ Find out what it takes to get a top rating. Understand that simply selling a lot doesn't cut it.

➠ Discover what you must know — and what rules you must follow — to avoid trading violations and to stay in eBay's good graces.

➡ See how you can connect to the people and happen-
ings on eBay through the navigation bar's handy
Community link. eBay has more than 100 million
members — a bigger population than some countries — but it can still have that small-town feel
through groups, chat rooms, and discussion boards.

Become a Top-Rated Seller

1. When you browse through the items on eBay, you're
bound to notice a Top-rated seller badge next to a member's user ID. To the uninitiated, this may look like an
award given to a used-car salesman for bullying hundreds
of people into expensive car leases — but it's not. The
Top-rated seller badge is given to only those PowerSellers
who uphold the highest levels of customer service on the
site. Take a look at mine in **Figure 10-1**.

The Top-rated seller badge of honor

Figure 10-1

2. The eBay Top-rated seller status rewards sellers who
create the best buyer experiences, including these:

- PowerSellers of all levels, from Bronze to Titanium (see **Table 10-1**), can qualify as eBay Top-rated sellers if they have at least 100 transactions and $3,000 in sales in the past year, and low Detailed Seller Ratings (DSRs) — where "low" means 1- and 2-star ratings — on no more than 0.5% of all transactions with U.S. buyers, in each of their four DSR categories.

- Low-volume sellers (fewer than 400 annual transactions) can also become Top-rated sellers if they have two or fewer instances of 1- or 2-star ratings on each of the four DSR categories. After 400 transactions, the 0.5% requirement is applied.

- The Top-rated seller DSR evaluation time period depends on your sales volume. For sellers with 400 or more transactions over the past three months, the time period evaluated is three calendar months. For all other sellers, it's 12 calendar months.

3. You may notice that many sellers on the site with feedback ratings in the tens of thousands do not have Top-rated seller badges on their listings. That's not because they're not good people; it's just that some of their transactions may have gone awry and resulted in negative feedback or low DSRs.

 Give sellers with high feedback ratings the benefit of the doubt. Be sure to check the seller's feedback and thoughtfully evaluate it. Many times, buyers don't read the seller's policies before they buy — and then give negative feedback (as in the case of buyers not reading the seller's warnings when buying liquidation merchandise).

Become an eBay PowerSeller

1. eBay PowerSellers have to maintain certain monthly levels of gross merchandise sales (total dollar amount of eBay sales — GMS in eBay-speak), and they get there by providing good items for sale and excellent customer service. When you're a PowerSeller, you will see the PowerSeller icon on your My eBay and Accounts pages. **Figure 10-2** shows you mine.

The PowerSeller icon

Figure 10-2

2. To become a PowerSeller on eBay, you must fulfill the following requirements:

- Be an active eBay member for at least 90 days.

- Rack up a minimum of $1,000 in sales or 100 items per month, for three consecutive months; OR an averaged minimum of 100 items sold on the site per month for the past three months.

- Meet the following average minimum sales requirements:

  Three-Month Requirement: A minimum of $1,000 in sales or 100 items per month, for three consecutive months.

  Annual Requirement: A minimum of $12,000 or 1,200 items for the prior twelve months.

- Achieve the following minimum average of items sold:

  Three-Month Requirement: 2 items sold per month for the past 3 months (6 items).

  Annual Requirement: 2 items sold per month for the past 12 months (24 items).

- Have a minimum overall feedback rating of 100.

- Maintain at least a 98 feedback percentage.

- Keep your eBay account current.

- Comply with all eBay policies.

- Maintain a rating of 4.5 or higher for the past 12 months in all four Detailed Seller Ratings (DSRs). (Top-rated sellers must maintain a 4.6 or higher).

3. eBay sends you a notification when you qualify for PowerSeller status. If you feel you have qualified and may have accidentally deleted the e-mail, find the PowerSeller's page from the Site Map link and attempt to log in with your regular user ID and password.

4. Being a PowerSeller gives you membership in an exclusive club. That club has five levels of membership, depending on your monthly sales (as shown in **Table 10-1**). Each PowerSeller tier gives the seller more privileges from eBay. One of the most valuable benefits is that when an issue needs to be addressed with eBay, PowerSellers can access priority customer-service support.

Table 10-1	PowerSeller Tiers with Benefits			
Tier	**Monthly GMS ($) or Items sold**	**Priority E-Mail Support**	**Toll-Free Phone**	**Manager Support**
Bronze*	$1000 or 100	Yes	No	No
Silver	$3000 or 300	Yes	Yes	No
Gold	$10,000 or 1,000	Yes	Yes	Yes
Platinum	$25,000 or 2,500	Yes	Yes	Yes
Titanium	$150,000 or 15,000	Yes	Yes	Yes
Diamond	$500,000 or 50,000	Yes	Yes	Yes

Bronze Tier PowerSellers get phone support if they meet the annual requirement of a minimum of $12,000 or 1,200 items for the prior twelve months.

 There's no official indication of it, but I'll bet if you're a Diamond-level PowerSeller that John Donahoe (eBay's CEO) will arrange babysitting for you when you're in a jam. Now I don't *know* it to be gospel . . . but I'm just sayin' . . . .

Know the PowerSeller Program Benefits

1. As a PowerSeller, you have access to some super-secret places on the eBay site reserved for PowerSellers! There's a PowerSeller newsgroup, PowerSeller discussion board, and even special items at the eBay store. You can find all this magic — as shown in **Figure 10-3** — at this URL:

```
pages.ebay.com/powerseller
```

Click for program benefits and requirements.

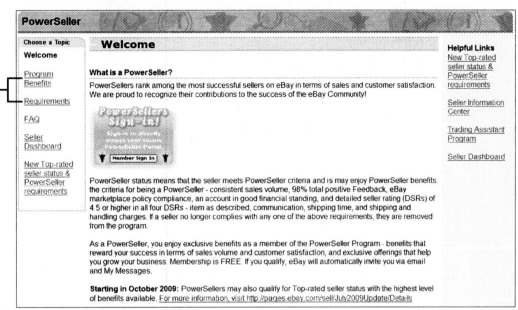

Figure 10-3

 You must log in to this area, and only PowerSellers are allowed to enter. Becoming an eBay PowerSeller is an important step to eBay professionalism. It's something worth aspiring to.

2. eBay has come to value that quality sellers not only sell a volume (of dollars and items), but also give people the best buying experience on the site. So they've devised a plan (tied into those gnarly Detailed Seller Ratings) to reward PowerSellers who play by the rules. In addition to receiving premium support, eBay PowerSellers get other benefits:

• **Increased visibility in Best Match search:** Now eBay gives the advantage to the listings of the upper half of sellers in terms of buyer satisfaction. Sellers with detailed seller ratings above 4.7 in the last 30 days will receive 5 to 25 percent more exposure than the average seller.

- **Discounts on Final Value Fees:** Now, this is a reward I can appreciate. eBay discounts the Final Value Fees on the monthly bill to PowerSellers who maintain high standards. (Your DSR ratings must be 4.6 or higher in all four categories to get the discount). See **Table 10-2** for the discount amounts.

- **Expanded seller protection from PayPal:** PowerSeller U.S. account holders are covered for eligible transactions in the event of an unauthorized payment or item-not-received claims, chargebacks, and reversals.

- **Approved use of PowerSeller logo:** eBay supplies PowerSellers with special templates so they may print custom business cards and stationery that include the official PowerSeller logo.

- **Unpaid Item Protection:** PowerSellers not only get Final Value Fee and listing credits when faced with a nonpaying buyer, they also get a credit for any Listing Upgrade Fees (for example, Buy It Now, Bold, or Subtitle) — you know, all those extras.

Table 10-2	eBay PowerSeller Discounts on Final Value Fees
DSR Percentage for past 30 days	**Percentage of Discount**
4.6	5
4.8	15
4.9	20

Think About Opening an eBay Store

1. Opening an eBay Store can expand your business. eBay stresses the fixed-price format on the site these days, and buyers are looking for that format. The more that savvy buyers learn about eBay Stores, the more popular they become. The more popular they become, the more people buy from them. Simple. An eBay Store provides you with your own little corner of eBay where you can make use of your good relationships with your customers and sell directly to them.

 If you're doing well selling your items on eBay auctions or fixed-price listings, you may wonder why you'd open an eBay Store. Well, in an eBay Store, all items are set at a fixed price and can remain online until cancelled (or can be listed for as few as 30 days), so it's kind of like a giant collection of Buy It Now featured items. If you've used the eBay Buy It Now feature in one of your listings and it worked for you, the eBay Store experience is similar.

2. If you're just beginning on eBay, the best advice I can give is to hold off on opening an eBay Store until your feedback rating is over 100. Participating in transactions on eBay is a natural teacher:

- You'll see mistakes that sellers make when they sell to you. Some sellers will send you e-mails that are plain unfriendly, and leave you with a truer understanding of how quality customer service — and common courtesy — will help you build your own business.

- You'll also learn from your own mistakes and be able to provide better service to your customers.

3. If you feel it in your gut and think you're ready to take the eBay Store leap, here's what you need to know. eBay has few requirements for opening an eBay Store:

- **Registered user:** You have to be a registered seller on the eBay site with a credit card on file.

- **Feedback rating:** You must have a feedback rating of 20 or higher, or be ID Verified, or have a PayPal account in good standing. You can also qualify without the 20 feedback if you are ID Verified — but you really won't have enough experience to run your store.

4. eBay's requirements are minimal, so meeting them seems pretty easy. Personally, I like to include these additional prerequisites to back you up for success:

- **PayPal account:** You need to have a business or premier PayPal account to accept credit cards. Accepting credit cards is a necessity for building sales, and PayPal is integrated into the site, as well as being widely accepted by buyers. (Find out about PayPal accounts in Chapter 2.)

- **Sales experience:** Having selling (and buying) experience over and above the 20 transactions required by eBay is a big plus. The best teacher (aside from this book) is the school of hard knocks.

- **Merchandise:** Opening an eBay Store with only one each of ten items isn't a good idea. You need to have enough merchandise to support consistent sales in your store.

- **Devotion:** You need to have the time to check into your eBay business *at least* once a day, and the time to ship the purchased merchandise in a prompt manner.

5. Before you open a store, understand how buyers must find your store merchandise. The items listed as store inventory will not come up in an eBay search unless eBay can come up with thirty (or fewer) of the item searched for in traditional listings. The only way new buyers can find your store inventory is by clicking the Find Items in eBay Stores link in eBay Search, by searching items on the store hub page (as shown in **Figure 10-4**), or by clicking from one of your auction pages to see what else you have on sale.

Find store items from the eBay Stores hub.

Figure 10-4

But eBay Stores are not a total solution, and having an eBay Store isn't a one-way ticket to Easy Street. I get e-mails all the time from people who open an eBay Store and are not successful in moving merchandise. Why? Because running an eBay Store takes an extra level of effort. Simple. No matter how many money-back guarantees you receive from online spammers promising magical success on eBay, the only magic is putting your shoulder, nose, and whatever else to the grindstone — and exerting the effort necessary to bring customers to your store.

Choose Between Store Types

1. All types of eBay Stores are on a level playing field. They're all equally searchable from the eBay Stores hub page, so you can be right up there with the big guys and compete. All eBay Stores have the following characteristics in common:

- **Listings:** All your eBay listings, whether auction, fixed-price, or store inventory, will appear in your eBay Store.

- **Custom URL:** Your eBay Store will have its own Internet address that you can use in links in promotional material — even to promote your store on the Internet.

- **Store search:** When customers visit your eBay Store, they will be able to search within your listings for their desired items — with your own personal search engine.

- **Cross-promotions:** You can insert thumbnail promotions for your store items within each of your items for sale on the regular eBay site.

- **Seller reports:** eBay sends you monthly reports on your store sales via e-mail.

2. A cost differential comes with the type of store you want to open. Although you will need to pay a small fee for each listing, eBay Store rental is available on three levels (outlined in **Table 10-3**).

Table 10-3	eBay Store Levels	
Level	*Cost per Month*	*What You Get*
Basic store	$15.95	All the benefits listed under Step 1.
Premium store	$49.95	All Basic store benefits, a link to your store from the store category page and randomly from the eBay Stores hub page, and more advanced sales reports.
Anchor store	$299.95	All Basic store benefits, your store logo rotating with others on the eBay Stores hub page, your logo randomly appearing on eBay's home page, your logo at the top of the category pages for store browsers.

There is no limit to the number of items you put up for sale in the Basic store. An Anchor store can have as few or as many items as the Basic store. Many high-level PowerSellers find that the Basic eBay Store fulfills their needs. Also, when people visit your eBay Store, they have no way of knowing whether you have a Basic, Premium, or Anchor store. The design of your store is up to you — you can make it as fancy as you want.

Know the eBay Store Fee Structure

1. When you have an eBay Store, other fees are involved (are you surprised?) in addition to the monthly rental fee: listing fees, options fees, and Final Value Fees. First up, start by understanding the listing fees, which are shown in **Table 10-4**.

Table 10-4	Store Inventory Listing Fees
Item Price	***Listing ($) per 30 days***
$1.00–$24.99	.03
$25.00–$199.99	.05
$200.00 and above	.10

2. As with listing fees, the optional listing-upgrade fees and Final Value Fees (FVFs) apply to eBay Store items, too. Although the fee structure is similar to that of items listed on the eBay site, the actual numbers and percentages are different. The difference in cost helps you decide which items to put in your store, in your auctions, or on your Web site. Knowing the prices in **Tables 10-5** and **10-6** up front helps you decide what sale price to assign to each item in the different sales formats.

Table 10-5	Store Inventory Listing Upgrades
Upgrade	***Cost per 30 Days of Listing Duration ($)***
Gallery Plus	0.35
Item subtitle	0.02
Listing Designer	0.10 (same as eBay core site)
Bold	1.00 (same as eBay core site)
Featured in search	9.95 to 24.95, based on starting price (same as eBay core site; for Top-rated sellers in a Best Match sort only)

Table 10-6	Store Final Value Fees
Final Item Price ($)	**Final Value Fee**
0.01 to 25.00	12% of the selling price
25.01 to 100.00	12% of the first $25.00 ($3), plus 8% of the remaining balance ($25.01 to $100.00)
100.01 to 1,000.00	12% of the first $25.00 ($3), plus 8% of $25.01 to $100.00 ($6), plus 4% of the remaining balance
1,000.01 and up	12% of the first $25.00 ($3), plus 8% of $25.01 to $100.00 ($6), plus 4% of $100.01 to $1,000 ($36) plus 2% the remaining balance

3. Listing your items for a l-o-o-o-n-g time may be tempting as a way to automate your listings — and it's a good strategy. However, there are restrictions on your listings that you have to remember:

- After someone makes a purchase from an item listing, you can make changes to most information, and you can update inventory. If you have a new picture or new ideas for a title or a description, you may want to close that listing and relist the item with the new information.

- If you have an unpaid item, you must close the store listing to file for your Final Value Fee refund.

Help eBay Be a Watchdog

1. The Security Center is where eBay's Trust and Safety gurus focus on protecting the Web site from members who aren't playing by the rules. Through this department, eBay issues warnings and policy changes — and in some cases, gives eBay bad guys the old heave-ho.

2. You can find eBay's Security & Resolution Center by clicking the Security Center link at the bottom of most eBay pages. Trust and Safety's Security & Resolution Center page (shown in **Figure 10-5**) is more than just a link to policies and information. It also connects you with a group of eBay staffers who handle complaints, field incoming tips about possible infractions, investigate infractions, and dole out warnings and suspensions via e-mail in response to the tips. eBay staffers look at complaints on a case-by-case basis, in the order they receive them.

Start here to resolve a problem.

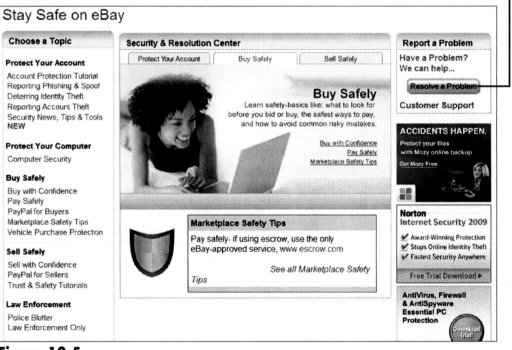

Figure 10-5

3. If you're on eBay long enough, you're bound to run across an abuse of the service. It may happen on an auction you're bidding on, or it may be one of the sellers whose auctions compete with yours. As a member of the eBay community, you can — and should — report bidding and selling abuses to the eBay staffers at the Security & Resolution Center. Be a good community member and be on the lookout for the following:

- **Shill bidding:** A seller uses multiple user IDs to place bids, or has accomplices place bids to boost the price of his or her auction items. eBay investigators look for six telltale signs, including a single bidder putting in a really high bid, a bidder with really low feedback but a really high number of bids on items, a bidder with low feedback who has been an eBay member for a while but who's never won an auction, or excessive bids between two users.

- **Auction interception:** An unscrupulous user, pretending to be the actual seller, contacts the winner to set up terms of payment and shipping in an effort to make off with the buyer's payment. This violation can be easily avoided by always paying with PayPal directly through the eBay site.

- **Fee avoidance:** A user reports a lower-than-actual final price or illegally submits a Final Value Fee credit.

- **Bid manipulation:** A user, with the help of accomplices, enters dozens of phony bids to make the auction appear to have a lot of bidding action. Let the experts at eBay decide on this one; but you may wonder what's up if loads of bids come in rapid succession but the price moves very little.

- **Bid shielding:** Two users work in tandem. User A, with the help of accomplices, intentionally bids an unreasonably high amount and then retracts the bid prior to the last 12 hours of an auction — leaving a lower bid (which the offender or an accomplice places) as the possible winning bid.

- **Bid manipulation (or invalid bid retraction):** A user bids a ridiculously high amount, raising the next highest bidder to his or her maximum bid. The manipulator then retracts the bid and rebids *slightly* over the previous high bidder's maximum.

- **Unpaid item (nonpaying bidder):** No matter how eBay chooses to couch it by fancy verbiage, I call these bidders deadbeats. The bottom line is that these people win auctions but don't pay.

- **Unwelcome bidder:** A user bids on a specific seller's auction despite the seller's warning that he or she won't accept that user's bid (as when a seller who has a no-international-sales policy receives international bids anyway). This practice is impolite and obnoxious. If you want to ban specific bidders from your auctions, you can exclude them in your My eBay area links.

4. All you have at eBay is your reputation, and that reputation is made up of your feedback history. eBay takes any violation of its feedback system seriously. Because eBay's feedback is transaction-related, unscrupulous eBay members can no longer manipulate the system. Here's a checklist of feedback abuses that you should report to Trust and Safety:

   - **Feedback extortion:** A member threatens to post negative feedback if another eBay member doesn't follow through on some unwarranted demand.

   - **Personal exposure:** A member leaves feedback for a user that exposes personal information that doesn't relate to transactions on eBay.

   - **–4 feedback:** Any user reaching a net feedback score of –4 is subject to suspension.

 Before you even consider blowing the whistle and reporting someone who gave you negative feedback to Trust and Safety, make sure that what you're encountering is *actually* a misuse of eBay. Some behavior isn't nice (no argument there), but it *also* isn't a violation of eBay rules — in which case, eBay can't do much about it. Stick with the primary reasons when you start a Trust and Safety investigation.

5. Who you are on eBay is as important as what you sell (or buy). eBay monitors the identities of its members closely — and asks that you report any great pretenders in this area to Trust and Safety. Here's a checklist of identity abuses:

- **Identity misrepresentation:** A user claims to be an eBay staff member or another eBay user, or registers under the name of another user.

- **False or missing contact information:** A user deliberately registers with false contact information or an invalid e-mail address.

- **Underage:** A user falsely claims to be 18 or older. (You must be at least 18 to enter into a legally binding contract.)

- **Dead or invalid e-mail address:** When e-mails bounce repeatedly from a user's registered e-mail address, chances are good that the address is dead. Usually returned e-mail indicates that the address is unknown.

- **Contact information:** One user publishes another user's contact information on the eBay site.

6. If you see someone trying to interfere with eBay's operation, eBay staffers want you to tell them about it. Here are two roguish operational abuses:

- **Hacking:** A user purposely interferes with eBay's computer operations (for example, by breaking into eBay's unauthorized files).

- **Spamming:** The user sends unsolicited commercial e-mail to eBay users.

7. The following are additional problems that you should alert eBay about:

- A user is threatening physical harm to another eBay member.

- A person uses racist, obscene, or harassing language in a public area of eBay.

8. Click the report item link on an item page or click the Resolution Center link on the bottom of all pages to report violators to eBay. For a complete list of offenses and how eBay runs each investigation, go to the following online address:

```
pages.ebay.com/help/buy/report-trading.
   html
```

Send VeRO to the Rescue

1. If you own intellectual property that you think is being infringed upon on the eBay site, you should take advantage of the eBay *Verified Rights Owner* (VeRO) program. Owners of trademarked or copyrighted items and logos, as well as other forms of intellectual property, can become members of this program for free.

2. You can find out more about the VeRO program by clicking the Help link on the main navigation bar. To get eBay's current VeRO policy, go to `pages.ebay.com/help/tp/vero-rights-owner.html`. Read the information, and if you qualify, click to download the form, fill it out, and fax it to eBay. Then you're on your way to protecting your intellectual property from being grabbed and auctioned off to the highest bidder without your consent.

   Remember, only *you* can stop the infringement madness. If eBay agrees with you that your intellectual property is being infringed upon, it invalidates the auction and informs the seller by e-mail that the auction "is not authorized." The high bidders in the auction are also notified and warned that they may be breaking the law if they continue the transaction. I am a member of the VeRO program. Should someone think it's a good idea to scan and sell pirate copies of my books, for example, I file my VeRO notice and the listing is removed within hours.

3. If eBay claims that an item you're selling is invalid because the item doesn't meet eBay's policies and guidelines, you can find out why by checking the page at `pages.ebay.com/help/sell/questions/listing-ended.html`. If you still feel you're in the right, scroll down the page to the Contact Us link. Click there to plead your case.

Avoid Trading Violations

1. Playing by eBay's rules keeps you off the Trust and Safety radar screen. If you start violating eBay policies, the company's going to keep a close eye on you. Depending on

the infraction, eBay may be all over you like jelly on peanut butter. Or you may safely lurk in the fringes until your feedback rating is lower than the temperature in Nome in November.

2. Avoid these trading violations (explained in the previous section), which are eBay no-no's that can get members keelhauled — or at least suspended:

- Feedback rating of –4

- Three instances of deadbeat bidding

- Repeated warning for the same infraction

- Feedback extortion

- Bid shielding

- Unwelcome bidding after a warning from the seller

- Shill bidding

- Auction interception

- Fee avoidance

- Fraudulent selling

- Identity misrepresentation

- Bidding when younger than age 18

- Hacking

- Physical threats

3. If you get a suspension but think you're innocent, respond directly to the person who suspended you to plead your case. Reversals do occur. But *don't* broadcast your suspicions on chat boards. If you're wrong, you may regret it.

 Be careful about accusing eBay members of cheating. Unless you're involved in a transaction, you don't know all the facts. Perry Mason moments are great on television, but they're fictional for a reason. In real life, drawing yourself into a possible confrontation is senseless. Start the complaint process (see the preceding section), keep it businesslike, and let eBay's staff figure out what's going on.

Join Community Boards, Chats, and eBay Groups

1. Start on the main page by clicking Community on the navigation bar. Now you can access more than three dozen category-specific chat and discussion boards, a bunch of general chat and discussion boards, and discussion boards that offer help with eBay difficulties. But there's a whole lot more to the eBay community. Take a little time to explore it for yourself. When you hover your mouse pointer over the Community box in the navigation bar on the eBay home page, you'll see a drop-down menu (shown in **Figure 10-6**).

Your gateway to the eBay community

	Buy Sell My eBay Community Help
Hi, marsha_c! (Sign out)	Announcements
You currently have $6 23 eBay Bucks!	Answer Center
All Categories ▾ Search Advanced Search	Discussion Forums
Categories ▾ Motors Stores Daily Deal	Neighborhoods
	Groups

Figure 10-6

2. From here you can get to the different eBay Community pages. The most important is the Announcement Board, the most important place to find out what's going on (directly from headquarters) on the Web site. **Figure 10-7** shows you eBay's general announcement board, complete with information that could affect your listings.

Keep up to date with changes on eBay.

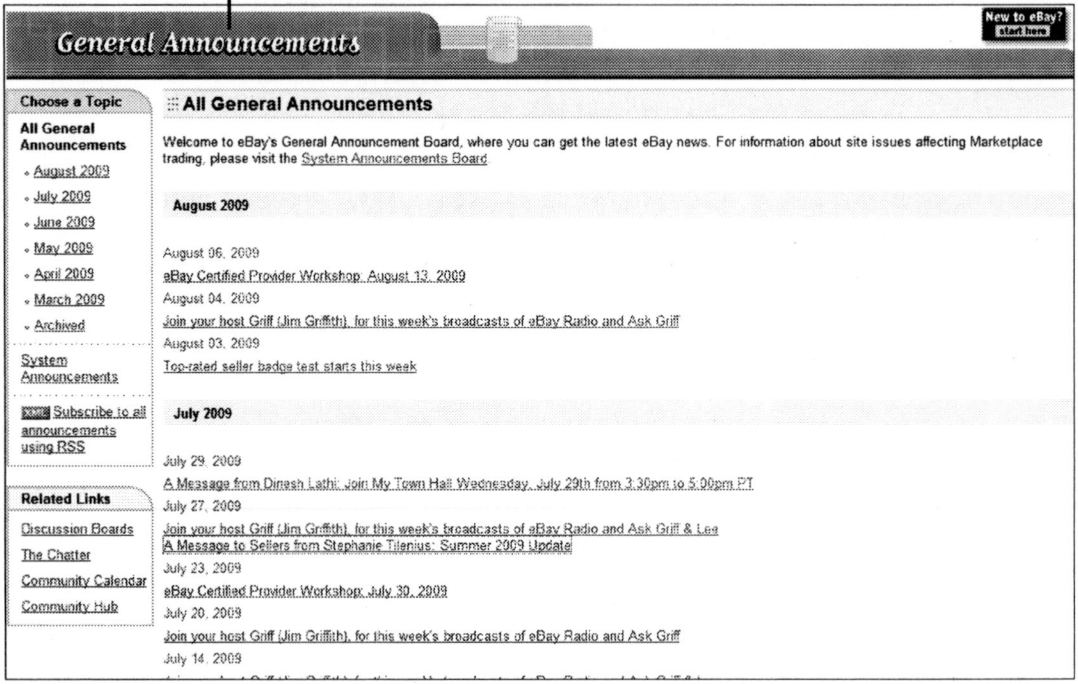

Figure 10-7

3. If you ever have specific eBay questions, you have several ways to get them answered:

- eBay discussion help boards on the Community: Chat page can help you. You can also go directly to the chat rooms to pose your question to the eBay members currently in residence. Chat rooms are full of people who are hanging out talking to each other online, all at the same time.

The one cardinal rule for eBay chat boards and discussion boards is: *No doing business on the board.* No advertising items for sale! Not now. Not ever. eBay bans any repeat offenders who break this rule from participating on these boards.

- Discussion boards work differently from chat rooms. Users of discussion boards tend to go in, leave a message or ask a question, and pop out again. Also, to get an answer in a message board, you have to start a thread by asking a question. Title your thread with your question, and you'll no doubt get an answer to your query posted swiftly.

 eBay newbies often find that the boards are good places to add to their knowledge of eBay. As you scroll on by, read the Q & A postings from the past; your question may already be answered in an earlier posting. You can even ask someone on the board to look at your auction listing and provide an opinion on your descriptions or pictures.

 If a new policy or some sort of big change occurs, the boards are most likely going to fill pretty quickly with discussion about it. On slow days, however, you may need to wade through personal messages and chatting with no connection to eBay. Many of the people who post on these boards are longtime members with histories (as well as feuds) that can rival any soap opera.

- Going to eBay's Answer Center can get most of your questions answered. You get there by clicking the Answer Center link in the Connect area on the main Community page. You then see questions covering almost any topic you can think of regarding listings on eBay. Just post your question and some kindly eBay member will probably suggest an answer.

4. Want to talk about Elvis, Louis XV, Sammy Sosa, or Howard the Duck? More than twenty category-specific chat boards are great for posting questions on items that you don't know much about. You can also find helpful sources for shipping information about items in that category (such as large furniture in the Antiques section or breakable items on the Glass chat board). You reach these boards by clicking Community on the main navigation bar and then clicking Chat Rooms in the Connect area.

 Don't be shy. As your second-grade teacher said, "No questions are dumb." Most eBay members love to share their knowledge.

5. If you're the friendly type and would like an instant group of new friends, I suggest you click the Groups link in the Connect area. Here you can find thousands of user groups (either public or private) hosted on eBay but run by eBay community members. They may be groups consisting of people from the same geographic area, folks with similar hobbies, or those interested in buying or selling in particular categories. Joining a group is easy: Just click any of the links on the main Groups page, and you're presented with a dizzying array of groups to join.

Communicate Graphically or Globally

1. When you visit the eBay boards, you may notice that many experienced posters to the board have cute little smiley icons (called *emoticons*) next to their posts to show emotion. Emoticons can help indicate whether the writer is being (for example) sincere, ironic, or goofy about what he or she just wrote. The following table shows how you too can doll up (or clarify) your posts with a little emotion.

2. You can type the keyboard shortcuts or use the HTML image links to display your chosen icon. Be sure not to put spaces between the characters in the key combinations. Using HTML is pretty easy; for example, you can use this command to insert a blushing smiley:

```
<img
    src="http://groups.ebay.com/images/
    emoticons/blush.gif">
```

Emoticon	Key Combinations	HTML Image Link
	X - (	http://groups.ebay.com/images/emoticons/angry.gif
	B -)	http://groups.ebay.com/images/emoticons/cool.gif
	] :)	http://groups.ebay.com/images/emoticons/devil.gif
	: D	http://groups.ebay.com/images/emoticons/grin.gif
	:)	http://groups.ebay.com/images/emoticons/happy.gif
	: x	http://groups.ebay.com/images/emoticons/love.gif
	:		http://groups.ebay.com/images/emoticons/plain.gif
	: (	http://groups.ebay.com/images/emoticons/sad.gif
	: O	http://groups.ebay.com/images/emoticons/shocked.gif

(continued)

(continued)

Emoticon	Key Combinations	HTML Image Link
😛	: p	http://groups.ebay.com/images/emoticons/silly.gif
😉	;)	http://groups.ebay.com/images/emoticons/wink.gif
😕	? : |	http://groups.ebay.com/images/emoticons/confused.gif
😊	: 8 }	http://groups.ebay.com/images/emoticons/blush.gif
😢	: _ |	http://groups.ebay.com/images/emoticons/cry.gif
😄	: ^ O	http://groups.ebay.com/images/emoticons/laugh.gif
😈	; \	http://groups.ebay.com/images/emoticons/mischief.gif

3. People from all around the world enjoy eBay. If you're considering buying or selling globally, visit the international discussion boards. They're a great place to post questions about shipping and payments for overseas transactions. Along with eBay chat, the international boards have discussions about current events and international politics.

> Got a seller or bidder in Italy? Spain? France? Translate your English messages into the appropriate language through the Web site at www.microsoft translator.com. If you venture into unfamiliar foreign tongues, I suggest you keep things simple. Don't try to get fancy with your verbiage — stick to standard phrases that can translate literally with minimum hassle.

Part III
Making Your Mark on eBay

The 5th Wave   By Rich Tennant

"Try putting a person in the photo with the product you're trying to sell. We generated a lot of interest in our eBay Listing once Leo started modeling my hats and scarves."

Seeing to Your Selling-on-eBay Homework

Chapter 11

*F*inding items to sell can be as easy as opening up your closet — or as challenging as acquiring antiques overseas. Either way, establishing yourself as an eBay seller isn't as difficult as you might think; you just need to do a bit of homework and get to know the ropes.

Most people starting a business have to worry about rounding up investment capital (startup money they may lose), building inventory (buying stuff to sell), and finding a selling location such as a booth at a swap meet or even a small store. Today, even a little home-based start-up can require a major investment. eBay has leveled the playing field; everybody can get an equal chance to start a small business with very little money.

A big plus to selling on eBay is wheeling and dealing from your home in sweats and slippers. But no matter where you conduct your business or how you dress, you'll find many more important big-time rewards for selling — for example, connecting with people from all over the world and getting to know about e-commerce from a personal point of view.

Get ready to...

In this chapter, you find out how to look for items under your own roof, figure out what they're worth, and turn them into ready cash. Also, I guide you on the logistics of selling, including how to research the competition and choose the proper time to sell. But before you pick your house clean and list your treasures on eBay, read up on the eBay rules of the road. Find out about the costs of selling on eBay, a seller's responsibilities to buyers, and, of course, what *not* to sell.

Start Small and Grow

1. Whether you just want to clear out 35 years of odd and wacky knickknacks cluttering your basement or you seriously want to earn extra money, you can find a place on eBay. The types of items sold, the benefits of selling, and the people doing the selling all reflect the diversity that is eBay. See what I mean in **Figure 11-1**.

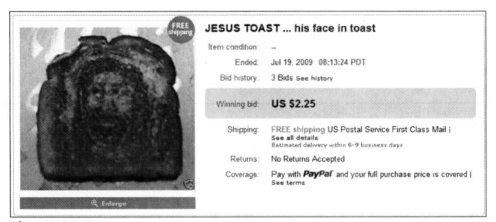

Figure 11-1

2. Get a few transactions under your belt. Buy something useful but inexpensive. This is a great way to become familiar with how eBay works, and you'll be gaining experience with leaving feedback — as well as building yours!

A fun way to get your feet wet on eBay is to buy some small items and build some feedback. When I say small, I *mean* it. Some of the least expensive items you can buy on eBay are recipes. Type **recipe** in the Search box and sort the results by Lowest Prices First. You'll find recipes for a dollar and under. You don't have to pay a shipping charge, either. The sellers usually e-mail the recipe direct to you after the auction.

3. Sell your old collection of postcards or your very own secret recipes. See how you like the responsibilities of marketing, collecting money, shipping, and customer service.

4. Grow a bit more, and you'll find yourself spotting trends, acquiring inventory, and marketing your items for maximum profit.

Scour Your House for Items to Sell

1. Finding merchandise to sell on eBay is as easy as checking your garage — and as tough as clambering up into the attic. Just about anything you bought and stashed away (because you didn't want it, forgot about it, or it didn't fit) is fair game.

 Think about all those birthday and holiday presents (hey, it was the thought that counted — and the givers may have forgotten about them, too). Now you have a place you can try to unload them for cash. They could even make somebody happy.

2. Look in your closet and find what's just hanging around:

- **Clothing** that no longer fits or is out of fashion. (Do you really want to keep it if you wouldn't be caught dead in it or you know it will never fit?) Don't forget that pair of shoes you wore once and put away.

- **Any name-brand item** with an intact label that's in new or almost-new condition.

- **Have some vintage magazines?** You can sell them whole or mount the ads in a matte and sell them as art. See **Figure 11-2**.

- **Kids' clothes.** (Kids outgrow things fast. Use profits from the old items to buy new clothes they can grow into. Now, *that's* recycling.)

 Have the articles of clothing in the best condition possible before you put them up for sale. For example, shoes can be cleaned and buffed till they're like new. According to eBay's policies, clothing *must* be cleaned before shipping.

Trade in old magazines for real money.

lot 9 BAZAAR VOGUE magazine 1945 1946 ad ads advertise

Item condition:	--
Ended:	Jul 12, 2009 19:44:05 PDT
Bid history:	26 Bids **See history**
Winning bid:	**US $89.00**
Shipping:	$9.99 US Postal Service First Class Mail | **See all details** Estimated delivery within 3-6 business days
Returns:	No Returns Accepted
Coverage:	Pay with **PayPal** and your full purchase price is covered | **See terms**

Figure 11-2

3. And consider putting what's parked in your basement, garage, or attic on the eBay auction block:

- **Old radios, stereo and video equipment, and 8-track systems:** Watch these items fly out of your house — especially the 8-track players (believe it or not, people love 'em). Check **Figure 11-3** if you don't believe me!

TSR-8 TASCAM 1/2" TAPE 8-TRACK RECORDER

Item condition:	Used
Time left:	16h 54m 46s (Jul 20, 2009 09:36:55 PDT)
Bid history:	12 Bids See history
Current bid:	**US $305.00**
Your max bid:	US $ [ ] **Place Bid**
	(Enter US $310.00 or more)
You can also:	**Watch this item**

You'll earn **$6.10** in eBay Bucks. See conditions

Shipping:	$102.23 UPS Ground	See all details
	Estimated delivery within 2-7 business days
Returns:	No Returns Accepted
Coverage:	Pay with **PayPal** and your full purchase price is covered	See terms

Figure 11-3

- **Books you finished reading long ago and don't want to read again:** Some books with early copyright dates or first editions by famous authors earn big money on eBay.

- **Leftovers from an abandoned hobby:** Who knew that building miniature dollhouses was so much work? And if you're into needlework, I'm sure you have one or two (three or four) unfinished projects hanging around. Look at **Figure 11-4**.

HUGE LOT OF NEEDLEPOINT YARN OVER 175 SKEINS

Item condition: --

Ended: Jul 17, 2009 09:36:37 PDT

Bid history: 6 Bids See history

Winning bid: **US $45.78**

Shipping: **$12.50** US Postal Service First Class Mail | See all details
Estimated delivery within 12-15 business days

Returns: 7 day money back, buyer pays return shipping | Read details

Coverage: Pay with **PayPal** and your full purchase price is covered | See terms

Figure 11-4

- **Unwanted gifts:** Have a decade's worth of birthday, graduation, or holiday gifts collecting dust? List them on eBay and hope Cousin Myra doesn't bid on them just because she thinks you need another mustache spoon!

4. Check for saleable stuff that might be lounging around in your living room or bedroom:

- **Home décor you want to change:** Lamps, chairs, and rugs (especially if they're antiques) sell quickly. If you think an item is valuable but you're not sure, get it appraised first.

- **Exercise equipment:** If you're like most people, you bought this stuff with every intention of getting in shape, but now all that's building up is dust. Get some exercise carrying all that equipment to the post office after you've sold it on eBay.

- **Records, videotapes, and laser discs:** Sell them after you've upgraded to new audio and video formats such as DVD (Digital Versatile Disc) or DAT (Digital Audio Tape). (Think Betamax is dead? You may be surprised.)

- **Autographs:** All types of autographs — from sports figures, celebrities, and world leaders — are popular on eBay. Here's a word of caution: A lot of fakes are on the market, so make sure that what you're selling (or buying) is the real thing.

 If you're in the market for an autograph, don't even consider bidding on one unless it comes with a *Certificate of Authenticity* (COA). Many sellers take authenticity so seriously that they give buyers the right to a full refund if any doubt about authenticity crops ups. **Figure 11-5** shows an item that comes with a COA from an auction on eBay. If you're planning on selling autographs on eBay, be sure to review the special rules that apply to these items. Here's where to find the rules:

```
pages.ebay.com/help/policies/
   autographs.html
```

Some items have special needs.

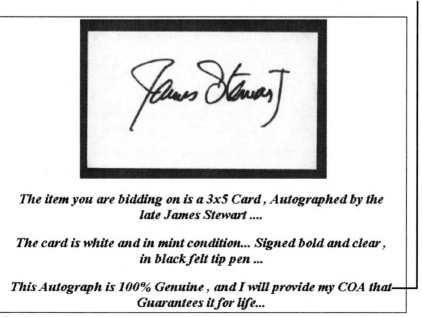

The item you are bidding on is a 3x5 Card, Autographed by the late James Stewart ....

The card is white and in mint condition... Signed bold and clear, in black felt tip pen ...

This Autograph is 100% Genuine, and I will provide my COA that Guarantees it for life...

Figure 11-5

Get the Facts About What You're Selling

1. If you haven't had to do a homework assignment in a while, it's time to dust off those skills. Before starting your auctions, do some digging to find out as much as you can about the items you intend to sell. Here are some ideas for ways to figure out what you have to sell:

- **Hit the books.** Check your local library for books about the item. Study historic guides and collector magazines.

     Even though collectors still use published price guides when they put a value on an item, so much fast-moving e-commerce is zipping by on the Internet that price guides often lag behind the markets they cover. Take published prices with a grain of salt.

- **Go Web surfin'.** Conduct a Web search and look for info on the item on other auction sites. If you find a print magazine that strikes your fancy, check to see whether the magazine is available on the Web by typing the title of the magazine into your browser's search window.

- **When the going gets tough, go shopping.** Browse local stores that specialize in your item. Price the item at several locations. When you get a feel for the demand for your product (whether it's a collectible or a commodity) and how much you can realistically ask for it, you're on the right track to a successful sale.

- **Call in the pros.** Need a quick way to find the value of an item you want to sell? Call a dealer or a collector and say you want to *buy* one. A merchant who catches a whiff of a possible sale will give you a current selling price.

- **eBay to the rescue.** eBay members often offer guidance for your research on the Community Boards and Chats. eBay has category-specific chat rooms, where you can read what other collectors are writing about items in a particular category.

2. Verify what you have — not only what it is and what it's for, but also *whether it's genuine.* Make sure it's the real deal. You are responsible for your item's authenticity; counterfeits and knock-offs are not welcome on eBay. In addition, manufacturers' legal beagles are on the hunt for counterfeit and stolen goods circulating on eBay — and they *will* tip off law enforcement.

Research Sales of Similar Items

1. Years ago, stores like Gimbel and Macy spied on each other, each looking for ways beat the other out. Today, in the world of e-commerce, the spying continues, and dipping into the intrigue of surveilling the competition is as easy as clicking your mouse.

2. To find out about the collectibles you gathered and now plan to sell, you can do some research on eBay. Start by conducting a Completed Items search on the Search page (as described in Chapter 5) to determine the following information:

   - Exactly how many of any collectible item has been sold in the past few weeks.

   - The high selling prices and how many bids the items received by the time the auctions were over.

   - When you repeat a completed search in a week or two, you can get at least a month's worth of data to use when pricing your item.

Figure 11-6 shows the results of a Completed Items search for collectible *Dukes of Hazzard* lunchboxes sorted by highest prices first.

3. The best deals for buyers (and for sellers to resell) often happen when the seller misspells a name or brand in the title. Conduct other searches that look for the same item, but with spelling errors.

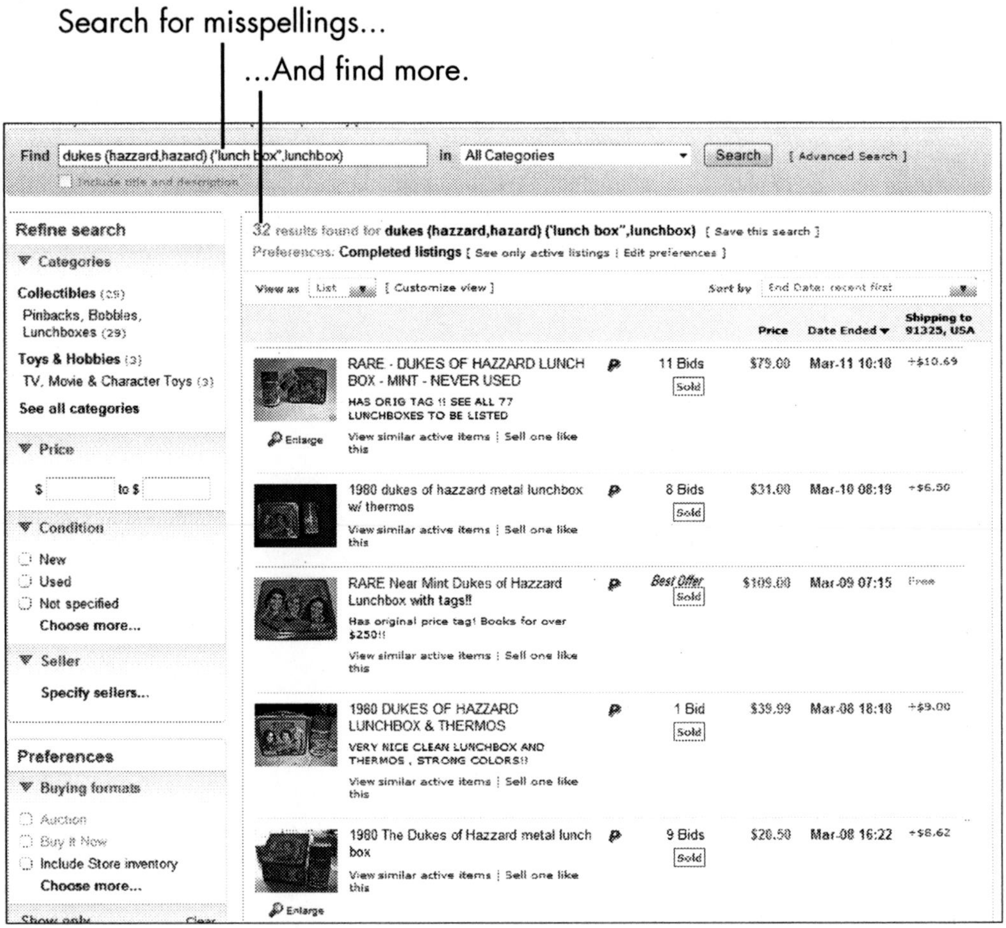

Search for misspellings...

...And find more.

Figure 11-6

You can use one of my favorite search tricks to look for these misspellings. The eBay search engine accommodates for one correction (as in *hazard* and *hazzard*) but when you want to check for two variations, you must input both. In the case of a *Dukes of Hazzard* lunchbox, type your search this way: **dukes (hazzard, hazard) ("lunch box",lunchbox)**. (Be sure that you drop the noise word *of*.) This way, you find all instances of *dukes hazzard lunchbox* and *dukes hazard lunch box*. Coincidentally, when I changed my search this way, my results went from 28 lunchboxes to 32!

4. Study the pictures you see in your search results! Look at the pictures on individual item pages for each item that your Completed Items search turns up. That way you can confirm that the items (lunchboxes, for example) are identical to the one you want to sell. And when you do your research, factor in your item's condition.

5. Read the individual item description. If your item is in better condition, expect more money for it; if your item is in worse condition, expect less. Also, note the categories in which the items are listed; they may give you a clue about where eBay members are looking for items just like yours.

6. Conduct the same search on Google.com or Bing.com. If you want to be extremely thorough in your comparison selling, go to a search engine to see whether the results of your eBay search mesh with the results you find elsewhere. If you find that no items like yours are for sale anywhere else online — and are pretty sure people *are* looking for what you have — you may just find yourself in Fat City.

Know What You Can't Sell

1. The majority of items sold on eBay are aboveboard. But sometimes eBay finds out about listings that are either illegal (in the eyes of the government) or prohibited by eBay's rules and regulations. In either case, eBay steps in, calls a foul, and makes the item's listing invalid.

 eBay doesn't have rules and regulations just for the heck of it. eBay wants to keep you educated so you won't unwittingly bid on, buy — or sell — an item that has been misrepresented. eBay also wants you to know what's okay and what's prohibited so you can help out fellow eBay members by reporting any item you run across that looks fishy. And eBay wants you to know that if you're selling knock-offs, getting your listing shut down is the least of your worries: You can be suspended if you knowingly list prohibited items.

2. You need to know about these three categories of items that can get you into trouble on eBay. Sometimes an item is okay to own but not to sell. Other times the item is prohibited from being *sold and possessed.* To complicate matters even more, some items may be legal in one part of the United States but not in others. Or an item may be illegal in the United States but legal in other countries.

- **Prohibited** lists the items that may *not* be sold on eBay under any circumstances. You may not even offer to give away a prohibited or an infringing item — that's right, it's off limits even if it's "for free" — nor can you give away a questionable item that eBay disallows; giving it away doesn't relieve you of potential liability.

- **Questionable** lists the items that may be sold under certain conditions. Just be quite sure you know *exactly* what those conditions are.

- **Potentially Infringing** lists the types of items that may be in violation of copyrights, trademarks, or other rights.

 Items that you absolutely *cannot* sell on eBay can fit into *all three* categories. Those items can be legally ambiguous at best — not to mention potentially risky and all kinds of sticky.

3. To find a detailed description of which items are prohibited on the eBay Web site, click the Policies link, which is on the bottom of all eBay pages, and you arrive at the friendly eBay Policies page.

4. Scroll to the Prohibited and Restricted items link and click. Ta-da! As shown in **Figure 11-7,** you are presented with the lists and links to help you decipher whether selling your item falls within eBay's policy boundaries.

5. Understand that *prohibited* on eBay does not necessarily mean *illegal*. Even though possessing (and selling) many of the items in eBay's prohibited list is legal in the United States and elsewhere, you are absolutely, positively *prohibited* from buying and selling them *on eBay*. See the appendix for a table of items prohibited on eBay.

 Ignorance of the Prohibited list is no excuse. If you list an item that's in any way prohibited on eBay, eBay will end your auction. If you have any questions, always check eBay's Trust & Safety department at `pages.ebay.com/help/policies/items-ov.html`.

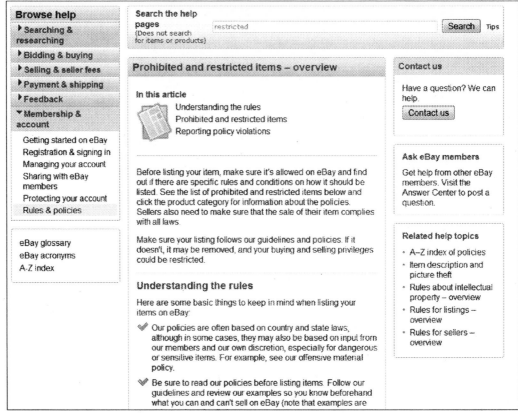

Browse help
▸ Searching & researching
▸ Bidding & buying
▸ Selling & seller fees
▸ Payment & shipping
▸ Feedback
▾ Membership & account
    Getting started on eBay
    Registration & signing in
    Managing your account
    Sharing with eBay members
    Protecting your account
    Rules & policies

eBay glossary
eBay acronyms
A-Z index

Search the help pages
(Does not search for items or products)
restricted   Search   Tips

Prohibited and restricted items – overview

In this article
Understanding the rules
Prohibited and restricted items
Reporting policy violations

Before listing your item, make sure it's allowed on eBay and find out if there are specific rules and conditions on how it should be listed. See the list of prohibited and restricted items below and click the product category for information about the policies. Sellers also need to make sure that the sale of their item complies with all laws.

Make sure your listing follows our guidelines and policies. If it doesn't, it may be removed, and your buying and selling privileges could be restricted.

Understanding the rules

Here are some basic things to keep in mind when listing your items on eBay:

✔ Our policies are often based on country and state laws, although in some cases, they may also be based on input from our members and our own discretion, especially for dangerous or sensitive items. For example, see our offensive material policy.

✔ Be sure to read our policies before listing items. Follow our guidelines and review our examples so you know beforehand what you can and can't sell on eBay (note that examples are

Contact us
Have a question? We can help.
Contact us

Ask eBay members
Get help from other eBay members. Visit the Answer Center to post a question.

Related help topics
• A-Z index of policies
• Item description and picture theft
• Rules about intellectual property – overview
• Rules for listings – overview
• Rules for sellers – overview

Figure 11-7

6. Recognize that eBay prohibits the selling of infringing items on its site. Profiting from a copy of someone else's legally owned *intellectual property* is an *infringement* violation. Infringement, also known as *piracy*, is the encroachment on another person's legal ownership rights on an item, a trademark, or a copyright. Check the appendix for a list of no-no items commonly found at the center of infringement violations.

 Trademark and copyright protection don't just cover software, music, and movies. Clothing, toys, sunglasses, and books are among the items covered by law. Intellectual property owners actively defend their rights and, along with help from average eBay users, continually tip off eBay to fraudulent and infringing auctions. Rights owners can use eBay's Verified Rights Owner (VeRO) program, as well as law-enforcement agencies.

7. Check eBay's policies regarding questionable items. Because some items are prohibited in one place and not another, eBay lists a few items that you can trade but that are restricted and regulated. As a member of eBay, you're responsible for knowing the laws and restrictions in your area — as well as those on the eBay Web site. It may be illegal to sell certain items (such as event tickets or alcohol) in one geographic area but not in another. See the appendix for a table of items that are questionable on eBay.

8. Another category you need to recognize are forbidden items. The folks on eBay didn't just fall off the turnip truck. eBay staffers have seen people try just about every scam imaginable to get around paying fees or following policy guidelines. Just so you know: The following items are definitely forbidden:

- **Raffles and prizes:** You need to sell something in your auction; you can't offer tickets or chances for a giveaway.

- **Want ads:** If you want something, you have to search for it. Don't try to run your needs as an ad thinly disguised as an auction. Visit eBay's Want-It-Now (pages.ebay.com/wantitnow/) section and legally post your wants and needs there.

- **Advertisements:** An eBay auction is not the place to make a sales pitch (other than attractive copy describing your item, that is). Some eBay bad guys list an auction and then use the auction to send bidders to some other auction or Web site.

The Real Estate category is one exception to the no-advertisements rule. You can run an ad there for your property. You can also use a Classified Ad listing format in some other categories. Check out `http://pages.ebay.com/help/sell/adformatfees.html` for more information.

- **Bait-and-switch tactics:** These are a variation on the old sales technique of pretending to sell what you're not really selling, and then flim-flamming the buyer into shelling out for something pricier. Some eBay users who are selling an unfamiliar brand of item try to snag bidders by putting a more familiar brand in the title. For instance, writing *Designer Chanel purse — not really, but a lot like it!* is a fake-out. eBay calls that little trick *keyword spamming.*

- **Mixing apples with oranges:** This gambit tries to attract more bidders to view an item by putting it in a high-traffic category where it doesn't belong. Forget it. eBay will move it for you if necessary, but keeping that rutabaga recipe book *away* from the list of auto-motive repair manuals is more considerate.

- **Catalogs:** "Buy my catalog so you can buy more stuff from me!" Uh-huh. I don't know why anyone would put a *bid* on a catalog (unless it's a Sears-Roebuck antique). If it's only a booklet that shows off all the cool junk you're selling, you can't offer it as an auction item.

Chances are good that if you try one of these scams, you'll get caught. Then eBay cancels the listing. Do it once, and shame on you. Do it a lot, and you're no longer welcome on eBay.

Know When to Sell Your Items

1. Experienced eBay sellers know that when planning a sale, timing is almost everything. Fur coats don't sell well in July, and as a collectible seller you don't want to be caught with 200 Nintendo games during a run on Xbox. But vintage games may still sell at any time. *Star Wars* action figures are traditionally good sellers — unless a new *Star Trek* movie is coming out.

 I'm about to hit you with some of my clichés: *Timing is everything. Sell what you know and know when to sell. Buy low and sell high. Fast quarters are better than slow dollars.* Granted, clichés may be painful to hear over and over, but they do contain nuggets of good information.

2. Timing your auctions and fixed-price listings is hardly an exact science. Rather, timing is a little bit of common sense, a dash of marketing, and a fair amount of diligent information-gathering, including

- **Research among your friends.** What are they interested in? Would they buy the items you're selling?

- **eBay Search as a research tool.** Search eBay's listings (see Chapter 4 for the how-to information) to see whether anyone's making money on the type of item you want to sell. If people are crazed for some fad item and you have a bunch, *yesterday* was the best time to sell (but *immediately* will do in a pinch).

3. Recognize that some items — such as good antiques, rugs, baseball cards, and sports cars — are timeless. But timing still counts. So do your research and follow these rules, even when you think you're selling a sure winner:

- Don't put your rare, antique paper-cutter up for auction if someone else is selling one at the same time. I guarantee that will cut into your profits.

- If the eBay market is already flooded with dozens of an item (as you see in **Figure 11-8**) and no one is making money on them, you can afford to wait before you plan your sale of the same item.

Just wait to sell if you have this much competition!

Figure 11-8

Understand the eBay Fees

1. The Cliché Police are going to raid me sooner or later, but here's one I'm poking a few holes in this time around: *You gotta spend it to make it.* This old-time business chestnut means that you need to invest a fair amount of money before you can turn a profit. Although the principle still holds true in traditional marketplaces, on eBay you don't have to spend much moola to run your business. eBay keeps fees low and volume high.

 Keeping costs low for sellers is one reason eBay has become one of the most successful e-commerce companies on the Internet and a darling of Wall Street.

2. But eBay does charge sellers for selling their wares on the site. The fees vary with the type of listing (auction, fixed-price, and so on), the type of product (media, vehicle, real estate, for example), and the special features used for a listing (bold typeface, extra pictures, and so on). There are three main types of eBay Fees (each of which has its own section in this chapter):

- **Insertion fees.** Every item listed on eBay is charged an insertion fee. There's no way around it. The insertion fee is calculated on a sliding scale based on the *minimum bid* (your starting price), your fixed-sale price, or the *reserve price* (the secret lowest price that you're willing to sell your item for) for your item. (Later in this chapter, in the section "Get a Grip on Insertion Fees," I explain how the reserve price affects what you eventually have to pay.)

- **Final Value Fees (FVFs).** If you follow the movie business, you hear about some big A-list stars who take a relatively small fee for making a film but negotiate a big percentage of the gross profits. This is known as a *back-end deal* — in effect, a commission based on how much the movie brings in. eBay does the same thing, taking a small insertion fee when you list your item — and then a commission on the back end when you sell your item. This commission is called the *Final Value Fee* and is based on the final selling price of your item. (You can find further explanation in this chapter's later task "Figure the Final Value Fees.")

- **Optional fees.** You don't have to pay a license fee and destination charge, but setting up your listing can be like buying a car. eBay has all sorts of options to spruce up your listing page. I explain how all these bells, whistles, and white sidewalls dress up your auction in Chapter 10 — and I explain the cost of the fancy stuff in the section "Plan for Optional Fees When Needed" later in this chapter.

Get a Grip on Insertion Fees

1. So what does the insertion fee buy you on eBay? These two essentials:

- A really snazzy-looking display page for your item that millions of eBay members worldwide can see, admire, and breathlessly respond to. (We can only hope.)

- The use of eBay services, such as the Trust & Safety program, which protects your selling experience.

2. Table 11-1 gives you a handy reference to eBay's current insertion fee structure ranging from $0.10 to $4.00 for a regular auction. (You don't need to memorize these fees; just refer to this table or find this information on eBay by searching the Help area for eBay fees.) The folks running eBay understand that there's not as much profit margin when you're selling media items (new or used books, music, DVDs, movies, and video games), so they have a lower listing fee to encourage you.

Table 11-1	Auction Insertion Fees	
Starting or Reserve Price	**Insertion Fee**	**Insertion Fee for Media**
$0.01–$0.99	$0.15	$0.10
$1.00–$9.99	$0.35	$0.25
$10.00–$24.99	$0.55	$0.35
$25.00–$49.99	$1.00	$1.00
$50.00–$199.99	$2.00	$2.00
$200.00–$499.99	$3.00	$3.00
$500–gazillions	$4.00	$4.00

3. If you're running a reserve-price auction, eBay bases its insertion fee on the reserve price, not the starting bid. eBay also charges an extra fee of $2.00 to run a reserve-price auction having a reserve price of $199.99 or less. Auctions with reserves over $200.00 have a fee of 1 percent of the reserve with a maximum of $50.00.

 Here's a snapshot of how a reserve price affects your insertion fee. If you set a starting bid of $1.00 for a gold Rolex watch (say what?) but your reserve price is $5,000.00 (that's more like it), you're charged a $4.00 insertion fee based on the $5,000.00 reserve price plus a $50.00 reserve fee (1 percent of the reserve price).

4. In the Automotive category, the first four listings are free (no insertion fee). Subsequent listings have a $20.00 insertion fee and motorcycles are charged only $15.00.

5. eBay has a different insertion fee structure for items that are listed as fixed-price sales. They are quite the bargain, so if you have multiples of a single item and know what you need to get for them, a fixed-price sale is a great way to go! Do know that there is a slightly higher final value fee for fixed-price listings (see the next section). **Table 11-2** shows you the insertion charges for a fixed-price listing that can stay on the site for as long as 30 days!

Table 11-2	Fixed-Price Insertion Fee	
Fixed Price	**Insertion Fee**	**Insertion Fee for Media**
$1.00 and more	$0.35	$0.15

Figure the Final Value Fees (FVFs)

1. In traditional situations where you pay sales commission on a big purchase (such as a house), you usually pay a fixed percentage on the entire amount. eBay's FVF (final value fee) structure for auctions is different: It's set up as a three-tiered system where you pay

- 8.75 percent of the closing bid amount for the first $25.00.

- 3.5 percent of the closing bid amount from $25.01 to $1,000.00

- 1.5 percent of the closing bid amount over $1,000.00

Table 11-3 covers the calculation of final value fees for auctions.

Because of the sliding percentages, the higher the final selling price, the lower the percentage of commission eBay charges. (I guess math can be a beautiful thing, when applied for my benefit.)

Table 11-3	Auction Final Value Fees
Closing Bid	**To Find Your Final Value Fee**
$0.01–$25.00	Multiply the closing bid by **8.75 percent.**
	For a closing bid of $25.00, you owe eBay $2.19.
	$25.00 × .0875 = $2.19
$25.01–$1,000.00	Multiply the first $25.00 of the closing bid by **8.75 percent.** Subtract $25.00 from your closing bid and then multiply this difference by **3.5 percent.** Add these two amounts.
	For a closing bid of $1,000.00, you owe eBay $36.32.
	$25.00 × .0875 = $2.19
	($1,000.00 – $25.00) × .035 = $34.13
	$2.19 + $34.13 = $36.32
$1,000.01 and over	Multiply the first $25.00 of the closing bid by **8.75 percent.** Multiply ($1,000.00 – $25.00) by **3.5 percent.** Subtract $1,000.00 from your closing bid and then multiply this difference by **1.5 percent.** Add these three amounts.
	For a final sale price of $3,000.00, you owe eBay $66.32.
	$25.00 × .0875 = $2.19
	($1,000.00 – $25.00) × .035 = $34.13
	($3,000.00 – $1,000.00) × .015 = $30.00
	$2.19 + $34.13 + $30.00 = $66.32

2. eBay doesn't charge a final value fee on an auction in the Real Estate/Timeshares category as they do in other categories; instead, they charge a flat *notice fee* of $35.00.

3. Instead of FVFs in the Automotive category, you pay a flat *successful listing fee* of $125.00 for passenger vehicles (the first four listings in a12-month period; $100.00 for the fifth and subsequent) and $100.00 for motorcycles (the first four listings in a 12-month period; $80.00 for the fifth and subsequent), if your auction ends with a winning bidder (and the reserve has been met).

4. Things get tricky when you're dealing with final value fees for fixed-price items; the FVFs differ by category. Checking out the costs involved in the individual categories may help you decide which type of items you choose to sell. **Table 11-4** is an attempt to clarify the tiers.

Table 11-4	Fixed-Price Final Value Fees	
eBay Category	**Selling Price**	**To Find Your Final Value Fee**
Consumer Electronics Video Game Systems, Cameras & Photo	$0.01–$50.00	**8%** of the selling price
	$50.01–$1,000.00	**8%** of the first $50.00, plus **4.5%** of the remaining selling price ($50.01–$1,000.00)
	$1,000.01 and over	**8%** of the first $50.00, plus **4.5%** of the amount up to $1,000.00, plus **1%** of the remaining selling price ($1,000.01 to the final sale amount)
Computers & Networking	$0.01–$50.00.00	**6%** of the selling price
	$50.01–$1,000.00	**6%** of the first $50.00, plus **3.75%** of the remaining selling price ($50.01–$1,000.00)
	$1,000.01 and over	**6%** of the first $50.00, plus **3.75%** of the amount up to $1,000, plus **1%** of the remaining selling price ($1,000.01 to the final sale amount)

eBay Category	Selling Price	To Find Your Final Value Fee
Clothing, Shoes & Accessories	$0.01–$50.00	**12%** of the selling price
	$50.01–$1,000.00	**12%** of the first $50.00, plus **9%** of the remaining selling price ($50.01–$1,000.00)
	$1,000.01 and over	**12%** of the first $50.00, plus **9%** of the amount up to $1,000.00 and then **2%** of the remaining selling price ($1,000.01 to the final sale amount)
Media (Books, Music, DVDs & Movies, Video Games)	$0.01–$50.00	**15%** of the selling price
	$50.01–$1,000.00	**15.00%** of the first $50.00, plus **5%** of the remaining selling price ($50.01–$1,000.00)
	$1,000.01 and over	**15.00%** of the first $50.00, plus **5%** of the amount up to $1,000.00, plus **2%** of the remaining selling price ($1,000.01 to the final sale amount)
All Other Categories	$0.01–$50.00	**12%** of the selling price
	$50.01–$1,000.00	**12.00%** of the first $50.00, plus **6%** of the remaining selling price ($50.01–$1,000.00)
	$1,000.01 and over	**12.00%** of the first $50.00, plus **6%** of the amount up to $1,000.00, plus **2%** of the remaining selling price ($1,000.01 to the final sale amount)

5. If you try to work out your own final value fees, you may get an extreme headache — and come up with fractional cents. Know that eBay rounds up fees of $0.005 and more — and drops any fees that are less than $0.005. These roundings are done on a per-transaction basis, and generally even out over time.

Plan for Optional Fees When Needed

1. eBay has options that you can use to get your listings noticed, for example, bold face titles (for appearance) and subtitles (for adding extra item information). The options you choose (and the price you're willing to pay) depend on the type and price of the items you plan to sell. **Table 11-5** lists the eBay listing options and what they'll cost you. (See Chapter 12 for more about your listing options.)

Table 11-5	eBay Optional-Feature Fees	
Option	**Fee (Auction or Fixed-Price) 3, 5, 7, 10 days**	**Fixed-Price Fee (per 30 days)**
Value Pack (Gallery Plus, Subtitle, and Listing Designer)	$0.65	$2.00
Boldface title	$2.00	$4.00
Featured First (for Top-rated Sellers)	$24.95	$74.95
List in two categories	Double-listing and upgrade fees	Double-listing and upgrade fees
10-day auction	$0.40	n/a
Listing Designer	$0.10	$0.30
Scheduled listings	$0.10	$0.10
Subtitle	$0.50	$1.50
Picture hosting	First picture free, each additional $0.15	
Auction BIN (Buy It Now) fee	(See Table 11-6)	
eBay Motors vehicle BIN fee	$1.00 for vehicles	
Passenger vehicle reserve fee		$7.00

2. eBay also charges an upgrade fee when you use the Buy-It-Now option on your listings. **Table 11-6** shows how Buy-It-Now upgrade fees break down.

Table 11-6	Buy-It-Now Fees
Buy-It-Now Price	**Fee**
$0.01–$9.99	$0.05
$10.00–$24.99	$0.10
$25.00–$49.99	$0.20
$50.00 or more	$0.25

Keep Current on Your Profits

1. When you've finished all the legwork needed to make some money, do some brain-work to keep track of your results. The best place to keep watch on your eBay sales is on your My eBay page, a great place to stay organized while you're conducting all your eBay business. For an example, see my My eBay page in **Figure 11-9**.

2. Use this checklist of what to watch out for after the listing closes:

- **Keep an eye on how much you're spending to place items up for sale on eBay.** You don't want any nasty surprises, and you don't want to find out that you spent more money to set up your listing than you received selling your item.

- **If you decide to turn your eBay selling into a business, keep track of your expenses for your taxes.** (I explain Uncle Sam's tax position on eBay next. Stay tuned.)

- **Make sure that you get refunds and credits when they're due.**

- **Double-check your figures to make certain eBay hasn't made mistakes.** If you have any questions about the accounting, let eBay know.

 Find an error or something that isn't quite right with your account on eBay? Use the form at `pages.ebay.com/help/contact_us/_ base/index_selection.html` to get your questions answered.

3. If your eBay business really takes off, you'll want to get more formal about tracking the money you make and spend. When it comes to calculating your bottom line, it's best to get comfortable with using an accounting program like QuickBooks. I recommend *QuickBooks For Dummies*, by Stephen L. Nelson (Wiley Publishing, Inc.).

Stay organized in the Sell area of My eBay.

Figure 11-9

Don't Forget the Taxes

1. As Ben Franklin knew (and we've all found out since), you can't escape death and taxes. (C'mon, it's not a cliché; it's "traditional wisdom.") Whether in cyberspace or face-to-face life, never forget that Uncle Sam is always your business partner. If you live outside the United States, check the tax laws in that country so you don't end up with a headache down the road.

2. I've heard some rumors about not having to pay taxes on eBay profits. If you hear any variation on this theme, smile politely and don't believe a word of it. Two of the more popular (and seriously mistaken) tax notions running around the eBay community these days go like this:

- Rumor #1: "E-commerce isn't taxed." They wish. One story claims that "there will be no taxes on e-commerce sales (sales conducted online) for three years." No one ever seems to know when those three years start or end.

 Some people confuse state-sales-tax issues with income-tax issues. You don't pay special Internet sales taxes, but that's not the same as not reporting income from the Internet or paying sales tax when you sell within your home state.

- Rumor #2: "Profits from garage sales are tax-exempt." The logic (such as it is) holds that "eBay is like a garage sale, and you don't have to pay taxes on garage sales." (Uh-huh. And the calories in ice cream don't count if you eat it out of the carton. Who comes up with this stuff, anyway?)

To get the reliable word, I checked with the IRS's e-commerce office. The good folks there told me that even if you make as little as a buck on any eBay sale after all your expenses (the cost of the item, eBay fees, shipping charges), you still have to declare it as income on your federal tax return.

3. Aside from any payroll taxes you pay for your employees, you'll have three main areas of taxes to keep track of:

- **Federal income taxes:** The rumor I refer to in the previous step is just an urban (or shall I say *suburban*) legend — somebody's wishful thinking that's become folklore. If you make money on a garage sale, you *do* have to declare it as income — just as you do with anything else you make money on. Most people never make any money on garage sales because they usually sell things for far less than they bought them for. However, the opposite is often true of an eBay transaction — people really do make money on many of the items they sell. If you have questions about eBay sales and your taxes, check with your personal accountant, call the IRS Help Line at 800-829-1040, or visit the IRS Web site at www.irs.ustreas.gov. And be friendly. (Just in case.)

Even if you lose money, *you may have to prove it to the government,* especially if you're running a small business. You most definitely should have a heart-to-heart talk with your accountant or tax professional regarding how to file your taxes. If something might look bad in an audit if you *don't* declare it, consider that a big hint about the wisdom of declaring it.

- **State income taxes:** Yes, it's true: Not only is Uncle Sam (way over in Washington, D.C.) looking for his slice of your eBay profits, but your state government may be hankering to join the feast. If you have a good accountant, give that esteemed individual a call. If you don't have one, find a tax professional in your area. Tax professionals actually do more than just process your income tax returns once a year; they can help you avoid major pitfalls even before April 15.

- **State sales tax:** If your state has sales tax, a *sales tax number* is required before you *officially* sell something. If sales tax applies, you may have to collect the appropriate sales tax for every sale that falls within the state that your business is in. A 1992 U.S. Supreme Court decision said that states can only require sellers that have *a physical presence in the same state as the consumer* to collect so-called use taxes — but don't just assume that little clause lets you off the hook. To find the regulations for your state, visit one of the following sites, which supply links to every state's tax board. The tax board should have the answers to your questions.

  www.taxsites.com/State-Links.html
  www.aicpa.org/yellow/yptstax.htm

Recognize That Other Laws Affect eBay Business

The U.S. government uses two laws on the books to go after eBay outlaws. One is the Federal Trade Commission (FTC) Act, which prohibits deceptive or misleading transactions in commerce. The other is the Mail or Telephone Order Merchandise Rule, which requires sellers to ship merchandise in a timely manner or offer to refund a consumer's money. The FTC is in charge of pursuing these violations. If you have a question about federal laws, you can find a lot of information online. For example, I found these three Web sites that keep fairly current lists of U.S. law and federal codes:

```
www.law.cornell.edu/uscode
www.ftc.gov
www.fourmilab.ch/ustax/ustax.html
```

Congress's Internet Tax Freedom Act stated that until October 2001, Congress and state legislatures couldn't institute *new* taxes on Internet transactions. President Bush signed a unanimously approved law that extended (through November 1, 2003) a ban on multiple and discriminatory Internet taxes and Internet-access taxes. (The moratorium did not apply to sales taxes or federal taxes.) The legislation also lengthened the "Sense of the Congress" resolution that there should be no federal taxes on Internet access or electronic commerce, and that the United States should work aggressively through the EU (European Union) and WTO (World Trade Organization) to keep electronic commerce free from tariffs and discriminatory taxes.

 Even though November 1, 2003, has passed, there's still discussion about the law. Some people want to exempt online merchants if they bring in less than $25,000 per year. Others say no taxes should be imposed unless the merchant has sales of $5 million a year. As of mid-2009, this issue still isn't resolved. Ask your tax pro how to proceed.

Something new is on the horizon: the *Streamlined Sales Tax Project* (SST). Although the name of this government project may make it sound like the states will be charging state sales tax on all e-commerce purchases, the reality isn't that simple. The battle is ongoing — and though I don't feel that eBay sellers with sales under $100,000 a year have much to fear, I still recommend that you do a Google search on the SSTA every once in a while to keep up to date.

As of this writing, the rules are up in the air. Please continue to check my Web site, `www.coolebay tools.com`, for news on the SSTA when it applies.

Getting Items Ready for Listing

You're on the threshold of adding your item to the hundreds of thousands that go up for sale on eBay every day (and perhaps also shedding some of those valuable things you haven't touched in years). Some items are so hot that the sellers sextuple their investments. Other items, unfortunately, are so stone cold that they may not register a single bid.

Once you decide what you want to sell, find out as much as you can about it and conduct a little research by searching for similar items on eBay. (See Chapters 4 and 11 to help with all that.) That homework should give you a good idea of the item's popularity and value. Then you need to decide what type of listing — traditional auction (with or without a reserve price), fixed-price, or Buy It Now — to try, what category to use, when to start and stop the listing, and so on.

Chapter 12

Get ready to...

The listing form (which I describe in this chapter and show you how to fill out in Chapter 13) may change in time, but the basic decisions I introduce here will not. In this chapter, I also give you some pointers on taking pictures of your item to include with the listing — it's a great way to attract buyers' eyes to your item. Rest assured that the selling philosophy laid out in this chapter should help you ride the wave of any changes on eBay.

Categorize and Describe Your Item

1. Before you list your item, find out where people will look for it. On eBay, that means the specific category under which you want the item listed. Selecting the exact category isn't crucial to achieving the highest price for your item. The bulk of buyers (who know what they're looking for) just input search keywords into eBay's search box and look for their items. Others, though, may select a category and peruse the items for sale to see whether a particular one strikes their fancy.

- Ask your friends or family where they'd look for such an item — and remember the categories you saw most frequently when you conducted your market research with the eBay search function.

- Investigate which category will pay off best for your item by running a search and then checking Completed Listings. See how many of this type of item are currently listed (and if people are actually bidding on it). Scroll down to the left of the search results page and click the Show Only Completed Listings box. Then sort your results by highest prices first — and look over the sales to see which categories they're listed in.

2. Decide what you want to say in your title and item description; jot down your ideas. Take a good look at your item and make a list of keywords that describe it. *Keywords* are single descriptive words that a buyer uses to find what you're selling: Keywords can make or break a findable title. The keywords for your title and description should include the following:

   - Brand name

   - Size of the item (citing measurements if appropriate)

   - Age or date of manufacture

   - Condition

   - Rarity

   - Color

   - Size

   - Material

 Think of your item title as a great newspaper headline. The most valuable real estate on eBay is the 55-character title of your item, as shown in **Figure 12-1**. *The majority of buyers do title searches, and that's where your item must come up to be sold!* Give the most essential information right away to grab the eye of the reader who's just browsing. Be clear and informative enough to get noticed by eBay's search engine.

Use your title's 55 words wisely.

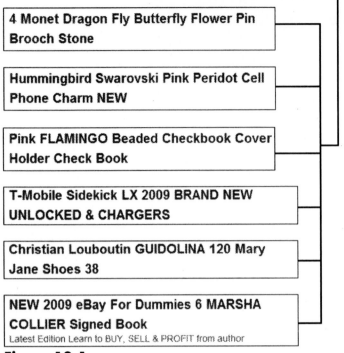

4 Monet Dragon Fly Butterfly Flower Pin
Brooch Stone

Hummingbird Swarovski Pink Peridot Cell
Phone Charm NEW

Pink FLAMINGO Beaded Checkbook Cover
Holder Check Book

T-Mobile Sidekick LX 2009 BRAND NEW
UNLOCKED & CHARGERS

Christian Louboutin GUIDOLINA 120 Mary
Jane Shoes 38

NEW 2009 eBay For Dummies 6 MARSHA
COLLIER Signed Book
Latest Edition Learn to BUY, SELL & PROFIT from author

Figure 12-1

 I know all about writer's block. Doing a little pre-work before you list makes the actual listing process so much easier.

3. Determine whether you want to attach an additional picture (or pictures) to your description. You can store such pictures online and link to them by using the Uniform Resource Locator (URL) for their location on the Web. Additional pictures help sell items, but you don't have to use them.

4. Decide on the price at which you think you can sell your item. Be as realistic as you can. (That's where your market research comes in.) Setting the right price is as important as your item description, and there is some strategy involved:

- eBay requires you to set a *starting price*, also called a minimum bid — the lowest bid allowed in an auction. You may be surprised to see stuff worth tens of thousands of dollars starting at just $0.99. No, these sellers haven't lost their minds. Setting an incredibly low minimum (just type it into the box *without* the dollar sign but *with* the decimal point) is a subtle strategy that gives you more bang for your buck.

 You can use a low starting price to attract more bidders who will, in turn, drive up the price to the item's real value — especially if, after doing your research, you know that the item is particularly hot.

- If you're worried that you'll have to sell your item for a bargain-basement price, you can set a *reserve price* to protect your investment. The best advice, if you choose this option, is to set a reserve price that is the lowest amount you'll take for your item — and then set a minimum bid that is ridiculously low. Use a reserve only when absolutely necessary because some bidders pass up reserve auctions.

 Before you set any starting or reserve price, do your homework and make some savvy marketing decisions. If your auction isn't going as you hoped, you *could* end up selling Grandma Ethel's Ming vase for a dollar. Think about your strategy, and see Chapter 13 for information on how you can make changes in your listing if you've made some egregious error.

Prepare a Picture of Your Item

1. The idea behind using images in your listings is to attract tons of potential buyers. With that goal in mind, you should try to create the best-looking images possible, no matter what kind of technology you're using to capture them. A point-and-shoot camera may be okay for a group shot at some historical monument, but illustrating your auction is a whole different idea. Whether you're using a traditional film camera (so you can scan your developed photographs later) or a digital camera to capture your item, some basic photographic guidelines can give you better results:

- **Do** take the picture of your item outside, in daylight, whenever possible. That way the camera can catch all possible details and color.

- **Do** forget about fancy backgrounds; they distract viewers from your item. **Figure 12-2** shows an example of what *not* to do. Put small items on a neutral-colored, nonreflective towel or cloth; put larger items in front of a neutral-colored wall or curtain. You'll cut out almost all the background when you prepare the picture on your computer.

- **Do** use extra lighting. You can do this with your camera's flash mode or with extra photo lighting on stands. Use extra lighting even when you're taking the picture outside. The extra lighting acts as *fill light* — it adds more light to the item, filling in some of the shadowed spots.

- **Don't** get so close to the item that the additional light washes out (overexposes) the image. The easiest way to figure out the best distance is by trial and error.

Start close and keep moving farther away until you get the results you want. This method can get pricey if you use film, but that's where digital cameras really shine: You can see the picture seconds after you shoot it, keep it and modify it, erase it, and start again.

Figure 12-2

- **Do** take two or three acceptable versions of your image; you can choose the best one later on your computer.

- **Don't** use incandescent or fluorescent lighting to illuminate the photos you plan to scan. Incandescent lighting tends to make items look yellowish, and fluorescent lights lend a bluish tone to your photos. Some sellers use GE Reveal incandescent bulbs; they throw a good-quality light which, when combined with natural daylight, produces an even tone.

- If your item relies on detail (for example, an engraved signature or detailed gold trim), **do** take a wide shot of the entire item — and then take a tight close-up or two of the detailed areas that you want buyers to see.

- **Do** make sure that you focus the camera; nothing is worse than a blurry picture. If your camera is a fixed-focus model (it can't be adjusted), get only as close as the manufacturer recommends. If you go beyond that distance, the item appears out of focus. (Automatic-focus cameras measure the distance and change the lens setting as needed.)

2. You can use a scanner to scan the box that the item came in, or if there's a photo of the item on the box, scan that portion of the box. If you have a three-dimensional item (such as a doll, jewelry item, or box) and you can't close the scanner lid, drape a black or white T-shirt over the item after you place it on the scanner's glass plate; that way you get a clean background and good light reflection from the scanner.

3. Follow this checklist of tried-and-true techniques for preparing fast-loading images to display at eBay:

- **Set your image resolution at 72 pixels per inch.** You can do this with the settings for your scanner. Although 72 ppi may seem like a low resolution, it shows up fast on a buyer's screen and looks great on eBay.

- **When using a digital camera, set the camera to no higher than the 800×600 format.** That's custom-made for a monitor. You can always crop the picture if it's too large.

- **Make the finished image no larger than 480 pixels wide.** When you size your picture in your image software, it's best to keep it no larger than 300×300 pixels or 4 inches square, even if it's a snapshot of a classic

4×4 monster truck. These dimensions are big enough for people to see without squinting, and the details of your item show up nicely.

- **Crop any unnecessary areas of the photo.** Just show your item; everything else is a waste.

- **Use your software to darken or change the photo's contrast.** When the image looks good on your computer screen, the image looks good on your eBay auction page.

- **Save your image as a .JPG file.** When you finish editing your picture, save it as a .JPG. (To do this, follow the instructions that come with your photo-editing software.) .JPG is the best format for eBay; it compresses information into a small file that appears quickly on-screen and reproduces nicely on the Internet.

Choose the Type of Listing

1. You have three ways to sell an item on eBay — auction, fixed price, and Buy It Now. You can decide which is best for you. An online auction is the tried-and-true traditional sale format on eBay. Many people look for single-item auctions; you can combine one of those with a Buy It Now option for potential buyers who want the item immediately. Often, if you're selling a collectible item, letting it go to auction may net you a much higher profit.

With Buy It Now (BIN), you can entice your bidders to pay just a tad more to have the satisfaction of walking away with the item free and clear (and *now*). Just specify the amount the item can sell for in the Buy It Now price area — the amount can be whatever you want, as long as it's at least 10 percent higher than the auction starting price. If you choose to take advantage of selling a hot item during the holiday rush, for example, you can make the BIN price as high as you think it can go. If you just want the item to move, make your BIN price the average price you see the item go for on eBay.

2. Here's a little secret about opting for an online auction: You can protect yourself from losing money on a valuable auction item with a *reserve price.* The reserve price is the lowest price that must be met before the item can be sold. You don't have to set a reserve price for your auction, but if you do, you can attract buyers by setting a lower starting bid. eBay charges an additional fee for the reserve price feature, and the fee varies depending on how high your reserve is.

As with everything in life, using a reserve price for your auctions has an upside and a downside. Many choosy bidders and bargain hunters blast past reserve-price auctions because they see a reserve price as a sign that proclaims "No bargains here!" Many bidders figure they can get a better deal on the same item with an auction that proudly declares *NR* (for *no reserve*) in its description. As an enticement to those bidders, you see lots of NR listings in auction titles. As a default, eBay includes titles in a search for NR that proclaim No Reserve. **Figure 12-3** shows just such a search.

On lower-priced items, I suggest that you set a higher starting price and set no reserve. Otherwise, if you're not sure about the market for your item, set a low minimum bid but set a high reserve to protect yourself.

3. A fixed-price sale is just like shopping at the corner store — so a fixed-price listing is easy for the buyer to comprehend and complete. Choose this type of listing when you have more than one of an item; that way you can run the listing for up to 30 days.

See several auctions that exclaim *NO RESERVE*.

GAS STATION FOR SALE BY OWNER! NO RESERVE! Take over payments		60 Bids	**$6,494.00**	4d 18h 16m	Not specified
Apple iPhone 16GB Unlocked Jailbroken NO RESERVE!		55 Bids	**$212.50**	15h 5m	+$5.99
Aladdin and the King of Thieves 1996 VHS Robin Williams	*Buy It Now or Best Offer*		**$5.00**	2d 18h 56m	+$3.00
18k Solid Yellow Gold Authentic Chanel Watch NO RESERVE		52 Bids	**$1,077.00**	46m	+$8.00
Hellsing Ultimate Series II Steelbook w/Art Book, 2 NEW Original 2-Disc Geneon 1st Press Limited Ed w/Art Book	*Buy It Now*		**$39.99**	5d 2h 52m	Free
DELL D800 15.4' WIFI Laptop "NO RESERVE"FREE SHIPPING"		45 Bids	**$151.99**	14m	Free
VHS Tape WD Pooh's Grand Adventure Christopher Robin	*Buy It Now or Best Offer*		**$5.00**	6d 15h 48m	+$2.99
Volkswagen : Golf GTI REPAIRABLE REBUILDABLE SALVAGE 5 SPEED RUNS NO RESERVE		51 Bids	**$1,525.00**	20h 29m	Not specified
MENS RAYMOND WEIL SPORT RW STEEL 8300-ST-20001 WATCH NR 100% AUTHENTIC FREE US SHIPPING 8300ST20001 BNIB $1195	*Buy It Now or Best Offer*		**$697.50**	13d 18h 47m	Free

Figure 12-3

A variation that I adore on a fixed-price listing is the *Best Offer* option. Adding this choice enables buyers to think they can get a great deal — but you have the opportunity to accept the offer or make a counteroffer. Cultural leanings toward bargaining mean some buyers prefer this method. You may not. But it can be fun — and it's an excellent way to spur sales in a slow retail environment (or if you'd like to offer some merchandise on the cheap and make some quick cash).

4. If you set up an eBay Store, you can, of course, sell items there. eBay Stores are a convenient place to sell many items, but the great thing about selling online is that having a store is certainly *not* necessary. You can always use fixed-price listings and save the cost of running a store. You may prefer setting up a store, however, if you have many items in large quantities. **Figure 12-4** shows the home page for eBay Stores.

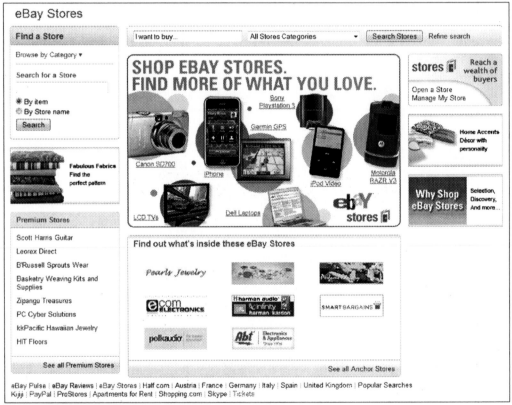

Figure 12-4

Know the Details of the Listing Process

1. You can find eBay's Sell an Item form by using either of these methods:

- Click the Sell link on the navigation bar at the top of the eBay home page. eBay allows you to select your category and download the Sell an Item page in seconds.

- Start your listing from your My eBay page. Just click the Sell Similar link (on the All Selling page) next to one of your existing items. Using the form that appears, you can change the item data.

2. At the top of the Sell an Item page, you see a link that invites you to a kinder, simpler listing form. *Please don't use it.* Yes, the form is simpler: It's a stripped-down version of the regular form — and though easier, it leaves off some important options that you will have to change from listing to listing. Besides, we're all grownups here; you don't need a "kindergarten" form to run your sales. Take your sales seriously and use the full listing form — that way you get all of eBay's benefits.

3. Take a minute to review **Table 12-1**, which outlines the info you're asked to fill out as you complete the listing form.

Table 12-1		Sell an Item Information
Form Element	*Required or Optional*	*What It Means / What It Costs*
Category	Required	The category under which you've decided to list your item.
Title	Required	The name of your item.
Description	Required	What you want to tell eBay buyers about your item.
eBay Picture Services	Optional	A way to upload a picture for your listing. Note that you get a free Preview picture at the top of your listing and Gallery in search.

(continued)

Table 12-1 *(continued)*

Form Element	Required or Optional	What It Means / What It Costs
Picture	Optional	By adding a picture, you can add your item's picture to eBay's search and the top of your listing. There's no charge to add the basic picture, but it will set you back $0.75 if you want a special picture that gets larger when a user drags his or her mouse pointer over it.
Picture URL	Optional	If you want to include an image that is hosted on another Web site, you must include the Web address of the JPEG image you want. If you just want to upload a picture from your computer, use eBay's Picture Service.
Item location	Required	The region, city, and country from which the item will be shipped
Quantity	Required	If your listing is an auction, the quantity is always one per listing.
Starting price	Required	The starting price (sometimes called a *minimum bid*) you set.
Selling price	Required	If this is a fixed-price listing, you have to post your selling price.
Best Offer	Optional	If you'd like to allow prospective buyers to make offers on your item, click this box.
Duration	Required	The number of days you want the listing to run.
Reserve price	Optional	A hidden target price you set, which must be met before the item can be sold. eBay charges you a fee for this feature.
Private auction	Optional	You can keep the identity of bidders secret with this option.
Buy It Now	Optional	You can sell your item directly to the first buyer who meets this price.
List item in two categories	Optional	If you want to double your exposure (and your listing fees), you can list your item in two categories.

Form Element	Required or Optional	What It Means / What It Costs
Featured First	Optional	Top-rated sellers only can have their auction appear at the top of the category when the listing displays in a Best Match sort. eBay charges $24.95 extra for this feature; $74.95 for a listing that lasts 30 days.
Boldface Title	Optional	A selling option to make your item listing stand out. eBay charges $2.00 ($4.00 for 30 days) extra for this feature.
Free Counter	Optional	If you want to have a free counter that counts off every visit to your listing, indicate so here.
Handling Time	Required	The maximum days you will let elapse between getting the money and shipping the item. Do yourself a favor — don't wait more than 48 hours. Buyers can get cranky.
Ship-to locations	Optional	Here's where you indicate where you're willing to ship an item. If you don't want to ship out of the United States, check that option. You can individually select different countries that you are willing to ship to.
Shipping and handling charges	Required	Your shipping charge. If your item isn't very large, list a flat shipping fee for your item. eBay takes that into account when deciding how your item shows up in Search and raises your visibility. For larger items, consider eBay's handy Shipping Calculator.
Payment instructions	Optional	You are required to accept PayPal. If you want to offer the option to pay with a different electronic payment service, mention that as well. This information appears at the top of your sale when the sale is completed, under the Shipping and Payments tab of the listing while it's active, and in the End of Listing e-mail.

(continued)

Table 12-1 *(continued)*

Form Element	Required or Optional	What It Means / What It Costs
PayPal and immediate payment	Optional	Fill in this area if you want to require the high bidder to pay through PayPal immediately when using Buy It Now. Add the Immediate Payment option if you know the shipping amount and would like the winner to pay with a click of the mouse.
Return policy	Required	Whether you do or don't accept returns, say so. You can give the customer as few as three days to return the item (that cuts down on spurious returns).

Constructing and Conducting Your Sale

Chapter 13

*I*f you're ready to create your listing and run your sale, then you already know what you're selling, how to title and describe it to attract buyers, what price you're asking, the type of listing that works for you, what payment methods you'll accept, as well as how you plan to ship the item to its buyer. *And* you have a great picture all prepared for your listing. If you're missing any of these pieces, check out Chapter 12 for a guide to the strategy of selling on eBay.

You're through with the decision making, and now it's time to get 'er done. This chapter helps you through the mechanics of creating the listing and running your sale.

The Sell an Item form looks daunting, but filling out its many sections doesn't take as long as you may think. Some of the questions you're asked aren't things you even have to think about; just click an answer and off you go. Other questions ask you to type information. Don't sweat a thing; all the answers you need are right here. In this chapter, I lead you through filling out all the required and optional stuff.

Get ready to...

Open the Form and Select a Category

1. Click the Sell link on the navigation bar at the top of the eBay Home Page. Then you simply start filling out the Sell an Item form that appears.

2. On the first page of the Sell an Item form, you need to select the main category for your item. If you want to search, type at least three keywords that best describe your item in the box provided and click Search. **Figure 13-1** shows you how the results come up after typing your words, making it easy to select a main category.

Type keywords here. Click here.

Find a matching category

Enter at least 3 keywords about your item to find a relevant category to list in.

For example: Amethyst gemstone rings

| star trek figure | Search |

Search categories | Browse categories | Recently used categories

Buyers will see your listing in the category that you select.

Toys & Hobbies
  Action Figures > TV, Movie & Video Games > Star Trek > Next Generation
  Action Figures > TV, Movie & Video Games > Star Trek > Star Trek (Original)
  Action Figures > TV, Movie & Video Games > Star Trek > Other
  Action Figures > TV, Movie & Video Games > Star Wars > Other
  Action Figures > Other
  Action Figures > TV, Movie & Video Games > Star Trek > Mixed Lots
  Action Figures > TV, Movie & Video Games > Star Wars > Episodes 4-6 (1977-1989) > Star Wars A New Hope
  Models & Kits > Science Fiction > Star Trek

Tip: Reach more buyers by selecting two categories (Fees apply)

Continue | Start over

Figure 13-1

 Your creativity can come into play for selecting a category. Who says that a box of Blue Dog (the famous doggie icon painted by Cajun artist George Rodrigue) note cards belongs in *Everything Else: Gifts & Occasions: Greeting Cards: Other Cards.* If you look

around, you may find a better category. The Find
Categories tool appears the second you open the Sell
an Item page. Check to see whether anyone else is
selling the item (and in which category) or just let
this tool help you pick a good category.

3. You can also browse the categories by clicking the aptly
named Browse Categories tab, which can help you select
your main category, and the thousands of subcategories.
eBay offers you this wealth of choices in a handy point-
and-click way. If you're unfamiliar with the types of items
you can actually *find* in those categories, you may want
to pore over Chapter 3 before you choose a category to
describe *your* item. **Figure 13-2** shows you how to manually narrow the subcategory listings on the Sell an Item
page. Here's the drill:

Choose the Browse Categories tab.

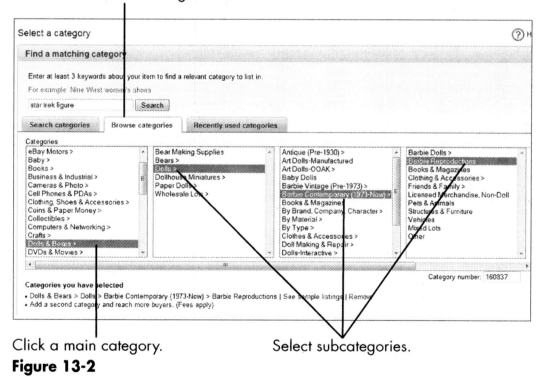

Click a main category.   Select subcategories.

Figure 13-2

1. *Click one of the main categories on the left. In the next box (to the right), you see a list of subcategories.*

2. *Select the most appropriate subcategory.*

3. *Continue selecting subcategories until you have narrowed your item listing as much as possible.* You know you've come to the last subcategory when you don't see any more right-pointing arrows in the Categories.

 Most bidders scan for specific items in subcategories. For example, if you're selling a Bakelite fruit pin, don't just list it under Jewelry; keep narrowing your choices. In this case, you can put it in a Costume Jewelry category that is especially for Bakelite. I guarantee that the real Bakelite jewelry collectors out there know where to look to find the jewelry they love. To narrow the category of your item, just keep clicking until you hit the end of the line.

Write a Good Title for Your Listing

1. After you figure out what category you want to list your item in, eBay wants to get down to the bare facts — what to call that thing you're trying to sell. Type the item name, or title, where prompted. eBay gives you 55 characters for this purpose. You want your title to use the item's common name and outline its age, condition, and any special features.

2. Avoid fancy punctuation or unusual characters, such as $, hyphens, and L@@K, because they just clutter up the title — and *buyers don't search for them.* Remember the keywords you used to find the item's category? That's what buyers will search for. Also avoid the following gaffes:

- If you've finished writing your item title and you have spaces left over, *please* fight the urge to dress it up with lots of asterisks and exclamation points!!!!!!!!!!!! (See how annoying that is?) The eBay search engine may overlook your item if the title is encrusted with meaningless **** and !!!! symbols. If bidders do see your title, they may become annoyed by the virtual shrillness and ignore it anyway!!!!!!!! (It's even more annoying the second time around.)

- Another distracting habit is overdoing capital letters. To buyers, seeing everything in caps is LIKE SEEING A CRAZED INFOMERCIAL SALESMAN SCREAMING AT THEM TO BUY NOW! Using all caps is considered *shouting*, which is rude and tough on the eyes. Use capitalization SPARINGLY, and only to finesse a particular point.

 Savvy buyers use the eBay search engine to find merchandise; if the name of your item is spelled wrong, the search engine can't find it. Poor spelling and incomprehensible grammar also reflect badly on you. If you're in competition with another seller, the buyer is likelier to trust the seller *hoo nose gud speling*.

3. Taking a crash course in eBay lingo can help bring you up to speed on attracting buyers to your item. Words and phrases — such as *mint, one of a kind, vintage, collectible, rare, unique, primitive, well-loved* — as well as the abbreviations in **Table 13-1** — are used frequently in eBay listings, and they can do wonders to jump-start your title.

Table 13-1		A Quick List of eBay Abbreviations
eBay Code	**What It Abbreviates**	**What It Means**
MIB	Mint in Box	The item is in the original box, in great shape, and just the way you'd expect to find it in a store.
MOC	Mint on Card	The item is mounted on its original display card, attached with the original fastenings, in store-new condition.
NRFB	Never Removed from Box	Just what it says, as in "bought but never opened."
COA	Certificate of Authenticity	Documentation that vouches for the genuineness of an item, such as an autograph or painting.
OEM	Original Equipment Manufacture	You're selling the item and all the equipment that originally came with it, but you don't have the original box, owner's manual, or instructions.
OOAK	One of a Kind	You are selling the only one in existence!
NWT	New With Tags	Item is new with store tags still on it.
NR	No Reserve Price	A reserve price is the price you can set when you begin your auction. If bids don't meet the reserve, you don't have to sell. Many buyers don't like reserve prices because they don't think that they can get a bargain. (For tips on how to allay these fears and get those bids in reserve-price auctions, see "Writing your description" later in this chapter.) If you're not listing a reserve for your item, let bidders know.
HTF, OOP	Hard to Find, Out of Print	Out of print, only a few ever made, or people grabbed up all there were. (HTF doesn't mean you spent a week looking for it in the attic.)

 Often you can rely on eBay slang to get your point across, but make sure that you mean it and that you're using it accurately. Don't label something MIB (Mint in Box) when it looks like it's been Mashed in Box by a meat grinder. You can find more abbreviations on my Web site, www.coolebaytools.com.

4. Add a subtitle, if you run out of title spaces and have more to say. eBay allows you to buy an additional 55 characters, which will appear under your item title in a search. The fee for this extra promotion is $0.50, and in a few circumstances, it is definitely worth your while, especially if there are other sellers selling the same item as you are. **Figure 13-3** shows some items with subtitles.

Limited Ed. Signed Remarked George Rodrigue Blue Dog NR
Hand drawn Blue Dog sketch with Blue Dog and Red Dog!

NEW 2009 eBay For Dummies 6 MARSHA COLLIER Signed Book
Latest Edition Learn to BUY, SELL & PROFIT from author

Black Orchid Voile De Fluer & Lotion of VoileDFluer
With travel black Orchid samples and White Patchulli

Auth.Manolo Blahnik Crocodile Leather Heels/Shoes 37/7
$1875.00 FROM BARNEY'S NEW YORK W/ BOX & DUSTBAG

0.10 CT ROUND COGNAC RED DIAMOND 14K GOLD STUD EARRINGS
Trusted Seller Over 33,000 Successful eBay Transactions

CCTV Sony 1/4 CCD 27x Zoom PTZ Dome D/N Outdoor Camera
Two Years Warranty!!! Heater&Fan Built-in, IR sensitive

New Laptop Battery for Dell Latitude D520 D600 D610
8 CELLS! EXTENDED BATTERY- 5 YEAR WARRANTY!

Figure 13-3

Any text that you put in a subtitle will really make your item stand out in the crowd — but (you knew there would be a *but,* didn't you?) those additional 55 characters won't come up in a title search. If you choose this option, choose attention-getting info that isn't absolutely needed for the title itself.

Add a Killer Item Description

1. After you hook potential bidders with your title, reel in buyers with a fabulous description. Don't think Hemingway here; think infomercial (the classier the better). **Figure 13-4** shows a great description of some silver dollars. You can write a magnificent description, as well — all you have to do is click in the box and start typing. Be sure to use the notes you've prepared ahead of time (see Chapter 12).

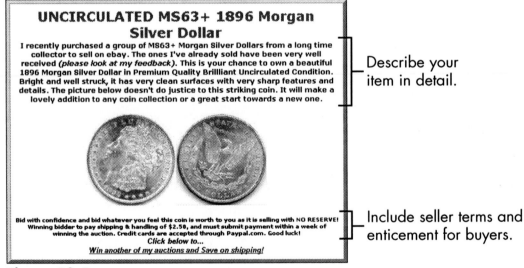

Describe your item in detail.

Include seller terms and enticement for buyers.

Figure 13-4

2. Include information about your item that accentuates the positive. Give the buyer a reason to buy your item — and be enthusiastic when you list all the reasons everyone should bid on it. Unlike the title, your info can take up as much space as you want. Even though you use a photo, be precise in your description — its size, color, kind of fabric, design, and so on.

3. Don't forget to include the negative facts, too. Don't hide the truth of your item's condition. If the item has a scratch, a nick, a dent, a crack, a ding, a tear, a rip, missing pieces, replacement parts, faded color, dirty smudges, or a bad smell (especially if cleaning might damage the item), mention it in the description. If your item has been overhauled, rebuilt, repainted, or hot-rodded, say so.

 Trying to conceal flaws costs you in the long run — you'll get tagged with bad feedback. And you run the risk of having the buyer file for a refund from PayPal because you weren't truthful about imperfections or modifications.

4. Promote yourself as a seller in your item description. As you accumulate positive feedback, tell potential bidders about your terrific track record. Add statements like "I'm great to deal with. Check out my feedback section." You can even take it a step further by inviting prospective bidders to your About Me page (where you may also include a link to your personal Web site — if you have one).

5. Add personal well-wishes for your potential bidders. Communication is the key to a good transaction, and you can set the tone for your auction and post-auction exchanges by including some simple phrases that show your friendly side. Invite potential bidders to e-mail you with questions, and offer the option of providing additional photos of the item if you have them.

6. You can (optionally) jazz up your item description with a bit of HTML coding, or you can use eBay's HTML text editor, shown in **Figure 13-5**. If you know how to use a word processor, you'll have no trouble touching up your text with this tool.

Use these tools to dress up your description.

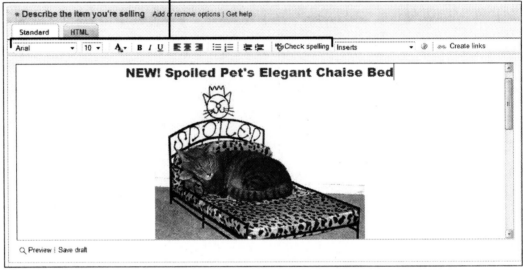

Figure 13-5

7. You can insert additional photos in your description and avoid eBay's additional photo charges by using the following line of HTML code. My example in Figure 13-5 uses this code:

```
<img src="http://www.collierad.com/
  catbed.jpg">
```

Just insert the URL of your hosted picture instead of my Web site (www.collierad.com), along with the picture's filename (in the example, it's catbed.jpg).

8. Occasionally, sellers offer an item as a *presell,* or an item that the seller doesn't yet have in stock but expects to. If you're offering this kind of item, make sure that you spell out all the details in the description. eBay policy states that you must ship a presell item within 30 days of the auction's end, so be sure you will have the item within that time span. Don't forget to include the actual shipping date.

 I have found that putting an item up for sale without having it in hand is a practice fraught with risk. The item you're expecting may not arrive in time or arrive damaged. I've heard of one too many sellers who have had to go out and purchase an item at retail for a buyer to preserve their feedback when caught in this situation.

Choose Duration and Timing for Your Listing

1. eBay gives you a choice to run your auction — 1, 3, 5, 7, or 10 days. Just click the number you want in the box. If you choose a 10-day auction, you add $0.40 to your insertion fee. My auction-length strategy depends on the time of year and the item I'm selling, and I generally have great success.

- If you have an item that you think will sell pretty well, run a 7-day auction (be sure it will cover a full week-end) so bidders have time to check it out before they decide to bid. However, if you know that you have a red-hot item that's going to fly off the shelves — say, a rare toy or a hard-to-get video game — choose a 3-day auction.

Eager bidders tend to bid higher and to beat out their competition more often if the item is hot and going fast. Three days is long enough to give trendy items exposure and ring up bids.

- Timing is not as important for fixed price listings as for auctions. It's generally accepted that you run a fixed-price listing with multiple items for 30 days. (If you have only one of an item, run an auction with the Buy It Now option).

2. With auctions running 24 hours a day, 7 days a week, you should know when the most bidders are around to take a gander at your wares. Here are some things to think about when you're choosing times on the Sell an Item form:

- **Saturday/Sunday:** Always run an auction over a weekend. People log on and off eBay all day.

- **Holiday weekends:** If a holiday weekend is coming up around the time you're setting up your auction, run your auction through the weekend and end it a day after the "holiday" Monday. This gives prospective bidders a chance to catch up with the items they perused over the weekend and plan their bidding strategies.

- **Time of day:** The best times of day to start and end your auction are during eBay's peak hours of operation, which are 5:00 p.m. to 9:00 p.m. Pacific Time, right after work on the West Coast. Perform your completed auction research, however, to be sure that this strategy applies to your item. Your timing depends on the item you're listing and whether "5:00 p.m. to 9:00 p.m. Pacific Time" is the middle of the night where you live.

Load Your Item's Image

1. Now you can put in the single picture to accompany your listing. Doing so also causes a postage-stamp-size version of your image to appear next to your listing in the category or search. Many buyers enjoy browsing the Gallery catalog-style, and it's open to all categories.

2. Click the Add Picture box and an Open File dialog box appears. Find your image file on your computer and click Open. The picture of your item appears in the image box. Add more pictures if you want (remember if you add them here, additional pictures cost $.15 each to post).

3. Click Submit Pictures and Continue. **Figure 13-6** shows the upload page — which is where you upload your image from the Sell an Item page. The best thing about using a picture in your listings is that it's *free* and it draws attention to your item on a search or category page. If you don't use a picture and just have an image in your description, your listing will get very few visitors.

Use at least one picture—it's free!

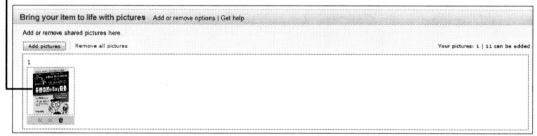

Figure 13-6

4. If you want to avoid extra eBay charges for additional pictures, put them in your description via the description's HTML tab. You've got to host your picture somewhere, though; it can't remain on your computer. Every additional picture needs to have an Internet address. Because your image needs an address, you have to find it a good home online. You have a couple of options:

- **Your ISP (Internet service provider):** All the big ISPs — AOL, Comcast, Road Runner, and Earthlink — give you space to store your Internet stuff. You're already paying for an ISP, so you can park pictures on your home-page area at no extra charge.

- **An image-hosting Web site:** Web sites that specialize in hosting pictures are popping up all over the Internet. Some charge a small fee; others are free. The upside here is that they're easy to use.

Get Fancy with Your Listing

1. How many times have you seen an item on eBay laid out on the page all pretty-like with a fancy border around the description? If that sort of thing appeals to you, eBay's Listing Designer will supply you with pretty borders for almost any type of item for $0.10. Selecting your design is as easy as clicking the menu (see **Figure 13-7**). You can designate where you'd like to place your image on the page relative to the description (left, right, top, or bottom).

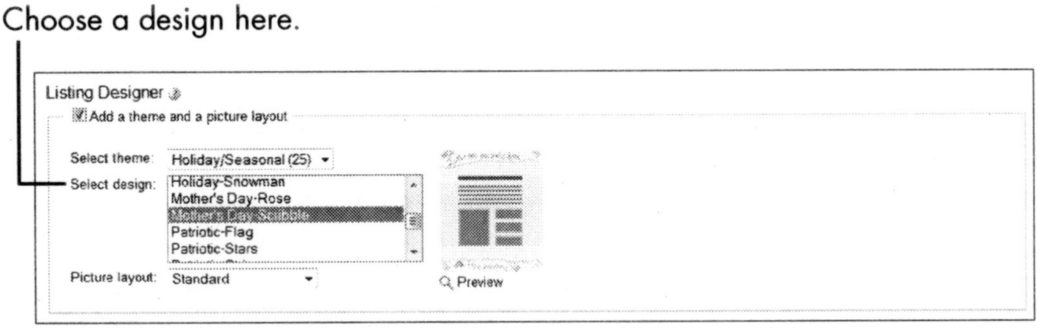

Choose a design here.

Listing Designer

☑ Add a theme and a picture layout

Select theme: Holiday/Seasonal (25) ▼

Select design:
Holiday-Snowman
Mother's Day-Rose
Mother's Day-Scribble
Patriotic-Flag
Patriotic-Stars

Picture layout: Standard ▼

🔍 Preview

Figure 13-7

Will the pretty borders increase the amount of bids your auction will get? It's doubtful. A clean item description with a few good clear pictures of your item is really all you need.

2. Consider a special combination deal called the Value Pack. For $0.65, you can place a subtitle on your listing, add a Gallery Plus picture, and doll things up with Listing Designer. All those features would normally cost $0.95, so the saving is clear if you run several listings a week.

 If you don't want to use the Listing Designer graphics to distract from your item, you can still get a discount. Just click the Listing Designer check box, but *don't* select a graphic pattern. You're still saving $0.30 over the price of a subtitle and Gallery (sneaky, huh?).

Let Buyers Know About Shipping

1. You need to decide where you are willing to ship your item. Here are the choices eBay offers on the Sell an Item form:

   - **Ship to the United States only:** This option is selected by default; it means you ship only domestically.

   - **Will ship worldwide:** The world is your oyster. I ship items every week to far-flung countries worldwide.

    When you indicate that you will ship internationally, your item shows up on the international eBay sites, which is a fantastic way to attract new buyers! eBay has lots of good international users, so you may want to consider selling your items around the world.

- **Will ship to United States and the following:** If you're comfortable shipping to certain countries but not to others, make your selections here; they show up on your listing page.

2. Traditionally, the buyer pays for shipping, and this is the point at which you must decide how much to charge. You also have to calculate how much this item will cost you to ship. If it's a small item (weighing under a pound or so), you may decide to charge a flat rate to all buyers. To charge a flat rate, click the Flat Shipping Rates tab and fill in the shipping amount. Before you fill in the amount, be sure to include your costs for packing (see Chapter 14 for more info on how much to add for this task) and insurance charges.

3. If your item weighs two pounds or more, you may want to use eBay's versatile Shipping Calculator. Because UPS and the U.S. Postal Service now charge variable rates for packages of the same weight, based on distance, using the calculator simplifies things for your customers (and you). The calculator automatically appears on the item page so that prospective buyers can type in their ZIP codes and immediately know how much shipping will be to their locations. **Figure 13-8** shows how simple the form is.

 Be sure you've weighed the item and know how much your handling charge will be. The calculator allows you to input a handling amount — and then adds it to the overall shipping total — but does not break out the amount separately for the customer.

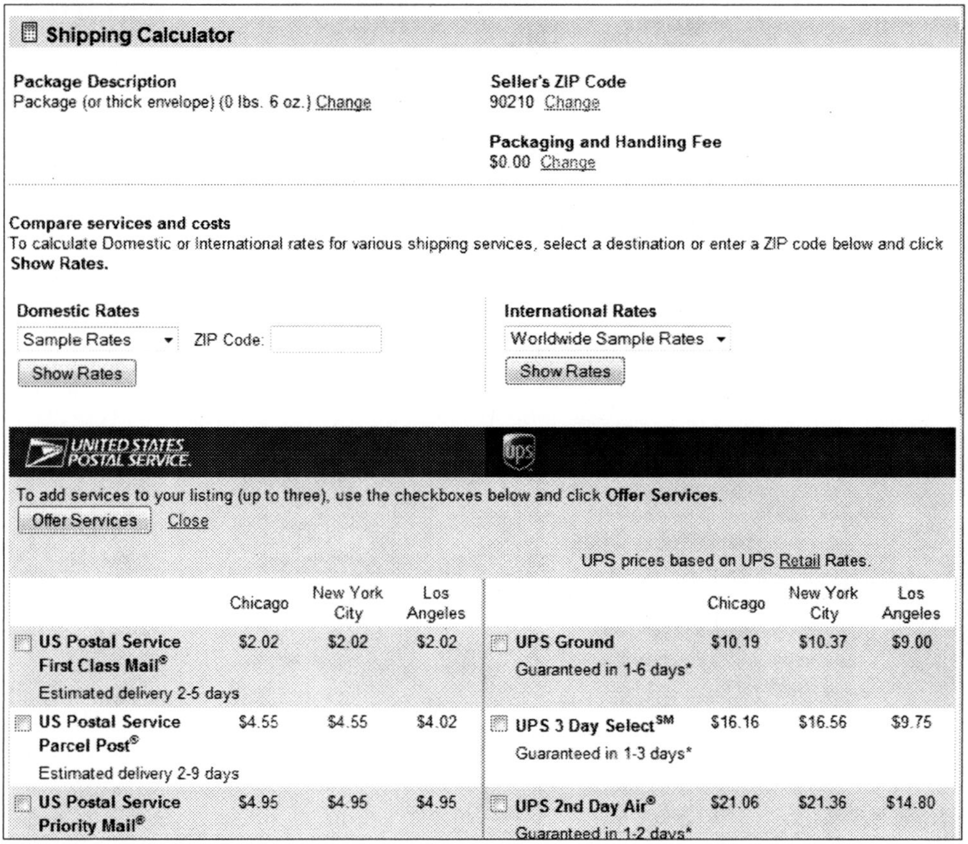

Figure 13-8

Add Options and Get Eyes on Your Item

1. Although eBay's display options aren't quite as effective as a three-story neon sign in Times Square, they do bring greater attention to your auction. Bold is a less-expensive option that affects the look of your title in searches. The eBay fee for bold is $2.00 ($4.00 for a 30-day listing). Bold type does catch your attention, as in **Figure 13-9,** but don't bother using it on items that'll bring in less than $25.00. Do use it if you're in hot competition with similar items and you want yours to stand out.

2. If you qualify, you can choose another (more expensive) option that affects where on eBay your item might be seen. If you are a Top-rated seller (see Chapter 10 for those requirements), you can add a Featured First option to your listing. When you do, your item listing appears at the top of its listing category when it is displayed in a Best Match sort. The charge for this option is $24.95 ($74.95 for a 30-day listing).

A bold title stands out.

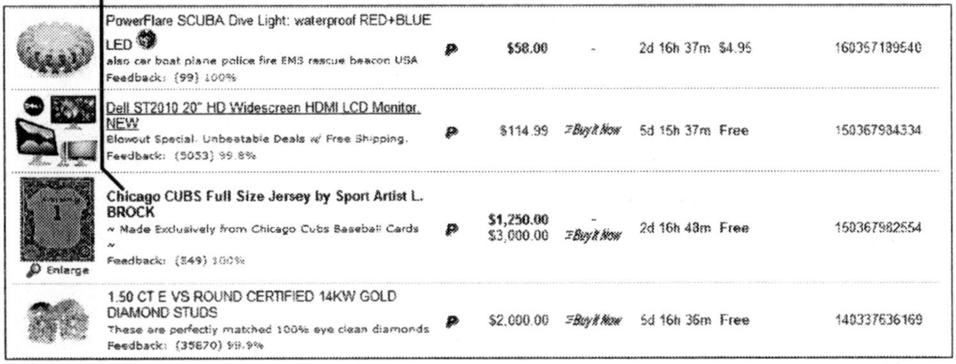

Figure 13-9

Preview and Review Your Listing

1. After you've filled in all the blanks on the Sell an Item form, you should take the opportunity to preview your listing. Scroll down the page and confirm that all the information you entered appears as you intended. If so, you're ready to join the world of e-commerce.

2. Under the heading How Your Listing Will Appear in Search Results, click the Preview Your Listing link shown in **Figure 13-10**.

3. A pop-up page opens showing you exactly how your listing will appear on eBay. This is the place where you can catch mistakes before your item is listed. The bottom of the Sell page shows you a condensed version of all your information and tallies how much eBay is charging you in fees and options to run this listing.

Click to preview your item's page.

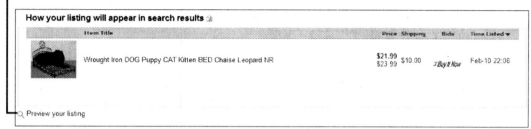

Figure 13-10

4. Check for mistakes. You also may find the preview page helpful as a last-minute chance to get your bearings. You can go back to any of the areas that need correcting by clicking the Edit Listings links on the Preview Your Listing page. Make category changes or any other changes and additions, and then head for the Preview Your Listing page again.

 Nitpick for common, careless errors; you won't be sorry. I've seen eBay members make goofs such as the wrong category listing, bad spelling, grammatical errors, and missing information about shipping, handling, and payment methods.

5. When you're sure everything's accurate and you're happy with your item listing, click the Submit button. A Confirmation page pops up. At that precise moment, your listing begins, even though it may be a few hours before it appears in eBay's search and listings updates. If you want to see your listing right away and check for bids, your Confirmation page provides a link for that purpose. Click the link, and you're there. You can also keep track of your auctions by using the My eBay page.

For the first 24 hours after your sale is underway, eBay stamps the Item page with a funky sunrise icon next to the listing. This is just a little reminder for buyers to come take a look at the latest items up for sale.

Make Mid-Course Corrections on Current Listings

1. Don't worry if you make a mistake filling out the Sell an Item page but don't notice it until after the auction is up and running. Pencils have erasers, and eBay allows revisions. You can make changes at two stages of the game: before the first bid is placed and after the bidding war is underway. The following steps explain what you can and can't correct — and when you have to accept the little imperfections of your item page.

2. Here's what you can change about your listing before bids have been placed (as long as the listing doesn't end within 12 hours):

- The title or description of your item

- The item category

- The item's starting price

- The item's Buy It Now price

- The reserve price (you can add, change, or remove it)

- The duration of your listing

- The URL of the picture you're including with your auction

- A private listing designation (you can add or remove it)

- Accepted payment methods, checkout information, item location, and shipping terms

3. When you revise a listing, eBay puts a little notation on your auction page that reads: Description(revised). (Think of it as automatic common courtesy.) To revise a fixed-price listing or any auction before bids have been received, follow these steps:

1. *Go to your My eBay page and find the item you want to revise.* Click the Revise link from the drop-down menu on the right side of the item (see **Figure 13-11**). If the item hasn't received any bids, a message appears on your screen to indicate that you may update the item, as in **Figure 13-12**.

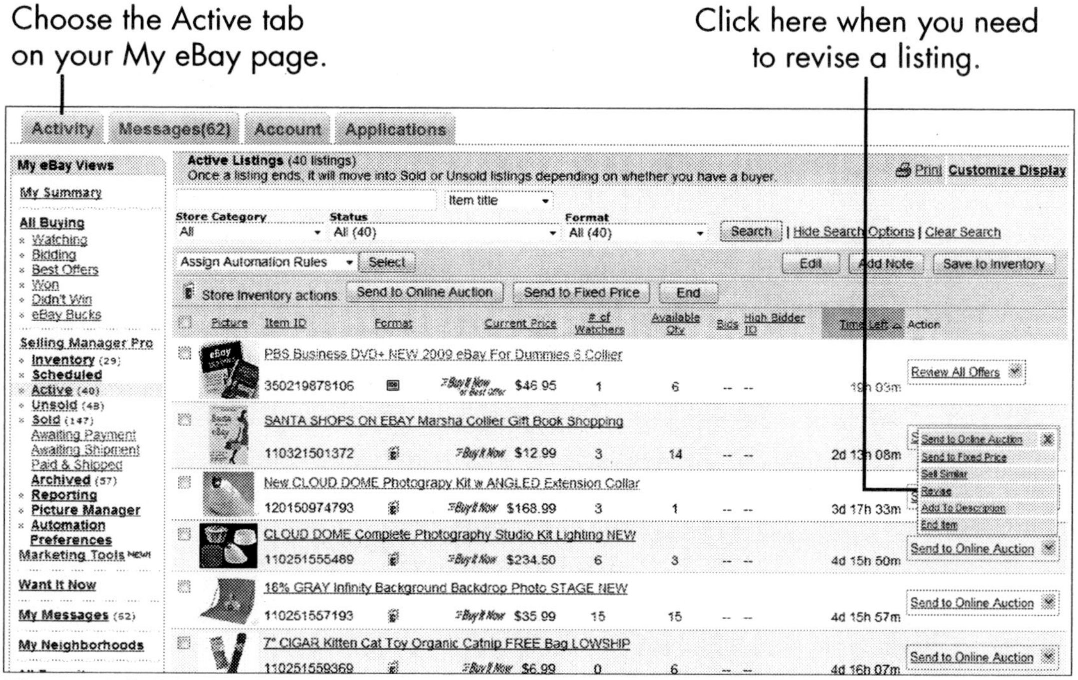

Choose the Active tab on your My eBay page.

Click here when you need to revise a listing.

Figure 13-11

Click here to revise.

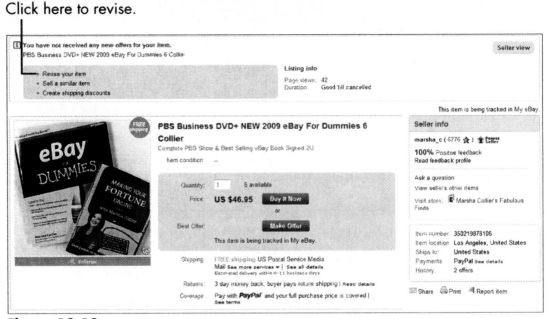

Figure 13-12

2. *You arrive at the Revise Item page, which looks like the Sell an Item form.* Make changes to the item information and then click the Save and Continue button at the bottom of the page when you're finished.

3. *A summary of your newly revised auction page appears on your screen. If you're happy with your revisions, click Save Changes.*

4. *You're taken to your newly revised item page, where you see a disclaimer from eBay that says you've revised the listing before the first bid.* If you want to make further revisions instead, click the Back button of your browser and redo the Edit your Listing page.

4. If your listing is up and running and already receiving bids, you can still make some slight modifications to it. Newly added information is clearly separated from the

original text and pictures. In addition, eBay puts a time stamp on the additional info in case questions from early bidders crop up later.

5. After your item receives bids, eBay allows you to add to your item's description. If you feel you were at a loss for words in writing your item's description, if you discover new information (that vase you thought was a reproduction is actually the real thing!), or if a lot of potential bidders are asking the same questions, go ahead and make all the additions you want. But whatever you put there the first time around stays in the description as well.

Always check your e-mail to see whether bidders have questions about your item. If a bidder wants to know about flaws, be truthful and courteous when returning e-mails. As you get more familiar with eBay (and with writing listing descriptions), the number of e-mail questions will decrease. If you enjoy good customer service in your day-to-day shopping, here's your chance to give some back.

Packaging and Shipping What You Sold

Chapter 14

Shipping can be the most time-consuming task for many eBay sellers, but it needn't be. It's your job as the seller to see that the item gets to the buyer in one piece. Your reputation is reflected in your professionalism at shipping.

This chapter briefs you on shipping etiquette, gives you details about the three most popular shipping options (the U.S. Postal Service, UPS, and FedEx Ground), and offers tips on how to make sure your package is ready to ride.

The best way to avoid shipping problems is to do your homework beforehand:

➠ Determine which method is likely to work best. Check out the three popular shippers I present in this chapter and decide which offers you the best in price and convenience.

➠ Spell out your shipping terms in your item description. Tell your buyers exactly how you intend to ship the item.

Get ready to...

Embrace Marsha's Tried-and-True Shipping Process

1. Before listing, get the package ready to ship. The time to think about packing and shipping is *before* you put the item up for sale — that way, last-minute shipping-related surprises are less likely to arise while your buyer waits impatiently for the item! The two critical factors in shipping are weight and time. The more a package weighs and the faster it has to be delivered, the higher the charge. So get the package ready to go first, and you have a head start on a timely and cost-effective delivery.

2. Know your carrier options and compare their costs and services. In the United States, the three main shipping options for most eBay transactions are the U.S. Postal Service, UPS, and FedEx. Later tasks in this chapter help you evaluate options from each service.

3. Before quoting the shipping fees, make sure that you include all appropriate costs. And do your best to cover your costs without burdening your buyers. Some eBay sellers inflate shipping and handling costs to make added profit. Purposely overcharging is tacky. (It's also a violation of eBay policy on circumventing fees and will penalize your listings in Best Match search.) The buyer also will figure it out after one look at the postage on the box.

- I recommend that you charge a nominal handling fee (up to $1.00 isn't out of line) to cover your packing materials, labels, and time, which can add up quickly as you start making multiple transactions. You should also include insurance and any delivery-confirmation costs in your handling fee.

- Post a flat shipping amount (or use the eBay online Shipping Calculator). This way, buyers can see this cost when they consider their bidding strategies. Figure out what the packed item will weigh and then give a good estimate; the online calculators can help.

 Occasionally, shipping calculations can be off-target, and you may not know that until after you take the buyer's money. If the mistake is in your favor and is a biggie, notify the buyer and offer a refund. But if shipping ends up costing you a bit more, take your lumps and pay it yourself. Consider it part of the cost of doing business. You can always let the buyer know what happened and that you paid the extra cost. Who knows, it may show up positively on your feedback from the buyer! (Even if it doesn't, spreading goodwill never hurts.)

4. E-mail the buyer and congratulate him or her on winning; reiterate what your shipping choice is, and how long you expect delivery will take. Make sure you're both talking about the same timetable. If the buyer balks at either the price or the shipping time, try working out an option that will make the buyer happy.

5. Send the package as soon as possible. Common courtesy says that you should ship the package as soon as the buyer has paid for the item and shipping charges. Ship that package no more than a few days after payment (or after the check clears) and remember to communicate:

   - E-mail the buyer as soon as you send the package and don't forget to put in a plug for positive feedback.

   - If you can't ship the package right away, immediately e-mail the buyer and explain the delay.

6. More often than not, you get an e-mail back from the
buyer to let you know the item arrived safely. If you
don't, it's a good idea to send another e-mail (in about a
week) to ask whether the item arrived in good condition.
It never hurts to take every opportunity to promote goodwill (and future business). Ask buyers whether they're
satisfied — and don't be bashful about suggesting that
they leave feedback for you. I show you an example of an
e-mail message I send in **Figure 14-1**.

Dear ▓▓▓▓,

Thank you for buying my Barbie WEDDING DAY Vintage Gown Ensemble #972 Repro
and paying so promptly! I want this to be a smooth transaction for you. Please
know that my goal is to give you the "five star service" that you deserve
as my customer. Your item will always reach you within a few days of your
purchase, since I use priority shipping.

I have inserted your package's Delivery Confirmation number into our transaction
on PayPal and on you My eBay Order Details page. Please note that if you
purchased shipping insurance, you will not see the insurance reflected on
the package, I insure my packages with a private insurance policy from U-Pic.

If there is any question when the package arrives, PLEASE email me immediately.
Your satisfaction is my goal, and I'm sure any problem can be easily taken
care of.

Marsha Collier
Author, "eBay for Dummies"
"Starting an eBay Business for Dummies"
Host of PBS Making Your Fortune Online
www.coolebaytools.com

Figure 14-1

Good communication throughout the shipping process is essential for demonstrating your professionalism as a seller. I include a thank-you note (a receipt would be a businesslike addition) in each package I send out. I appreciate when I get one in eBay packages, and it always brings a smile to the recipient's face. Also, when you communicate with your buyers after they receive their packages, remind them that you'll be leaving positive feedback for them. Leave the feedback right away so you don't forget.

Identify Shipping Supplies You Need

1. When the item's ready to go, you're ready to pack it. (This may sound obvious, but you'd be surprised …) Any list of packing material should start with a box. But you don't want just any box — you want one that's larger than the item. If you still have the original shipping container for such things as electronic equipment, consider using it, especially if it still has the original foam inserts (they were designed for shipping, and when you reuse them, they avoid cluttering up the environment awhile longer).

2. If the item is extremely fragile, I suggest you use two boxes, with the outer box about three inches larger on each side than the inner box that holds the item, to allow for extra padding between the boxes to accommodate any bumps it receives on its way. As for padding, **Table 14-1** compares the most popular types of box-filler material.

Table 14-1	Box-Filler Materials	
Type	**Pros and Cons**	**Suggestions**
Bubble wrap	**Pros:** Lightweight, clean, cushions well **Cons:** Cost	Don't go overboard taping the bubble wrap. If the buyer has to battle to get the tape off, the item may go flying and end up damaged. And for crying out loud, don't pop all the little bubbles, okay?
Newspaper	**Pros:** Cheap, cushions **Cons:** Messy, and adds considerable weight to the package	Seal fairly well. Put your item in a plastic bag to protect it from the ink. I like shredding the newspaper first. It's more manageable and doesn't seem to stain as much as wadded-up paper. I spent about $30.00 at an office-supply store for a shredder. (Or find one on eBay for much less.)
Cut-up cardboard	**Pros:** Handy, cheap **Cons:** Transmits some shocks to item, hard to cut up, heavy	If you have some old boxes that aren't sturdy enough to pack in, this is a pretty good use for them.
Styrofoam peanuts	**Pros:** Lightweight, absorb shock well, clean **Cons:** Environmentally unfriendly, annoying	Your item may shift if you don't put enough peanuts in the box, so make sure to fill the box. Also, don't buy these — instead, recycle them from stuff that was shipped to you (plastic trash bags are great for storing them). And never use plastic peanuts when packing electronic equipment, because they can create static electricity. Even a little spark can trash a computer chip.
Air-popped popcorn	**Pros:** Lightweight, environmentally friendly, absorbs shock well, clean (as long as you don't use salt and butter, but you knew that), low in calories **Cons:** Cost, time to pop	You don't want to send it anywhere there may be varmints who like it. The U.S. Postal Service suggests popcorn. Hey, at least you can eat the leftovers!

3. Evaluate the item you're shipping, and choose packing materials specific to the item's requirements. Make your packing do all the little things that you'd want done if you were the buyer — use double boxes for really fragile items, wrap lids separately from containers, and fill hollow breakables with some kind of padding. Here are a few other items you need:

- **Plastic bags:** Plastic bags protect your item from moisture. I once sent a MIB doll to the Northeast, and the package got caught in a snowstorm. The buyer e-mailed me with words of thanks for the extra plastic bag, which saved the item from being soaked along with the outer box. (Speaking of boxes, if you send an item in an original box, bag the item inside to protect it.)

 For any small items, such as stuffed animals, you should always protect them in a lunch baggie. For slightly larger items, go to the 1-quart or 1-gallon size. Be sure to wrap any paper or cloth products, such as clothing and linens, in plastic before you ship.

- **Bubble-padded mailers:** The shipping cost for a package that weighs less than 13 ounces (First-Class mail) is considerably cheaper than Priority. Many small items, clothing, books, and so on will fit comfortably into the many available sizes of padded envelopes. You can find them made of Kraft paper or extra sturdy vinyl. A big plus is that they weigh considerably less than boxes — even when using extra padding. See **Table 14-2** for standard sizes.

- **Labels:** You'll need extras because it's always a good idea to toss a duplicate address label inside the box, with the destination address and a return address, in case the outside label falls off or becomes illegible.

- **Shipping tape, 2- or 3-inches in width:** Make sure that you use a strong shipping tape for the outside of the box. Clear plastic will do just fine. There is also box-color tape that works very well for recycling boxes (taping over old shipping information). Remember not to plaster every inch of box with tape; leave space for those *Fragile* and *Insured* rubber stamps.

- **Hand-held shipping tape dispensers:** It's quite a bit easier to zzzzzip! tape from a tape dispenser than to unwind it and bite it off with your teeth. Have one dispenser for your special shipping tape and one for your clear tape.

- **Scissors:** A pair of large, sharp scissors. Having a hobby knife to trim boxes or shred newspaper is also a good idea.

- **Handy liquids:** Three that I like are GOO GONE (which is available in the household supply section of most retail stores and is a wonder at removing unwanted stickers and price tags); WD-40 (the unstick-everything standby that works great on getting stickers off plastic); and Un-Du (the best liquid I've found to take labels off cardboard).

- **Rubber stamps/stickers:** Using custom rubber stamps or stickers can save you a bunch of time when preparing your packages. I purchased some return address self-inking rubber stamps. I use these stamps to stamp all kinds of things that require my identification. I often also use fluorescent red SCAN NOW stickers next to my Delivery Confirmations.

- **Thermal label printer:** Once I thought this was a flagrant waste of money, but now I wouldn't be without one (I have two). When you begin shipping several packages a week, you'll find it far more convenient to use a printer for postage, addressing and delivery confirmations all on one label.

 Dymo offers a workhorse of a printer, the LabelWriter 4XL. If you want to get industrial, try one of the Zebra thermal printers (I use the LP2844). These printers can print labels for Fed Ex and UPS as well as USPS (you can buy used ones on eBay).

- **Black permanent marker:** These are handy for writing information ("Please leave on porch behind the planter") and the all-important "Fragile" all over the box or "Do Not Bend" on envelopes. I like the big, fat Sharpie markers.

Table 14-2	Standard Bubble-Padded Mailer Sizes	
Size	*Measurements*	*Suggested items*
#000	4" x 8"	Collector trading cards, jewelry, computer discs, coins
#00	5" x 10"	Postcards, paper ephemera
#0	6" x 10"	CDs, DVDs, Xbox or PS2 games
#1	7¼" x 12"	Cardboard sleeve VHS tapes, jewel-cased CDs and DVDs
#2	8½" x 12"	Clamshell VHS tapes
#3	8½" x 14½"	Toys, clothing, stuffed animals
#4	9½" x 14½"	Small books, trade paperbacks
#5	10½" x 16"	Hardcover books
#6	12½" x 19"	Clothing, soft boxed items
#7	14¼" x 20"	Much larger packaged items, framed items, plaques

4. If you plan to sell on eBay in earnest, consider adding a 10-pound weight scale (for weighing packages) to your shipping department. I got a 25-pound scale free when I purchased a shipping package from Endicia (an online postage vendor).

 Whatever materials you use, make sure that you pack the item well and that you secure the box. Many shippers will contest insurance claims if they feel you did a lousy job of packing.

Find Packing Materials

1. The place to start looking for packing material is the same place you should start looking for things to sell on eBay: your house. Between us, I've done over eight thousand eBay transactions and rarely pay for a carton. I buy most of my stuff from catalogs and online companies (I love e-commerce) and save all the boxes, bubble wrap, padding, and packing peanuts I get in the mail. If you recently got a mail-order shipment box that was used only once — and it's a good, sturdy box with no dents or dings — there's nothing wrong with using it again.

2. You can go beyond the house to rustle up some packing stuff. Go to your local supermarket, department store, or drugstore; you won't be the first person pleading with a store manager for boxes. (Ah, fond memories of moving days past.) Stores like giving them away because it saves them the work of compacting the boxes and putting them in the trash or recycling bin.

3. Contact shippers such as UPS, FedEx, and the U.S. Postal Service. These shippers offer all kinds of free supplies as long as you use these supplies to ship things with their service. If you want, the Postal Service also ships free boxes, labels, and shipping forms for Express Mail, Priority Mail, and Global Priority Mail to your house. In the United States, you can order by phone (800-222-1811) or online (shop.usps.com). When placing a USPS order:

- **Specify the service** (Priority Mail or Express Mail, for example) you're using because the boxes and the labels all come with the service name printed all over them, and you can use them only for that specific service. The boxes come flat, so you have to assemble them. Hey, don't look a gift box in the mouth — they're free!

- **Order in bulk,** for example, address labels come in rolls of 500 and boxes in packs of 25.

4. Shop for supplies with eBay and online sellers. Many terrific eBay sellers are out to offer you really good deals. (You can't beat eBay sellers for quality goods, low prices, and great service.) I recommend the following family-run eBay stores:

- **Royal Mailers** is where I buy my padded paper envelope mailers for my eBay sales. This company also sells Tyvek envelopes, vinyl bubble mailers, zipper-lock plastic bags, air pillows, box-sealing tape, and lots more. They ship from various places and they offer *free shipping* (so shipping costs are not an issue) and a discount of 5% to my readers if you use this code: COOLEBAY. Visit their Web site at www.royal mailers.com.

- **Bubblefast** — an eBay seller from the Chicago area — sells tons of reasonably priced bubble wrap, mailers, and more. **Figure 14-2** shows some of the products that Bubblefast sells.

Figure 14-2

- **Melrose Stamp** (melrose_stamp on eBay) is based in New York (but its items are tiny, so shipping isn't a huge issue). Melrose Stamp mainly sells custom and stock message rubber stamps. They also sell rolls of package-identification labels such as Fragile, Scan Me, First Class, Media Mail, and Airmail.

 Notice that I mention where vendors are located. When ordering a large shipment, the distance it has to travel from the vendor's place to yours can tack on quite a bit of cash (and time) to your shipping costs!

Prepare Your Items and Shop for a Shipper

1. Before you package it, give your item the once-over. Here's a checklist of what to consider about your item before you can ship it:

- **Is your item as you described it?** If the item has been dented or torn somehow, e-mail the winning bidder immediately and let them know. If you sell an item with its original box or container, don't just check the item, make sure the box is in the same good condition as the item inside. Collectors place a high value on original boxes, so make sure the box lives up to what you described in your listing. Pack to protect it as well.

- **Is the item dirty or dusty, or does it smell of smoke?** Buyers may complain if the item they receive is dirty or smelly, especially from cigarette smoke. Make sure the item is fresh and clean, even if it's used or vintage. If something's dirty, check to make sure you know how to clean it properly (you want to take the dirt off, not the paint), and then give it a spritz with an appropriate cleaner or just soap and water. If you can't get rid of the smell or the dirt, say so in your item description. Let the buyer decide whether the item is desirable with aromas and all.

   If the item has a faint smell of smoke or is a bit musty, a product called Febreze may help. Just get a plastic bag, give your item a spritz, and keep it in the bag for a short while. *Note:* This is not recommended for cardboard. And, as with any solvent or cleaning agent, read the label before you spray. Or, if you're in a rush to mail the package, cut a 2-by-2-inch piece of sheet fabric softener and place it in a plastic bag with the product.

2. If only you could transport your item the way they did on *Star Trek* — "Beam up that cashmere sweater, Scotty!" Alas, not so. Later tasks in this chapter outline shipping with the major carriers, but here's a quick list to get you thinking about which shipper is right for you:

- Parcel Post and Priority Mail via the U.S. Postal Service (USPS) is pretty much the eBay standard if you're shipping within the United States. (International First Class for shipments up to 4 pounds to Canada.) Sellers also rely on the USPS to ship internationally as well.

- Larger packages (over five pounds) are generally cheaper to ship through FedEx Ground or UPS. (As of this writing, FedEx is cheaper unless you're shipping a hundred packages a week).

- Whether you're at the post office, UPS, FedEx, or your doctor's office, be ready, willing, and able to wait in line. If you decide to go with USPS, why not save yourself the time and stress by giving your packages to your letter carrier — or by requesting a free carrier pickup from the Post Office Web site (`www.usps.com/pickup/`) if you can ship from home.

 Be sure to visit my Web site, `www.coolebaytools.com`, for introductory offers for much of the software and services that I mention in this chapter.

Ship with the U.S. Postal Service

1. The U.S. Postal Service (USPS) is the butt of many unfair jokes and cheap shots, but when it comes right down to it, I think the USPS is still the most efficient and inexpensive way to ship items — eBay or otherwise. It also supplies free boxes and labels for Priority and Express Mail packages.

2. Priority Mail is the standard method of shipping for eBay users. I love the flat-rate free envelopes and boxes, plus I like the rates. The promised delivery time is two to three days, although I've experienced rare delays of up to four days during peak holiday periods. As of this writing (rates are always subject to change), the current rates and options include

- $4.95 for a 1-pound package. Over a pound, the charge is calculated according to weight and distance.

- $4.95 for a flat-rate Priority envelope is also available. You can ship as much stuff as you want — as long as you can fit it into the supplied $9\frac{1}{2}$ x $12\frac{1}{2}$ envelope. (You'll be surprised how much stuff you can jam into those envelopes.) You can reinforce the envelope with clear packing tape.

- Reduced flat rates on Priority Mail boxes that come in three sizes. Order the boxes directly from the USPS, as **Figure 14-3** shows.

 If you print your postage electronically, through a service such as Endicia or PayPal, you get a discount on your Priority Mail postage. You also get a free Delivery Confirmation code.

3. Express Mail is your choice if the item needs to be delivered the next day. The Postal Service promises delivery no later than noon the following afternoon (even on weekends or holidays). And you can get free boxes. Express Mail costs run

- $13.05 for packages 8 ounces and under.

- $17.50 for a flat-rate envelope, which is the same size as the Priority flat-rate envelope. (You get a 5% discount when purchasing your postage electronically.)

Order Priority Mail boxes from USPS.

Figure 14-3

 Get to know your letter carriers and have your parcels ready and stacked up for them when they make the regular stop at your home. They will be happy to take your packages back to the post office at no additional charge. (A bottle of icy-cold water for your letter carrier on hot days will go a long way in your relationship!)

4. First-Class Mail is an option if your item weighs 13 ounces or less. First-Class Mail is considerably cheaper than Priority. I try to ship as much as I can via First Class mail so I can have the edge on other sellers by offering lower shipping prices.

5. Media Mail is a popular option among those who sell books on eBay. It's the new name for two older products, Book Rate and Special Standard Mail. Media Mail rates start at $2.23 for the first pound and increase by $0.35 for each additional pound.

6. Check out the USPS Web site (www.usps.com) for an overview of the U.S. Postal Service rates so that you can see all your options. It sure beats standing in that endless line! For a complete explanation of domestic rates, check out www.usps.com/prices/.

 USPS has a page that can help you determine exactly what your item costs to mail (after you've packaged it and weighed it, of course). Start at the Rate Calculator page at postcalc.usps.gov and follow the instructions.

7. One of the options that the Postal Service offers is delivery confirmation (DC), which buys you the knowledge of when and where your item was delivered. Not only that, but if buyers report to PayPal that they want a refund because they never received an item, the scan on the delivery confirmation code prevents you from getting a chargeback. You can add this service to Priority Mail, as well as with other mailing services such as First Class or Parcel Post. The cost is a mere $0.75 — and it's free when you buy postage online (see the later task, "Buy Postage Online" for details).

 You can't accurately track your package with a DC; instead, it serves as proof that the package was mailed and delivered. You can check on whether the package was delivered (or whether an attempt was made to deliver it) by typing in the number online at www.usps.com/shipping/trackandconfirm.htm.

Ship with UPS

1. Understand that the folks in the brown UPS trucks love eBay. The most popular option for eBay sellers is Ground service. UPS also takes many of the odd-shaped large boxes, such as those for computer equipment, that the U.S. Postal Service won't. UPS makes pickups, but you have to know the exact weight of your package so you can pay when the UPS driver shows up. UPS charges for this service unless you have a Daily Pickup account and ship a minimum number of packages with UPS per week.

2. If you're going to use UPS regularly, be sure to set up an account directly with UPS. The rates for the same UPS shipment can vary based on whether you have a business account with UPS, whether the package goes to or is picked up at a residence, and whether you use the right kind of form. Although UPS offers "discounts" to eBay PowerSellers, don't be fooled. If you ship mostly small packages, you'd have to ship truckloads of goods on a daily basis to compete with USPS rates.

3. Check out the UPS home page at www.ups.com. For rates, click the Shipping tab and then click Calculate Time and Cost on the left side of the page, which gives you estimated prices based on ZIP codes and package weights (see **Figure 14-4**). Note the ominous word "estimated" and also be aware that the UPS.com quick cost calculator prices are based on what UPS charges its regular and high-volume users. When you get to the counter, the price may be higher than what you find on the Web.

 My favorite link on the UPS site is the transit map that shows the United States and how long it takes to reach any place in the country (based on the originating ZIP code). If you're thinking of shipping that compact refrigerator to Maine, you can check out this fun and informative page at www.ups.com/using/services/servicemaps/service maps.html.

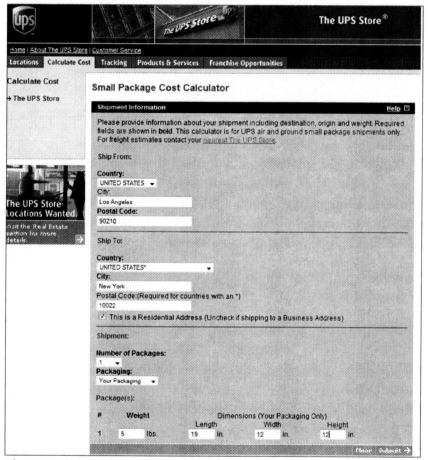

Figure 14-4

Ship Via Federal Express

1. FedEx Ground service has competitive prices and carries all the best features of FedEx. I use FedEx Ground for items that are heavy or extremely large, because FedEx ships anything up to 150 pounds in a single box — 80 more pounds than the U.S. Postal Service takes. FedEx also delivers on Saturdays — which UPS won't — but charges $4.00 to pick up items from shippers who ship less than $60.00 in weekly package charges.

2. When choosing your shipper, consider how FedEx stacks up against the others. The FedEx Ground Home Delivery service is a major competitor for UPS. The rates are competitive, and FedEx offers a money-back guarantee (if it misses the delivery window) for residential ground delivery. Some other facts to note:

   • For residential delivery, FedEx charges an additional $2.30 to $2.40 per package. A 2-pound package going from Los Angeles to a residence in New York City takes five days and costs $8.71 including the Home Delivery fee. FedEx includes online package tracking and insurance up to $100.00 in this price.

   • You have to be a business to avail yourself of home delivery — but plenty of home businesses exist.

3. When compared with FedEx Ground Home Delivery, the same 2-pound U.S. Postal Service Priority Mail package with $100.00 insurance and a delivery confirmation costs you $11.50. (But remember, you know how to get free delivery confirmation forms, and insurance can cost much less with private package insurance!)

   • With USPS, the package is supposed to arrive within two to three days. But FedEx Ground *guarantees* a five-day delivery, and I've had a few Priority Mail packages take up to a week.

   • When you drop off your box at UPS, you can get five-day service for $11.53.

- FedEx Ground won't supply boxes for you, so you're on your own there.

4. FedEx offers other services besides FedEx Ground. I use FedEx Express Air all the time for rush business, but Express seems rather expensive for my eBay shipping. However, if the buyer wants it fast and is willing to pay, I'll send it by FedEx overnight, you bet. I also like the FedEx boxes. But just like the boxes you get from the USPS, don't think of using these boxes to ship with another service. (The FedEx logo is plastered all over every inch of the freebies, and the company may get seriously peeved about it.) Also, you can't use those fancy free boxes for Ground service.

 You can find the FedEx home page at www.fedex.com/us. The link for rates is conveniently located at the top of the page.

Consider Shipping Internationally

1. Many sellers are afraid to ship internationally and list "I don't ship overseas" on the item page. Of course, sending an item that far away may be a burden if you're selling a car or an exercise bicycle (they don't fit in boxes too well), but I've found that sending a package across the Atlantic can be just as easy as shipping across state lines.

2. When you ship internationally, you need to tell what's inside the package. Be truthful when declaring value on customs forms. Use descriptions that customs agents can figure out without knowing eBay shorthand terms. For example, instead of declaring the contents as "MIB Barbie," call it a "small child's doll." Some countries require buyers to pay special duties and taxes, depending on the item and the value. But that's the buyer's headache.

3. Wherever you send your package (especially if it's going to a country where English is not the native language), write legibly. (Imagine getting a package from Russia and having to decipher a label written in the Cyrillic alphabet. *'Nuff said.*)

The one downside I've found to international shipping: My shipper of choice, the U.S. Postal Service, does not insure packages going to certain countries, so I use private shipping insurance with U-PIC.

Ship Directly from PayPal

1. I consider PayPal shipping to be required for all beginning eBay sellers. By using PayPal, a seller can streamline the buyer's shopping experience, making it simple to buy, click, and pay. Those out in the eBay world who haven't used PayPal find the service to be a life-changing experience. Because you don't need to use additional software or sign up with an additional service, shipping with PayPal is a convenient system for those who don't have to ship many packages each week.

2. When you're ready to deal with shipping, you simply sign on to your PayPal account and handle it right on the site. You can also click the Print Shipping Label link from the item's page to start the process. When you do, you see the page shown in **Figure 14-5**. There's no charge for the service, and you have a choice of U.S. Postal Service or UPS (sorry, no FedEx Ground).

As of this date, PayPal will not print postage for First Class Mail International; it prints postage only for the far more expensive Priority or Express. If you plan on doing business overseas (as I do), be competitive with your shipping costs. It will bring you more business from savvy international buyers.

Figure 14-5

Buy Postage Online

1. Isn't technology great? You no longer have to schlep to the post office every time you need stamps. What's even better, with the new print-it-yourself postage, you can give all your packages directly to your mail carrier. You can print postage for First Class, Priority, Express, and Parcel Post, and additional postage for delivery confirmation and insurance. Several vendors of Internet-based postage exist, but Endicia Internet Postage and Stamps. com are the most popular.

 If your printer mangles a sheet of labels or an envelope, you can send the printed piece to your Internet postage provider for a refund.

2. When you install your Internet postage software, you apply for a USPS postal license that allows you to print your own *Information Based Indicia* (IBI) for your postage. IBI is a bar code printed either on labels or directly on an envelope and has both human- and machine-readable information about where it was printed and security-related elements. IBI provides you, and the post office, with a much more secure way of getting your valuable packages through the mail.

3. Take a look at the DAZzle software in **Figure 14-6**. DAZzle — combined with the patented Dial-A-Zip — became the basis for the software that comes free with the Endicia Internet Postage service. There isn't a more robust mailing program on the market. Endicia has all the basic features and more:

   • **Prints postage for all classes of mail, including international:** From Anniston, Alabama, to Bulawayo, Zimbabwe, the DAZzle software not only prints postage but also lists all your shipping options and applicable rates. For international mailing, Endicia advises you about any prohibitions (no prison-made goods can be mailed to Botswana), any restrictions, any necessary customs forms, and areas served within the country.

```
DAZzle Designer - zebra small first class mail international shipping label

File   Edit   Insert   Layout   Postage   Help

Print    $ Buy   Postage Options

Design   Address Book   Postage Log
```

$10.30   US POSTAGE
* SAMPLE *   Mailed from ZIP 91325
1 lb First-Class Intl Parcel Rate

LJ 210 775 709 US

VOID - DO NOT MAIL

USPS First-Class International

ITN/Exemption Code:
NOEEI 30.37(a)

endicia.com   071V00506289

Customs Declaration	CN 22				From:	Marsha Collier

Contents:
Gift ☐   Commercial Sample ☒
Documents ☐ Other ☐

From: Marsha Collier
The Collier Company, Inc.
My Address
Studio City, CA 91604-
US

Detailed description of contents:	Qty	Weight lb oz	Value (US $)
Descriptions are printed here.	1	0	$0.00

To: Patrice Barker
     Schoppers 44
     9461EN GIETEN
     NETHERLANDS

HS tariff number and country of origin:

Total Wt 1 0   Total Value $5.00

I, the undersigned, whose name and address are given on the item, certify that the particulars given in this declaration are correct and that this item does not contain any dangerous article or articles prohibited by legislation or by postal or customs regulations.

Sender's signature.   Date:

PS Form 2976-FCMi Do not duplicate this form without USPS approval. The item/parcel may be opened officially

Mailing Office Date Stamp

FEB 5 2009
91325

Account 506289 is active, Balance: $21.09   ZDesigner LP 2844 on USB001

Figure 14-6

- **Provides free delivery confirmation on Priority Mail:** You can print electronic delivery confirmations for First Class, Parcel Post, and Media Mail for only $0.18 each (a substantial savings of from the Postal Service counter purchase).

- **Enables you to design mail pieces:** The software enables you to design envelopes, postcards, and labels with color graphics, logos, and text messages. You can print your labels with postage and delivery confirmation on anything from plain paper (tape it on with clear tape) to 4-by-6 labels in a label printer.

- **Integrates with U-PIC private insurance:** If you're saving time and money using a private package insurer, you can send your monthly insurance logs electronically to U-PIC at the end of the month.

4. Endicia offers two levels of service. All the preceding features come with the standard plan for $9.95 a month. The premium plan adds special features, customizable e-mail, enhanced online transaction reports and statistics, business reply mail, return shipping labels (prepaid so your customers won't have to pay for the returns), and stealth indicia for $15.95 a month. For a free 60-day trial (30 days longer than offered to anyone else), go to www.endicia.com/coolebaytools.

 Stealth indicia (also known as postage-paid indicia) can be an awesome tool for the eBay seller. By using this feature, your customers can't see the exact amount of postage that you paid for the package. This way, you can add reasonable shipping and handling costs and not inflame buyers when they see the final label.

Insure Your Package (and Your Peace of Mind)

1. Sure, "damaged in the mail" is an excuse we've all heard hundreds of times, but despite everyone's best efforts, sometimes packages (and their contents) do get damaged or misplaced during shipment. That's what insurance is for. Since eBay doesn't allow you to charge the buyer for insurance and the cost is on the seller, I still purchase it on expensive items, one-of-a-kind items, or very fragile items.

2. The major shippers all offer forms of insurance that's fairly reasonably priced, so check out their rates on their Web sites. Pack carefully so your buyer gets what's been

paid for. Be mindful that shippers won't make good on insurance claims if they suspect you of causing the damage by doing a lousy job of packing.

 But don't forget to read the details of the shipper's insurance coverage. For example, many items on eBay are sold MIMB (Mint in Mint Box). True, the condition of the original box often has a bearing on the final value of the item inside, but the U.S. Postal Service insures only what is *in* the box. So, if you sold a Malibu Barbie mint in a mint box, USPS insures only the doll and not the original box.

3. Alternatively, when you're selling on eBay in earnest, you can purchase your own parcel protection policy from a private insurer like U-PIC.com (shown in **Figure 14-7**). When you use this type of insurance, combined with pre-printed electronic postage, you no longer have to stand in line at the post office to have your insured package logged in by the clerk at the counter.

4. Some sellers also offer their own form of *self-insurance*. Realize that I use the term "self-insurance" as a descriptive phrase only. You may not charge your buyer for insurance unless you are actually paying for insurance from a licensed third-party insurance company. Charging and not fulfilling insurance is a violation of state law. Here's what I offer my buyers at no cost to them:

- On lower-priced items, I am willing to refund the buyer's money if the item is lost or damaged.

- On some items I sell, I have a *risk reserve*. That means I have more than one of the item I sold. If the item is lost or destroyed, I can send the backup item as a replacement.

Insure with U-PIC for one package or many.

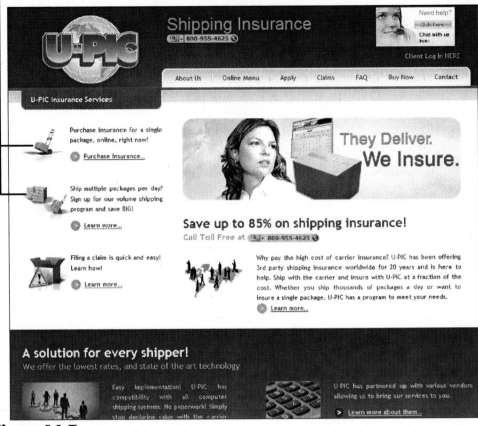

Figure 14-7

5. Understand that insurance only protects you so much.
Even though your buyer is not paying extra for the insurance, you are *still responsible* for making sure that the item
arrives at the buyer's door. Federal mail-order laws state
that when an item is paid for, it must be delivered to the
buyer within 30 days unless there has been an agreement
between the buyer and the seller for other arrangements.

 Delivery confirmation (DC) is useful when you try
to collect insurance for an item that was never delivered or if the buyer says the item was never delivered.

If your package gets lost in the mail for a few weeks, the delivery-confirmation number rarely acts as a tracking number and won't reveal the location of your package until it's delivered. But it can serve as proof from the Postal Service that the item was sent.

Part IV
Taking the Plunge: Running a Sale

The 5th Wave   By Rich Tennant

"Oh, we're doing just great. Philip and I are selling decorative jelly jars on eBay. I manage the listings and Philip sort of controls the inventory."

eBay's No-No Items

*e*Bay has its rules about the types of items you can sell. Sometimes owning, selling, or buying a particular item is perfectly legal, but you still can't do the buying or selling on eBay. And other times, you can sell certain "questionable" items — but only under certain circumstances.

Here are some examples:

➠ Selling a used original CD, cassette tape, commercial VHS movie, DVD, or CD-ROM is perfectly legal. Some television shows have sold episodes on tape; you can sell those originals as well. But if you're tempted to sell a personal copy that you made of an original, you are committing an infringing violation.

➠ If you're planning to sell event tickets, visit `pages.ebay.com/help/policies/event-tickets.html` for details. This page has details featuring the various states' legal requirements. Be sure to double-check this page to be certain you're following the appropriate laws for your area.

➡ If you want to sell collectible alcohol or wine, you must be sure that the buyer is at least 21 years old. Also, you must be sure that the sale complies with all laws and shipping rules. Every state has its own laws about shipping alcohol and wine. Some states require licenses to transport it; some limit the amount you can ship. You're responsible for knowing what your state laws are (and you're expected to conduct your auctions accordingly).

Chapter 11 encourages you to know what you can and can't sell. And this appendix gives you a bit more detail about some of the prohibited, potentially infringing, and questionable items that make up the no-no list on eBay.

eBay Prohibited Items

Item	Including	Comments
Firearms and accessories	Antique, collectible, sport, or hunting guns; air guns; BB guns; silencers; converters; kits for creating guns; gunpowder; high-capacity ammunition magazines; and armor-piercing bullets	You can't even sell a gun that *doesn't* work, but you *can* buy and sell single bullets, shells, and even antique bombs and musket balls — as long as they have nothing explosive in them.
Military weapons	Bazookas, grenades, and mortars	
Police and other law-enforcement badges and IDs	U.S. federal badges or imitation badges, federal agency identification cards, credential cases, or those really cool jackets they use in raids	Selling a copy or reproduction of any of these items is prohibited, too.
Replicas of official government identification documents or licenses	Birth certificates, drivers' licenses, and passports	

Item	Including	Comments
Vehicle license plates	Current plates or plates that claim to resemble current ones	Expired license plates (at least 5 years old) are okay to sell because they're considered collectible — as long as they are no longer valid for use on a vehicle.
Locksmithing devices		These items can be sold only to authorized recipients. Federal law prohibits the mailing of such devices.
Human parts and remains	Organs such as kidneys, sperm, eggs, blood, or anything else you manage to extricate from your body	You can't even *give* away any of these items as a free bonus with one of your auctions.
Drugs or drug paraphernalia	Narcotics, steroids or other controlled substances such as gamma hydroxybutyrate (GHB), and items primarily intended or designed for use in manufacturing, concealing, or using a controlled substance	For example, you can't sell 1960s-vintage cigarette papers, bongs, or water pipes.
Anything that requires a prescription from a doctor, a dentist, or an optometrist to dispense	Any drug that's legal to use but requires a prescription from a medical professional	If you're looking for Viagra listings on eBay, don't even *go* there.
Stocks, bonds, or negotiable securities	Stock in new companies, investment property you may own, or offers of credit	Note that antiques and collectible items, such as antique stock certificates, *are* permitted.
Bulk e-mail lists	E-mail or mailing lists that contain personal identifying information, and tools or software designed to send unsolicited commercial e-mail	

(continued)

eBay Prohibited Items (continued)

Item	Including	Comments
Pets and wildlife, including animal parts from endangered species	Any live pets or wildlife or dead endangered animals (such as stuffed spotted owls or rhino-horn love potions)	
Child pornography	All materials	You can sell other forms of erotica. (See the section later in this appendix about questionable items.)
Forged items	Autographs from celebrities and sports figures, for example	Don't even consider bidding on an autographed item unless it comes with a *Certificate of Authenticity* (COA).
Items that infringe on someone else's copyright or trademark	See the next section for details on infringing items	
Satellite and cable TV descramblers	All hardware and instructions on how to get around cable TV scrambling	Bypassing scrambling is illegal.
Stolen items	Any stolen items	Need I say more?

eBay Infringing Items

Item	Including	Comments
Re-recorded music, movies, or television shows	Any entertainment media that's been re-recorded from an original source	For music, an original source would be a compact disc, cassette tape, or record; for movies, an original DVD, laser disc, or commercial VHS tape; for television shows, an original network, cable, or satellite service airing.

Item	Including	Comments
Copied software and computer games	Any such programs that have been copied from CD-ROMs or disks (and that includes hard drives — anybody's)	
Counterfeit items (also called *knock-offs*)	Clothes, accessories, and jewelry that have been produced, copied, or imitated without the permission of the manufacturer	Bart Simpson knock-off T-shirts abounded in the early '90s.

eBay Questionable Items

Item	Including	Restrictions
Event tickets	Concerts, sporting events, plays, and so on	Laws regarding the sale of event tickets vary from state to state, even city to city. Some laws prohibit reselling the ticket for a price higher than the amount printed on the face of the ticket. Some states limit the amount you can add to the ticket's face value.
Wine and alcohol	Wine and alcohol products, kits or ingredients for making alcoholic beverages, food with alcoholic ingredients	eBay does not permit sales of any alcohol products unless they are sold for their "collectible" containers (and there are several restrictions on the containers and their values). You may sell wine for consumption if you have a liquor license and are preapproved by eBay.
Erotica	To see what forms of erotica eBay allows and what it prohibits, type `pages.ebay.com/help/policies/adult-only.html` into your browser.	One thing that's definitely illegal, wrong, and criminal is child pornography. If someone reports that you're selling child pornography, eBay forwards your registration information to law enforcement for criminal prosecution.

# Index

Symbols

• A •

• C •

• G •

• H •

• I •

Business/Accounting & Bookkeeping

Bookkeeping For Dummies
978-0-7645-9848-7

eBay Business
All-in-One For Dummies,
2nd Edition
978-0-470-38536-4

Job Interviews
For Dummies,
3rd Edition
978-0-470-17748-8

Resumes For Dummies,
5th Edition
978-0-470-08037-5

Stock Investing
For Dummies,
3rd Edition
978-0-470-40114-9

Successful Time
Management
For Dummies
978-0-470-29034-7

Computer Hardware

BlackBerry For Dummies,
3rd Edition
978-0-470-45762-7

Computers For Seniors
For Dummies
978-0-470-24055-7

iPhone For Dummies,
2nd Edition
978-0-470-42342-4

Laptops For Dummies,
3rd Edition
978-0-470-27759-1

Macs For Dummies,
10th Edition
978-0-470-27817-8

Cooking & Entertaining

Cooking Basics
For Dummies,
3rd Edition
978-0-7645-7206-7

Wine For Dummies,
4th Edition
978-0-470-04579-4

Diet & Nutrition

Dieting For Dummies,
2nd Edition
978-0-7645-4149-0

Nutrition For Dummies,
4th Edition
978-0-471-79868-2

Weight Training
For Dummies,
3rd Edition
978-0-471-76845-6

Digital Photography

Digital Photography
For Dummies,
6th Edition
978-0-470-25074-7

Photoshop Elements 7
For Dummies
978-0-470-39700-8

Gardening

Gardening Basics
For Dummies
978-0-470-03749-2

Organic Gardening
For Dummies,
2nd Edition
978-0-470-43067-5

Green/Sustainable

Green Building
& Remodeling
For Dummies
978-0-470-17559-0

Green Cleaning
For Dummies
978-0-470-39106-8

Green IT For Dummies
978-0-470-38688-0

Health

Diabetes For Dummies,
3rd Edition
978-0-470-27086-8

Food Allergies
For Dummies
978-0-470-09584-3

Living Gluten-Free
For Dummies
978-0-471-77383-2

Hobbies/General

Chess For Dummies,
2nd Edition
978-0-7645-8404-6

Drawing For Dummies
978-0-7645-5476-6

Knitting For Dummies,
2nd Edition
978-0-470-28747-7

Organizing For Dummies
978-0-7645-5300-4

SuDoku For Dummies
978-0-470-01892-7

Home Improvement

Energy Efficient Homes
For Dummies
978-0-470-37602-7

Home Theater
For Dummies,
3rd Edition
978-0-470-41189-6

Living the Country Lifestyle
All-in-One For Dummies
978-0-470-43061-3

Solar Power Your Home
For Dummies
978-0-470-17569-9

Internet
Blogging For Dummies,
2nd Edition
978-0-470-23017-6

eBay For Dummies,
6th Edition
978-0-470-49741-8

Facebook For Dummies
978-0-470-26273-3

Google Blogger
For Dummies
978-0-470-40742-4

Web Marketing
For Dummies,
2nd Edition
978-0-470-37181-7

WordPress For Dummies,
2nd Edition
978-0-470-40296-2

Language & Foreign Language
French For Dummies
978-0-7645-5193-2

Italian Phrases
For Dummies
978-0-7645-7203-6

Spanish For Dummies
978-0-7645-5194-9

Spanish For Dummies,
Audio Set
978-0-470-09585-0

Macintosh
Mac OS X Snow Leopard
For Dummies
978-0-470-43543-4

Math & Science
Algebra I For Dummies
978-0-7645-5325-7

Biology For Dummies
978-0-7645-5326-4

Calculus For Dummies
978-0-7645-2498-1

Chemistry For Dummies
978-0-7645-5430-8

Microsoft Office
Excel 2007 For Dummies
978-0-470-03737-9

Office 2007 All-in-One
Desk Reference
For Dummies
978-0-471-78279-7

Music
Guitar For Dummies,
2nd Edition
978-0-7645-9904-0

iPod & iTunes
For Dummies,
6th Edition
978-0-470-39062-7

Piano Exercises
For Dummies
978-0-470-38765-8

Parenting & Education
Parenting For Dummies,
2nd Edition
978-0-7645-5418-6

Type 1 Diabetes
For Dummies
978-0-470-17811-9

Pets
Cats For Dummies,
2nd Edition
978-0-7645-5275-5

Dog Training For Dummies,
2nd Edition
978-0-7645-8418-3

Puppies For Dummies,
2nd Edition
978-0-470-03717-1

Religion & Inspiration
The Bible For Dummies
978-0-7645-5296-0

Catholicism For Dummies
978-0-7645-5391-2

Women in the Bible
For Dummies
978-0-7645-8475-6

Self-Help & Relationship
Anger Management
For Dummies
978-0-470-03715-7

Overcoming Anxiety
For Dummies
978-0-7645-5447-6

Sports
Baseball For Dummies,
3rd Edition
978-0-7645-7537-2

Basketball For Dummies,
2nd Edition
978-0-7645-5248-9

Golf For Dummies,
3rd Edition
978-0-471-76871-5

Web Development
Web Design All-in-One
For Dummies
978-0-470-41796-6

Windows Vista
Windows Vista
For Dummies
978-0-471-75421-3

Printed in the United States of America
ED-10-30-11